Foreword

The symposium on Building Preservation and Rehabilitation was held in Bal Harbour, Florida on 17 Oct. 1983. The American Society for Testing and Materials' Committee E-6 on Performance of Building Constructions sponsored the symposium. Gerald Davis, TEAG—The Environmental Analysis Group, and William F. Westcott, Westcott Associates, presided as symposium cochairmen.

Related
ASTM Publications

Building Security, STP 729 (1981), 04-729000-10

Building Air Change Rate and Infiltration Measurements, STP 719 (1980), 04-719000-10

Durability of Building Materials and Components, STP 691 (1980), 04-691000-10

Masonry: Research, Application, and Problems, STP 871 (1985), 04-871000-07

A Note of Appreciation
to Reviewers

The quality of the papers that appear in this publication reflects not only the obvious efforts of the authors but also the unheralded, though essential, work of the reviewers. On behalf of ASTM we acknowledge with appreciation their dedication to high professional standards and their sacrifice of time and effort.

ASTM Committee on Publications

ASTM Editorial Staff

David D. Jones
Janet R. Schroeder
Kathleen A. Greene
Bill Benzing

Contents

Overview

This volume contains papers about the preservation and rehabilitation of buildings. The papers are in two groups: Theme A, to improve overall building performance, and Theme B, for historical buildings and building materials. The thirteen papers included here were among those presented at a symposium held at Bal Harbour, Florida on 17 Oct. 1983, sponsored by ASTM Committee E-6 on Performance of Building Constructions, with leadership from what have since become Subcommittees E06.24 and E06.25.

For Theme A, the scope and structure of total building performance is explained, several approaches to functional and technical evaluation are presented, and the differences in overall building performance that are required by an organization at various stages of its life history are considered. Although the subjects of total building performance and building diagnostics have been addressed at previous technical conferences, such as those of the International Council for Building Research, Studies and Documentation (CIB), the U.S. National Institute of Building Sciences, and the U.S. National Research Council's Advisory Board on the Built Environment (ABBE), this was the first symposium leading to standards development for measuring overall *functional* performance.

Theme B deals with a more established field: historical buildings and building materials. The properties of masonry, stone, and wood and their rehabilitation are discussed, and two approaches to nondestructive testing are presented. The two final papers discuss energy conservation, rehabilitation, and damage to the building fabric.

The symposium was organized for two main purposes: to elicit new methods and data and to provide a starting point for standards development work on the two themes. It was successful in both efforts. Immediately following the symposium, a decision was made to establish ASTM Subcommittee E06.25 on Overall Performance of Buildings, with the task group that had led Theme A providing charter members. Contributors to Theme B have been active in the standards development work of ASTM Subcommittee E06.24 on Building Preservation and Rehabilitation.

This book gives convenient access to the new ideas presented at the symposium and to those papers which contain reference information, checklists, procedures, and the like. It therefore will appeal to three groups:

1. Those concerned with the methods and materials of building preservation and rehabilitation, for whom all the papers in Theme B should be helpful.

2. Those who are developing standard guides and procedures in this area, who will find all the papers in Theme B to be useful, plus some of the papers in Theme A, particularly those by Jockusch, Stern, and Farbstein et al.

3. Those who are developing methods and standard guides for evaluating or improving overall performance of buildings, for whom the material in Theme A will be of primary importance, but for whom all the material in Theme B also will be relevant.

Although the papers in this book present the state of the art for many aspects of the practice and technology of building preservation and rehabilitation, they do not provide a comprehensive review of the subject.

Overall performance of buildings is covered at the general level, but specific methods for assigning comparative numerical performance scores are not covered. Life safety issues are mentioned in several papers, but rating overall life safety performance for purposes of building regulation is not discussed. The papers in Theme B discuss the testing and preservation of masonry and stone facades, and wood structures and structural members, but there are many other building materials which are not considered. Two papers describe experiences in improving energy conservation and raise issues for consideration, but a comprehensive framework for energy management in rehabilitation projects is not included.

From the material presented at the symposium and printed in this volume, it is evident that, though the technology of building preservation and rehabilitation is sophisticated, there is not yet a general framework of standard guides for improving overall performance of existing buildings through preservation and rehabilitation. That work is now proceeding within ASTM Subcommittees E06.24 and E06.25.

Gerald Davis

TEAG—The Environmental Analysis Group, New Canaan, CT 06840; symposium co-chairman and editor.

Building Preservation and Rehabilitation for Better Overall Building Performance

Volker H. Hartkopf,[1] *Vivian E. Loftness,*[1] *and*
Peter A. D. Mill[2]

The Concept of Total Building Performance and Building Diagnostics

REFERENCES: Hartkopf, V. H., Loftness, V. E., and Mill, P. A. D., **"The Concept of Total Building Performance and Building Diagnostics,"** *Building Performance: Function, Preservation, and Rehabilitation, ASTM STP 901*, G. Davis, Ed., American Society for Testing and Materials, Philadelphia, 1986, pp. 5-22.

ABSTRACT: This paper introduces the concept of total building performance and the diagnostic tools for measuring and assessing this performance. It emphasizes the need: (1) to fully address the fundamental building performance mandates of thermal comfort, acoustic comfort, air quality, lighting comfort, spatial comfort, and building integrity; (2) to define their physiological, psychological, sociological, and economic limits of acceptability; and (3) to clarify their relationships with each other. Integrated within the building delivery process, these performance mandates and the associated diagnostic measurement and assessment tools suggest new quality assurance procedures for providing suitable and reliable conditions for occupancy comfort in new as well as in existing buildings.

KEY WORDS: total building performance, building diagnostics, comfort, building measurement, case studies, quality assurance, building delivery process

Total Building Performance

In recent years, the international emphasis on resource management—specifically, energy and economic resources—has put a new stress on the building industry in excess of the traditional building demands of health, safety, and welfare. This sudden elevation of a single building requirement has in turn triggered a series of measurable building failures. In some cases, design for energy conservation has led to intermittent high velocity air supply systems, with serious consequences to acoustic comfort. A demand for air tightness has raised questions of air quality and building inadequacies regarding

---

[1]Associate professor and adjunct associate professor, respectively, Department of Architecture, Carnegie-Mellon University, Pittsburgh, PA 15213.
[2]Director, Architectural and Building Sciences, Public Works Canada, Ottawa, Canada.

human health. A major increase in enclosure insulation has led to unexpected levels of condensation and eventual enclosure degradation. It is not the recent focus on energy conservation or other resource management efforts that is at fault for these building failures, however, but the lack of transdisciplinary understanding of the impact each building performance mandate has on the other performance areas. It is the challenge of the 1980s and 1990s, therefore, to understand the critical balance needed to simultaneously ensure all building performance mandates: thermal comfort, acoustic comfort, visual comfort, air quality, spatial comfort, and building integrity.

Building Performance Mandates

It is critical to begin with a complete definition of the building performance mandates to be assiduously met by building policy makers, programmers, architects, engineers, contractors, owners, and managers. For the sake of discussion, this definition can be divided into two areas. First, there has been a fundamental mandate over the centuries for building enclosure integrity—protection of the building's visual, mechanical, and physical properties [1] from environmental degradation through moisture, temperature, air movement, radiation, chemical and biological attack, and environmental disasters (such as fire, flood, earthquake). Established by concerns for health, safety, welfare, resource management (energy, money), and image, the requirements for building integrity are set by the limits of "acceptable" degradation (of the visual, mechanical, and physical properties), ranging from slight decay to debilitation in the ability to provide weather tightness or environmental conditioning for the function to total devastation or destruction. Second, there are a series of mandates relating to interior occupancy requirements (human, animal, plant, artifact, machine) and the elemental parameters of comfort—thermal comfort, acoustic comfort, visual comfort, air quality, and spatial comfort—dependent on physiological, psychological, sociological, and economic values.

In attempting to put forward a discrete list of performance mandates of equal weight and of primary concern for the building industry, an outline has been developed (Table 1) with admittedly lopsided emphasis given to building integrity (protection from degradation), reflecting in turn the industry's focus on building failures in this area.

Limits of Acceptability

Each building performance mandate has a "comfort zone" establishing the limits of acceptability for the type of occupancy concerned. These limits, often translated into standards and codes, budgets, and guidelines, are established by the physiological, psychological, sociological, and economic [3] requirements of the occupancy. The limits must be established for the range of

TABLE 1—*Building performance mandates.*

1. Building integrity (versus degradation of the structure, enclosure, interior, and servicing assemblies)
   (*a*) moisture: rain, snow, ice, vapor
       (i) penetration
       (ii) migration
       (iii) condensation
   (*b*) temperature
       (i) insulation effectiveness
       (ii) thermal bridging
       (iii) freeze-thaw cycle
       (iv) differential thermal expansion and contraction
   (*c*) air movement
       (i) air exfiltration
       (ii) air infiltration
   (*d*) radiation and light
       (i) environmental radiation
       (ii) solar radiation, for example, ultraviolet
       (iii) visible light spectrum
   (*e*) chemical attack
   (*f*) biological attack
   (*g*) firesafety
   (*h*) disaster: earthquake, flood, hurricane, etc.
2. Thermal comfort
   (*a*) air temperature
   (*b*) radiant temperature
   (*c*) humidity
   (*d*) air speed
   (*e*) occupancy factors and controls
3. Acoustic comfort
   (*a*) sound pressure level and frequency
   (*b*) reverberation and absorption
   (*c*) speech privacy, articulation index
   (*d*) vibration
   (*e*) occupancy factors and controls
4. Visual comfort
   (*a*) ambient and task levels: artificial and daylight
   (*b*) contrast, brightness ratios (glare. . .)
   (*c*) color rendition
   (*d*) occupancy factors and controls
5. Air quality
   (*a*) ventilation rate: fresh air supply, circulation
   (*b*) mass pollution [2]: gases, vapors, microorganisms, fumes, smokes; dust
   (*c*) energy pollution: ionizing radiation; microwaves; radio waves; light waves; infrared
   (*d*) occupancy factors and controls
6. Spatial comfort
   (*a*) work station layout: space; furniture—surface, storage, seating; ergonomics
   (*b*) work group layout: adjacencies; compartmentalization; useable space; circulation/
       accessibility/way finding/signage; indoor-outdoor relationships
   (*c*) conveniences, services: sanitary; electrical; security; telecommunications; circulation/
       transportation
   (*d*) amenities
   (*e*) occupancy factors and controls

building or space functions and the range of occupancy types and factors (age, metabolic rate, clothing, etc.).

In regards to human occupancy, physiological requirements aim to ensure the physical health and safety of the building occupants, sheltering basic bodily functions—sight, hearing, breathing, feeling, movement, etc.—from wear or destruction over time against such conditions as fire, building collapse, poisonous fumes, high and low temperatures, and poor light. Psychological requirements aim to support individual mental health through appropriate provisions for privacy, interaction, clarity, status, change, etc. Sociological requirements (also referred to as sociocultural requirements) aim to support the well-being of the community within which the individuals act, relating the needs of the individuals to those of the collective. Finally, economic requirements aim to allocate resources in the most efficient manner to serve user needs within the wider social context.

The interdependencies of these four limits of acceptability might be best illustrated through an acoustic performance example. Guidelines, codes, and standards have been developed to protect the human against excessive noise. To mitigate physiological hearing damage, both noise intensity and duration are considered. To mitigate psychological discomfort, noise frequency (even beyond the known hearing threshold) is evaluated to eliminate the distraction of low frequency rumbles and high frequency hisses. To mitigate sociological hearing discomfort, consideration is given to speech articulation to help ensure privacy in offices or between apartments. Finally, the availability of resources (financial, technical, energy) superimposes another layer of requirements, establishing limits of feasibility alongside the limits of acceptability. Decision, however, must be tempered with the full understanding of resources over time, evaluating allocations necessary for initial outlay, operating costs, maintenance costs, eventual replacement or conversion costs, and associated personnel costs.

Terms of Evaluation

The performance concept establishes that the primary goals of buildings are to serve user needs in the broadest sense: occupancy needs (human, animal, plant, artifact) as well as the needs of the surrounding community [4]. The limits of acceptability are defined by the individual's and the community's physiological, psychological, sociological, and economic needs, requiring a sophisticated understanding of the complex term *comfort*. Instead of prescriptive specifications for component selection, this concept emphasizes the specification of the desired performance of the whole system (building and community) and the resulting demands on component parts.

When evaluating such a system of building and community, performance can be stated and alternatives compared in terms of suitability, reliability, and flexibility [5]. *Suitability* is a measure of the degree to which a building and its component parts serve user needs in the present and near future. *Reli-

ability is expressed as the probability that the service will continue to perform as intended throughout the life of the facility, given appropriate maintenance and use. *Flexibility*, including adaptability, is a measure of the systems ability to accommodate changing functions and occupancies and the continuing effort and resources required during the building life cycle to maintain suitability.

Interrelationships of Building Performance Mandates

Performance requirements in each of the six categories cannot be understood in isolation from the other. First of all, they are related in a complex manner through their physiological, psychological, sociological, and economic values. For instance, the concept of privacy has acoustic, spatial, visual, and olfactory (air quality) dimensions.

Second, in trying to fulfill the requirements of one performance mandate, side effects are created which impinge upon the fulfillment of another. The need for acceptable air quality, for example, may lead to a ventilation rate which will affect both thermal and acoustic comfort.

Third, performance requirements are related to each other through the multiple effects of building component choice. The selection of a ceiling light fixture has implications in terms of heat as well as light, noise as well as radiation. Although the building component may provide adequate performance in one dimension, it may fail in other areas due to specification, context, or maintenance.

To deliver a project that is acceptable in all the performance areas, therefore, conflicts must be resolved between performance mandates and limits, and priorities must be set, based on the building or space function. Then, total building performance evaluation techniques are needed to consider these complex interrelationships in the conception, design, specification, installation, and use of components and assemblies within buildings, techniques which are the focus of building diagnostics.

Component Interfaces and Total Building Performance

The materials, components, and assemblies synergistically designed to create buildings also must be synergistically designed to fulfill the basic performance mandates for building integrity, thermal comfort, acoustic comfort, lighting comfort, spatial comfort, and air quality. For the sake of discussion, building materials and components can be grouped into four assembly categories: load-bearing structure, exterior enclosure, interior enclosure, and servicing.

1. Examples of load bearing structural assemblies include suspension structures, with tension cables and compression masts as components, as well

as frame structures with vertical columns, horizontal beams, and diaphragms as components.

2. The exterior enclosure assembly incorporates roof, exposed exterior walls and floors, below grade exterior walls and floors, and connective components such as parapets. Then, within the broad component classification of exterior wall exist secondary components such as windows and tertiary components such as mullions, eventually arriving at aluminum as a material.

3. Interior enclosure is composed of fixed spatial components such as walls, ceilings, and floors and furnishings such as chairs, desks, and movable partitions.

4. Servicing assemblies include mechanical (HVAC), electrical (lights, power), vertical transport (elevators, stairs, escalators), sanitary (plumbing), fire safety, and telecommunications.

There is no question that one component may be serving a dual function: for example, a load-bearing structure acting as an exterior enclosure or interior definition or both; servicing assemblies acting as an interior definition or an exterior enclosure [4]. In fact, the richer building designs capitalize on this multiple function as a design approach. What is critical to the concept of total building performance, however, is the understanding that these four assembly categories are often only designed to their respective component performance requirements, resulting in the inability of two assemblies (component-to-component interfaces) to sustain all six performance mandates. For example, a roof membrane carefully designed to roofing component performance specifications may itself be watertight, but the elevator shaft, designed to other component specifications, may penetrate the membrane without adequate detailing to guarantee the air, vapor, or water seal required to withstand differential expansion and contraction and chemical compatibilities.

Traditionally, the performance of individual components is measured and predicted in isolation from other components, often in the laboratory. Today, this is slowly giving way to integrated performance measurements and assessments. The suitability, reliability, and flexibility of components and their interfaces in providing for the basic performance requirements of the occupancy is best evaluated under conditions of that occupancy. It is the dynamic environment created by the managers and users of buildings which provides the realistic basis for appraisal.

Building Diagnostics Tools

Definition

Building Diagnostics is the measurement and assessment of a building's ability to provide thermal comfort, acoustic comfort, lighting comfort, air quality, and functional comfort for its occupancy, as well as to provide building integrity versus debilitation. Effective diagnostics implies that the measurements and assessments must be completed in a transdisciplinary manner for each of the six performance areas, in relation to established standards or limits of acceptability, for the specific occupancy and function. Building diagnosis establishes at various stages during the building delivery process [6], the suitability of a building and its component parts to serve occupant needs in the present, the reliability or probability that the service will continue to be suitable throughout the life of the building (dependent on the appropriateness of the maintenance and operation practices), and the flexibility or adaptability of the building and its component parts to provide long-term suitability given changing occupancies and functions.

Illustration

To begin with, the building diagnostician must establish the relevant performance requirements and their limits of acceptability before measuring a specific material, component, or assembly. When measuring the performance of light fixtures, for example, the visual comfort mandate and the client's limits of acceptability (or standards) must be established, as well as related acoustic, thermal comfort, and radiant/health standards. Then, as outlined in the IES standards [7], a comprehensive in-place testing procedure is necessary to establish the suitability, reliability, and flexibility of the lighting fixture/assembly.

To establish the suitability of the lighting assembly in providing the accepted range of foot candles on the task surface without jeopardizing other comfort requirements, the fixtures must be measured within the overall assembly of ceiling, floor, wall, furniture, partitions, and occupants at various times of the day. Lighting suitability is as dependent on the position and color of partitions, the position and color of furniture, and the fixtures interference with acoustic comfort or thermal comfort as it is dependent on the manufacturer's labelled footcandle levels.

To establish the reliability of the lighting assembly in providing visual comfort over time requires measurement and comparison of the long-term quality of the ballasts and starters, the tubes and bulbs, the lenses and reflectors, etc. Acrylic lenses provide suitable light transmission at installation but are not necessarily reliable since they often yellow when exposed to light. Establishing reliability also depends on the measurement and assessment of the maintenance effort that can be reasonably expected, including cleaning schedules, replacement schedules, etc.

To establish the ability of the lighting assembly to sustain visual comfort over time given changing occupancy, function, and use, flexibility measurement must identify the range of conditions under which the system will maintain suitability or the investments necessary for adaptation. This measure anticipates new office planning in which functions may change from drafting to lounge areas, in which increased density and major partitioning may divide light fixtures, or in which dark painted walls may reduce reflectivities. Flexibility and adaptability, then, is a measure of the level of effort and resources necessary to sustain suitability over changes in occupancy, function, or use.

Diagnostic Measurement—Equipment and Procedures

Increasing expectations and demands for building enclosure integrity and occupancy "comfort" has spurred an unprecedented growth in instrumentation and measurement techniques for buildings. Parallel and interwoven advances in the behavioral and social sciences [8], combined with the expansion of scientific engineering and medical testing [9], has greatly enhanced our understanding of the way in which buildings affect occupant physiological, psychological, sociological, and economic comfort. The result is a range of diagnostic tools, equipment, and procedures capable of determining the suitability, reliability, and flexibility of building components and component interfaces in providing total building performance. Five categories are defined in an attempt to capture the various forms of diagnostic measurement approaches used today (Table 2).

Further classification of measurement equipment and procedures should focus on the performance mandate being evaluated and the accuracy and precision needed for the desired level of evaluation. "A performance testing method must be looked upon in exactly the same way as any other test method. This means that the general rules of statistics should be used to deal with problems of sampling, repeatability, and reproducibility. This may lead to expensive testing programs when simpler methods would be more realistic. In such cases, simple cost/benefit analysis may reveal the most realistic test procedures" [4]. This precision filtering would allow the assemblage of diagnostic packages for simultaneously measuring thermal comfort, acoustic comfort, lighting comfort, functional comfort, air quality, and building integrity versus degradation for several levels of assessment, over time, within a building. Care should be taken not to identify the various measurement approaches with individual components and assemblies (in isolation), such as roof, wall, and heating installation, since it is often the interactions of these components/assemblies which fail. It is equally important that the various diagnostic tools do not become identified with subsets of the different performance mandates such as vapor pressure, insulation, and wet bulb/dry bulb, since again it is the interaction that ensures comfort. These disassociations will not only limit the application of the tools, they will often result in incomplete data bases and eventually inaccurate conclusions regarding the ability of the total building system to meet the fundamental performance mandates.

Even the diagnostic packages, however, will not resolve the historic conflict between unidisciplinary or multidisciplinary performance testing and the

TABLE 2—*Diagnostic measurement.*

1. Plan/archive analysis
   (*a*) plans, specifications, photographs
   (*b*) building budgets, implementation history
   (*c*) occupancy/management records
2. Occupancy and use analysis
   (*a*) questionnaire
   (*b*) interview
   (*c*) behavioral mapping, photographing
   (*d*) annotated plans
3. Expert walk-through analysis
   (*a*) ear: listening
   (*b*) eye: seeing
   (*c*) nose: smelling
   (*d*) hand, body: touching, feeling
   (*e*) mouth: tasting
4. Simple instrumentation analysis
   (*a*) measuring component and component interfaces
   (*b*) measuring space types/functions
   (*c*) measuring combined stressors (for example, privacy)
   (*d*) measuring retrofit packages
   (*e*) measuring transdisciplinary hypotheses (for example, productivity)
5. Complex instrumentation analysis
   (*a*) measuring component and component interfaces
   (*b*) measuring space types/functions
   (*c*) measuring combined stressors (for example, privacy)
   (*d*) measuring retrofite packages
   (*e*) measuring transdisciplinary hypotheses (for example, productivity)

transdisciplinary diagnostics recommended today. Performance testing was initially developed within the laboratory, measuring the unidisciplinary performance (acoustic or thermal or degradation, etc.) of a single component. This evolved into field test methods focusing on component assemblies, allowing component-to-component interfaces to be assessed, but still measuring unidisciplinary performance. Today, however, we are at the threshold of developing total building performance measurement and assessment procedures for the occupied building as a total system.

These transdisciplinary procedures would allow the measurement of one performance mandate to be related to the measurement of all other areas of performance, evaluating in place the components and component interfaces as well as the interrelated occupancy. For this reason it is suggested that diagnostic measurement approaches be primarily classified as archival, behavioral, sensory, simple and complex instrumentation, and laboratory testing. The present-day capabilities of each of these tools in measuring each of the six performance mandates can be then described, leaving room for innovative transdisciplinary packaging and use.

Diagnostic Assessment—Procedures and Equipment

While diagnostic measurement implies the collection of relevant data and the equipment, expertise, and methods necessary for this collection, diagnostic assessment refers to the generation of recommendations from this data and the equipment (for example, computers), expertise (for example, algorithms), and methods necessary for that interpretation. Indeed, the weakest links in evaluating total building performance today are the procedures for diagnostic assessment. Given the body of data produced by diagnostic measurement, a diagnostic assessment and eventual "diagnosis" including recommendations only can be made based on the comparative performance of the measurements to the standards or limits of acceptability. However, both the standards or limits of acceptability and the range of assessment procedures in use today have shortcomings in their ability to deal fully (in a transdisciplinary manner) with all performance variables (Table 3).

These assessment procedures are independent of the equipment used for diagnostic assessment, equipment ranging from hand calculations and plots to simple graphic plotters to calculators and microcomputers to large-scale computers. The simplest of scales or algorithms can be read into the most complex equipment. Although further development in assessment hardware will be beneficial to building diagnosis, it is the algorithms that form the basis of the assessment procedure which need the greatest emphasis and development.

To begin with, the algorithms that form the basis of the assessment procedure often avoid the full set of performance indexes and the performance-to-performance conflicts. Despite the comprehensiveness reflected in the American Society of Heating, Refrigerating and Air-Conditioning Engineers' (ASHRAE) Thermal Comfort Standard 55-81 [10], thermal comfort (as controlled by thermostats) is often assessed by building operators and users given air temperature measurement alone, with no call for radiant temperature conditions, air movement, clothing, or metabolic rate. Even when all thermal comfort factors are accounted for, action often is recommended despite the implications it will have on other performance mandates, such as air quality or acoustic comfort. Before transdisciplinary actions can be effectively recommended from diagnostic measurement, stronger assessment algorithms must be developed, fully defining the six performance mandates, their limits of ac-

TABLE 3—*Diagnostic assessment procedures.*

1. Informed judgment (unidisciplinary or transdisciplinary)
2. Mock-up sensory assessment (transdisciplinary)
3. Pattern/statistical assessment (transdisciplinary)
4. Simple unidisciplinary algorithms
5. Complex unidisciplinary algorithms [4], p. 20
6. Transdisciplinary algorithms

ceptability (guidelines, codes, and standards), and their relationships to each other. With the computer available as an assessment tool, we now have the capability of storing broad measurement data bases, assimilating assessment algorithms for several performance mandates, and finally diagnosing for total building performance.

Introducing Building Diagnostics into the Building Delivery Process

Building Delivery Process or Project Delivery System [6]

Building diagnostics (measurement and assessment) has the potential of rapidly becoming a major tool in building appraisal to evaluate suitability, to anticipate long-term performance and the resources necessary to sustain this performance, and to assess risk. Upon reviewing the various types of measurement equipment and procedures available, it should be clear that this ability to appraise performance and risk will be available to most of the building decisionmakers throughout the building delivery process.

The building delivery process, already defined by many groups (Fig. 1; Refs 6,11), incorporates at a minimum the following ten stages: (1) problem identification; (2) feasibility assessment; (3) project programming; (4) design, including working drawings; (5) tendering and procurement; (6) construction; (7) initial occupancy; (8) operation and maintenance; and the two final alternatives over time: (9) adaptive reuse or (10) demolition. Although the implications of building diagnostics for appraising performance and risk throughout this building delivery process should be explored more fully, its value in measuring and diagnosing component failure, occupant discomfort and stress, and operational costs should be apparent already to the associated building decisionmakers.

Development of Knowledge and Feedback Within the Project Delivery System

One of the greatest advantages of building diagnostics is the ability to measure and assess the transdisciplinary performance of a full range of existing building types for feedback into the project delivery system. Evaluating the suitability, reliability, and flexibility of a building in meeting its function(s) over time will enable the building community to anticipate and prevent failure as well as to improve overall performance.

In pursuit of accomplishing this feedback, there is a serious need for knowledge development and packaging, including: refining the limits of acceptability (or standards) for performance, given varying occupancy types and environmental conditions; establishing the terms of evaluation dictating these standards; defining the interrelationships (and conflicts) between different performance mandates; discovering the critical component interfaces

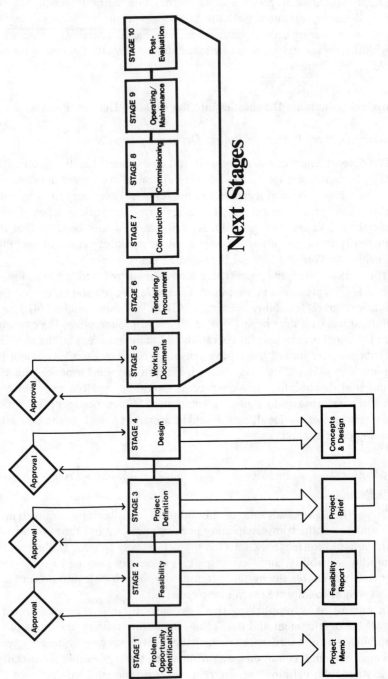

FIG. 1—*The project delivery system, Public Works Canada [6].*

affecting each performance mandate; developing the "diagnostic" measurement equipment and procedures for evaluating transdisciplinary as well as unidisciplinary performance; developing the "diagnostic" assessment procedures and equipment; and establishing education and training programs aimed directly at each major decision-making group in the building delivery process.

Structuring and Recording Case Studies

One of the most critical knowledge packages for ensuring information feedback and development is the case study. Properly documented case studies illustrate the transdisciplinary nature of failures and successes, point out the series of decisions and decision-making disciplines (within the building delivery process) which led to the success or failure, and allow for future identification, repetition, or prevention.

The effective structuring of transdisciplinary case studies is still in the evolutionary stages (Table 4). It necessitates a strategic combination of diagnostic measurement equipment and procedures and diagnostic assessment procedures and equipment. These diagnostic packages must be suitable for the building function, the level of evaluation needed, and the finances and resources available. The packages will need continual refinement to improve the timing, the scale, the depth, and the pertinent output of the various measurement and assessment procedures.

The effective recording of transdisciplinary case studies centers around feedback into each stage within the building delivery system to each decision maker. This information transfer, intended to improve the quality of future buildings as well as the buildings in question, would be primarily sorted by building function and space function. Secondary classifications would deal with disciplinary recommendations (thermal, lighting, acoustic, air quality, function, building integrity), yet emphasizing recommendations that accommodate reinforcements or conflicts between two or more disciplines. To anticipate future computer (or other objective) diagnostic approaches, however, a third approach to case study recording is needed, that of recommendations pertaining to components and component interfaces.

To accomplish a computer (or objective) identification of possible performance stresses occurring throughout the building delivery process, the performance successes and failures should be documented by a precise set of physical descriptors of the components *and their interfaces*. For example, the recognition of a rain penetration failure will not foretell a similar failure in another building unless the component and component interface that failed is identified, as well as the conditions under which it failed. It is only the identification of the interface that failed (between load-bearing structure, exterior enclosure, interior enclosure, and servicing assemblies), the specifications of

TABLE 4—*Structure for programming, evaluating, and recording case study buildings.*

Limits of Acceptibility, Guidelines, Codes, & Standards	Terms of Evaluation	Interrelationships of Performance Mandates	Component & Component Interfaces	Building Diagnostics		Political Structure	Structuring & Recording Case Studies
				Measurement Equipment & Procedure	Assessment Equipment & Procedure	Knowledge Development & Feedback into the Building Delivery System	
1	2	3	4	5	6	7	8
Physiological, Psychological, Sociological, Economic (Resource Management)	Suitability, Reliability, Flexibility	Priorities & Conflicts Established by Function & Occupancy Type	Structure, Exterior Enclosure, Interior Enclosure, Servicing	Occupancy & Use, Sensory Walkthru, Handheld, Transportable, Model Testing, Laboratory	Informed Judgment Mock Up Sensory, Statistical, Unidisciplinary Algorithm, Transdisciplinary Algorithm	Conception, Assessment, Programming, Design, Procurement, Construction, Occupancy, Operation & Maintenance	Recording by: Function, Discipline, Physical Descriptors

Performance
mandates
Thermal comfort
Acoustic comfort
Lighting comfort
Air quality
Functional
comfort
Building integrity
versus
debilitation

that interface, and the external and internal conditions that will allow another designer, contractor, or manager to identify potentially parallel building performance failures. Table 5 exemplifies this "physical descriptor" approach to recording performance failures (and eventually the diagnostic equipment and procedures that can predict or ascertain these failures). This table identifies failures occurring between servicing components [heating, ventilating, and air-conditioning (HVAC), lighting, vertical transport, water, etc.] and interior enclosure components (walls, ceilings, floors, partitions, furnishings). This failure classification would include, for example, thermal comfort failures resulting from air diffusers (mechanical services) that have been blocked by movable partitions (furnishings). Ten tables of this simple data base management type, ideally contained within a computer assessment program, would catalog performance failures between structure and exterior, structure and interior, exterior and interior, exterior and servicing, interior and servicing, servicing and structure, as well as failures within assemblies.

Many building failure records are presently organized by singular component (roof, window, HVAC) or by material (steel, concrete, plaster), ostensibly focusing on building integrity failures. These records do not clearly identify the component-to-component interfaces, and their respective specifications, that are ultimately responsible for failure, nor do they record other performance mandate failures, now identified as transdisciplinary failures. As a result, there is most often an inadequate historic data base for future action. In addition, case studies often do not address the full set of building decision makers who affect total building performance. It is recommended, therefore, that future documentation of building failures and successes provide full lists of recommendations to each of the decision makers within the building delivery process, first by building and space function, then by performance disciplines and combinations thereof, and finally by component and component interfaces.

Conclusion

This paper introduces the concept of total building performance and the building diagnostic tools for measuring and assessing this performance. Integrated with the present building delivery process, these tools offer new quality assurance procedures for providing suitable, reliable, and sustainable conditions for occupancy comfort (defined in physiological, psychological, sociological, and economic terms). The paper establishes the importance of understanding component-to-component interfaces within the occupied building in contrast to studying discrete materials, components, and assemblies. Above all, however, the paper attempts to stress the importance of transdisciplinary knowledge, empirical and deductive, for ensuring total building performance.

TABLE 5—*Physical descriptor approach to recording building performance failures for computerized databases.*

	HVAC (Heating, Ventilation, Cooling)	Electrical (Lighting, Electricity)	Transport (Elevators, Stairs, Escalators)	Water (Sanitary)	Fire Safety
Components Within Servicing Assemblies	Fixed Def. (Walls, Floors, Clgs.) Movable Def.	Fixed Def. (Walls, Floors, Clgs.) Movable Def.	Fixed Def. (Walls, Floors, Clgs.) Movable Def.	Fixed Def. (Walls, Floors, Clgs.) Movable Def.	Fixed Def. (Walls, Floors, Clgs.) Movable Def.
Components Within Interior Assemblies	(Partitions, Furniture)	(Partitions, Furniture)	(Partitions, Furniture)	(Partitions, Furniture)	(Partitions, Furniture)

BUILDING PERFORMANCE MANDATES IN RELATION TO:

1. BUILDING INTEGRITY[a]
1.1 Moisture: rain, snow, & vapor
1.1.1 penetration
1.1.2 migration
1.1.3 condensation
1.2 Temperature
1.2.1 insulation effectiveness
1.2.2 thermal bridging
1.2.3 freeze-thaw cycles
1.2.4 differential thermal, expansion/contraction
1.3 Air movement
1.3.1 air exfiltration
1.3.2 air infiltration
1.4 Radiation
1.4.1 solar, including ultraviolet radiation
1.4.2 environmental radiation (that is, radon)

1.5 Chemical compatabilities
1.6 Biological health
1.6.1 fungi
1.6.2 animals (insects, rodents)
1.7 Fire/earthquakes/floods/hurricanes
2. THERMAL COMFORT[b]
2.1 Air temperature
2.2 Radiant temperature
2.3 Humidity
2.4 Air speed
3. ACOUSTIC COMFORT
3.1 Noise control
3.2 Speech privacy
4. VISUAL COMFORT
4.1 Ambient lighting levels
     (artificial & daylighting)
4.2 Brightness ratios (including glare)
4.3 Color rendition
5. AIR QUALITY
5.1 Ventilation rate
5.2 Pollution
6. FUNCTION
6.1 Proxemics
6.2 Ergonomics
6.3 Conveniences (hot water, sanitary, electricity)

[a]The first major performance mandate relates to the integrity of the building enclosure.
[b]The next five performance mandates relate directly to human occupancy requirements.

References

[1] Fix, W. and Rubben, A. "A New Approach for Calculating Time Dependent Effects in Polymer Building Materials," in *Proceedings*, Performance Concept in Building, Third ASTM/CIB/RILEM symposium, Lisbon, Portugal, 1982.

[2] Woods, J. E. "Do Buildings Make You Sick?", in *Proceedings*, Third Canadian Buildings Congress Achievements and Challenges in Building, 1982, No. 21158, National Research Council, Washington, DC, 1982.

[3] Blanchere, G., "The Notion of Performance in Building: Building Requirements," and "What are the Natures of Performance and Evaluation for the Three Levels: Building, Component, Materials?" in *Proceedings*, Performance Concept in Buildings, NBS 361, National Bureau of Standards, Gaithersburg, MD, 1972.

[4] "Working with the Performance Approach in Building" CIB Report Publication 64, Centre Internationale du Batiment, Jan. 1982, pp. 5, 10, 17, 20.

[5] Lemer, A. C. and Moavenzadeh, F., "Performance of Systems of Constructed Facilities," in *Proceedings*, Performance Concept in Buildings, 1972, NBS 361, National Bureau of Standards, Gaithersburg, MD.

[6] "The Project Delivery System" of Public Works Canada, Stages 1 to 10, Public Works Canada, Ottawa, Oct. 1978.

[7] "Practice for Office Lighting," in *IES Lighting Handbook*, J. Kaufman, Ed., Illuminating Engineering Society, New York, 1981.

[8] Zeisel, J., *Inquiry by Design: Tools for Environment-Behavior Research*, Brooks/Cole Publishing Co., Monterey, CA, 1981.

[9] Mill, P. A. D., "Thermography—a New Building Science Tool," Report Series No. 29, Public Works Canada, Ottawa, 1979.

[10] "Thermal Environmental Conditions for Human Occupancy," Standard 55-1981, ANSI/ASHRAE, Atlanta, GA, 1981.

[11] Vonier, T., "Preventative Medicine," *Progressive Architecture Magazine*, April 1983.

Pleasantine Drake,[1] Polly Welch,[2] and John Zeisel[3]

The Role of Occupancy Analysis in Diagnosing Total Building Performance

REFERENCE: Drake, P., Welch, P., and Zeisel, J., **"The Role of Occupancy Analysis in Diagnosing Total Building Performance,"** *Building Performance: Function, Preservation, and Rehabilitation, ASTM STP 901*, G. Davis, Ed., American Society for Testing and Materials, Philadelphia, 1986, pp. 23-38.

ABSTRACT: There is a crisis of premature building deterioration due, at least in part, to inadequate performance. This crisis has been particularly notable in office buildings. In addition, there are apparently conflicting demands in office environments: to reduce the energy consumption of buildings, to maintain or improve the productivity of employees accommodated, to satisfy their demands for a degree of environmental choice and control, and to respond to increased consumer awareness about the quality of such environmental attributes as air and lighting levels.

The approach taken in building diagnostics is highly innovative. In order to solve the complex problems being encountered, investigators have to diagnose buildings in transdisciplinary ways. This approach to problem solving requires that each disciplinary subgroup keep in mind a larger shared picture of the team's joint goals, that data are gathered concurrently and analyzed so as to test the findings and implications of decisions in each area, and that recommendations be examined that minimize negative side effects.

Occupancy analysis is one aspect of a transdisciplinary approach. It focuses on issues of environmental effectiveness, user well-being and control, and change (incremental and major) by probing patterns of, and attitudes towards, occupancy and use. This paper presents a case study in which this approach was applied. Occupancy analysis data, gathered with concurrent base technical testing of ambient environmental conditions, was used to focus more detailed technical testing in specific areas as necessary, thus reducing the enormous costs of blanket technical testing. Occupancy analysis provided critical data on perceived environmental comfort and effectiveness to be compared with the actual measurement of environmental conditions. The objective of this diagnostic project was to improve energy performance without diminishing environmental quality within office areas.

Increasingly it is being realized that unless all participants in building design, operation, and maintenance have an improved collective understanding of how to design and control the technical systems and layouts in buildings over time, new problems or negative

[1]Principal, Architectural Diagnostics, Ottawa, Ontario, Canada KIN 8V3.
[2]Principal, Welch & Epp Associates, Arlington, MA 02174.
[3]Principal, Building Diagnostics, Inc., Cambridge, MA 02138.

side effects may be unintentionally created by unidisciplinary action. Diagnostic studies explore the possibility that improvement can be achieved by nurturing a sense of collective competence and well-being of occupants rather than the current sense of environmental deprivation, while minimizing operating and maintenance costs as well as building deterioration.

KEY WORDS: total building performance, building diagnostics, building effectiveness, energy efficiency, occupancy analysis, collective competence

Total Building Performance: The Issues

Loss of Building Effectiveness

There is an unprecedented crisis of premature building degradation throughout North America. More invidious, though, is the loss of building effectiveness from an occupancy perspective. A building loses effectiveness when its use or occupancy is restricted by inappropriate or inadequate performance of one or more environmental attributes, such as ventilation, lighting, or temperature. Poor performance in one area, such as ventilation, may be the result of a conflict in performance requirements between several attributes, such as is presented in the case study section of this paper. The cumulative effect of less than satisfactory performance in several different areas culminates in environmental stresses perceived by the occupants. Where once total building performance focused on interactive forces causing building envelope degradation, such as cladding panels falling off or windows popping out, total building performance now addresses the more complex issues of reduced building effectiveness. Since 1980, the joint work of Architectural and Building Sciences Directorate, Public Works Canada, with private consultants, has been responding to immediate acute problems and concerns [1].

One dramatic example of the loss of building effectiveness is the now commonplace problem of air quality, which reduces effective occupancy. This problem has been labeled as the "tight building syndrome" [2]. The frequency of "tight building syndrome" has increased dramatically as building materials have changed, as windows have been sealed, and as mechanical ventilation systems are used to control fresh air supply within the buildings. Evidence indicates that the accumulation and recirculation of contaminants overlaid on deficiencies in the actual distribution and circulation of air throughout the buildings may be a cause of tight building syndrome symptoms, such as eye and throat irritations, headaches, and respiratory problems among office workers [3]. This syndrome is an example of the consequences of design and operation decisions based on energy conservation overlaid on decisions about materials, finishes, and layout. Cumulatively, these decisions reduce the effective occupancy of the building.

This crisis of building effectiveness has been particularly notable in office buildings. Sealed office buildings with mechanical ventilation and centrally controlled systems, and particularly those with large open office areas, offer instructive examples of what the fragmentation of design decision-making implies for occupancy. They underline the necessity for a diagnostics that takes a broader perspective on assessing interactive aspects of buildings. The case study presented in the second half of the paper demonstrates that although the air handling system may provide the intended quantity of air at the diffuser, the combination of the integrated ceiling system with the layout and type of screens may prevent air from ever reaching occupant nose level. Thus, diagnosis for building effectiveness is not a question of assessing whether standards have been met, but whether, in fact, actual building performance sustains reasonable occupancy and use in terms of individual and organizational well-being, health, and productivity. Any building in which the staff dozes or is groggy for 1 h every afternoon as a result of energy conserving measures is too expensive to operate. Energy savings achieved by reducing fresh air ventilation are offset by the negative effects on occupants.

Collective Competence

Unless all participants in building design, operation, use, and maintenance have an improved collective understanding of how to design and control the mechanical and electrical systems and the layouts in buildings over time, new problems or negative side effects may be unintentionally created by unidisciplinary action. Each individual undertaking an action, either official or unofficial, believes that she is improving her environment. This may or may not be the case. A partition moved to accommodate an increase in staff or a screen moved to give more privacy may reduce air circulation. A thermostat lowered to reduce heat from one air handling system may trigger increased hot water flowing through an adjacent perimeter heating system. Higher temperature settings on the air handling systems to reduce energy costs may increase perceived ventilation problems. A covered diffuser or crimped air duct to prevent drafts may lead to stale, stuffy air. In addition, in office environments there are apparently conflicting demands to reduce the energy consumption of buildings, maintain or improve the productivity of employees accommodated, satisfy their demands for a degree of environmental choice and control, and respond to increased consumer environmental awareness about the quality of such attributes as air and lighting levels.

We can no longer assess buildings as if they were empty shells. Occupants in buildings produce dynamic environments. Design, operation, use, and maintenance all influence performance. Furthermore, in an increasing number of new and renovated office buildings, occupants issue a steady stream of complaints, petitions, and union objections from the time of first move in. Occasionally these complaints culminate in walkouts or lawsuits. People often bring in their own fans, heaters, and air ecologizers to increase their individual comfort. They tamper with mechanical systems and achieve their own comfort without realizing that they have done so at the expense of discomfort for others elsewhere in the system and, usually, at the expense of the energy budget. Management within the organizations occupying these buildings has begun to acknowledge cumulative environmental inadequacies and to question links between productivity of staff and their environmental satisfaction and comfort.

The Office Challenge

Office buildings are strategic research sites for the study of total building performance, offering excellent examples of the problems of collective competence. General purpose office buildings tend to be master-planned rather than designed. The lack of specific programmatic direction prior to design of the office building becomes an excuse for not anticipating occupancy needs. This emphasizes the need for more extensive space planning and mechanical and electrical fit-up prior to move in. Building designers give little or no guidance as to how to adapt systems to particular requirements.

Those who do the space planning and layouts for the office areas often are not well-informed about how to achieve an effective fit with the mechanical and electrical systems. Often interior space planners do not consult the architect or engineer prior to making space planning and fit-up decisions. The result is that many fit-up decisions are implemented which contradict initial design decisions and contribute to poor systems performance and poor quality environments unresponsive to basic occupancy requirements. As a further complication, this process is cyclical as layouts in offices are constantly being modified over time without proper space planning, fit-up, and consideration of the environmental consequences.

Furthermore, office buildings contain a diverse range of ancillary spaces which may have special requirements quite different from the standard environmental requirements for office space per se. These spaces include computer rooms, laboratories, courtrooms, public meeting spaces, equipment spaces, interview rooms, testing rooms, audio visual rooms, lounge/break areas, print shops, cafeteria, and kitchens. Many problems arise from the lack of anticipating these special requirements in designing or adapting the mechanical and electrical systems.

Operators and managers of office buildings also make decisions which may be based on erroneous assumptions and which may negatively impact environmental quality and comfort. Mechanical systems in many buildings are operated on a schedule which assumes 9:00 a.m. to 5:00 p.m. occupancy patterns, Mondays through Fridays, even though there have been substantial shifts in work patterns including flextime, compressed work weeks, work out of the office, and evening and weekend use.

Existing problems of marginal ambient environment conditions in office buildings are exacerbated by the introduction of information technology and office automation [4]. New equipment places additional demands on building systems, which, if not met, greatly increase environmental discomfort and stress for occupants [5]. This, in turn, can increase health hazards and decrease productivity. New technologies require that the original requirements for heating/cooling, lighting, acoustic, and space be reassessed. Sensitive equipment with which occupants tend to have less contact, such as large computer installations, receives special attention, being placed in isolated, cooled, dust-free, specially lit rooms. Yet, most office automation equipment is introduced to the **workplace** with little or no modification to the environment. Spaces in which computer terminals are grouped and at which individuals sit for 7 to 8 h per day receive no special treatment. Indeed, much of the new technology is being installed in existing buildings with little or no adaptation to existing lighting or mechanical systems, although studies indicate that many office buildings will not reasonably accommodate office automation and information technology without substantial modifications to environmental control and electrical systems [6, 7].

Building Diagnostics

A Total Building Performance Diagnostic Model

To gain insight into the many complex problems encountered in buildings, we have developed a model of total building performance focusing on occupancy-based performance issues. These issues, which have received inadequate attention in most contemporary office buildings, are effectiveness, component efficiency, occupancy well-being, and management control.

Effectiveness—Design, planning, engineering, construction, staffing, and other such building decisions are made on the basis of explicit and implicit cost benefit analyses. Trade-offs are made between how well a particular component will perform (component efficiency), the impact the component and its performance will have on the individual and group users of the building (occupancy well-being), and the ability to organize and manage the relationship between component efficiency and well-being (management efficiency).

For example, using these concepts, the effectiveness of a conference room in an office building might be described as follows. A heating, ventilating, and air conditioning (HVAC) system is first evaluated for its efficiency, its low initial and life cycle costs, and a specified number of air changes per hour (ACH). The second evaluation component is how conference room users react to the way the heat and smoke are actually exhausted when the room is in use. If lingering smoke cuts meetings short or reduces the use of the room, then its effectiveness has been affected. The third criteria for evaluation of the effectiveness of the room is in terms of users' ability to manage and control the room, such as to boost the exhaust system as deemed desirable by users.

Component efficiency refers to the degree to which a particular environmental or physical component of a building meets the performance, specific to a particular condition, for which it was designed at the least cost. Thus, an assessment of ventilation efficiency would compare the cost of HVAC systems to the ACH and distribution characteristics various systems achieve. Space efficiency is measured in terms of the number of usable square feet compared to the total square footage. "Effectiveness," as distinct from efficiency, takes the actual effects on occupancy more into account in the cost benefit equation.

Occupancy well-being refers to the qualities of life provided for building occupants and users, including mutual effects of environmental satisfaction, job performance, organizational productivity, and physical health. Illumination levels which are inappropriate for specific tasks or which produce glare may diminish the well-being of occupants in terms of health and job performance.

Management efficiency refers to the way in which a building is run, how it is managed and controlled to maximally accommodate and respond to the needs of building users. Management is a major theme in total building performance because it constitutes a complex set of regulatory and control mechanisms that keep the building functioning. Who controls is an important issue. Degree of control appears to influence occupant perceptions of environmental performance and satisfaction.

Component efficiency, occupancy well-being, and management efficiency help to describe a building's performance and effectiveness at a particular time. Actual occupancy and use means dealing with a dynamic environment that changes over time. Two time dimensions must be added—incremental change and major shifts—to complete the picture of total building performance. These two themes stress the ability of a building to maintain the required level of performance as natural and successive changes occur. *Incremental change* refers to the ability of a building to be easily adapted to meet small-scale changes which continually occur within the uses of any building, such as shifts in work group layout. *Major shifts* refers to shifts of knowledge, technology, or use to which a building may be subject. In recent times, major shifts which have had significant impacts on building performance include energy conservation measures, solar technology, interior space planning, and office automation.

A Transdisciplinary Approach

Diagnostic methodologies have been developed to measure and assess total building performance of actual occupied conditions, that is, to ascertain the integral performance of building systems, elements, occupants, and operations. The work, part of which is described in following paragraphs, is unique in that it blends assessment of specific detailed systems performance with that of user satisfaction and other aspects of occupancy performance. Both quantitative and qualitative data and information on the workplace are included.

The approach taken in building diagnostics is highly innovative. In order to solve the complex problems being encountered, investigators have to diagnose buildings in transdisciplinary ways. Such an approach requires developing new methods and techniques to assess:

1. Building quality in terms of balancing fuel expenditures with the impact of air and lighting quality on productivity;

2. Desired environmental performance criteria expressed in terms of the impact on workers in their workplaces, rather than in more traditional abstract quantitative modes, such as ACH;

3. Relationships between interior layouts, employee control over their privacy and territory, and questions of productivity and satisfaction.

A transdisciplinary approach to problem solving requires that each disciplinary subgroup not only achieve expert understanding of the problem within their own discipline, but that they also keep in mind a larger shared picture of the team's joint goals. Data must be gathered concurrently and analyzed to test findings and implications of decisions in each area. Recommendations must be developed to minimize negative side effects to the total building's performance and effectiveness. A transdisciplinary building diagnostic team includes building scientists, sociologists, psychologists, architects, engineers, building managers, and occupants. The team must have a collective competence in acoustics, lighting, ventilation, air quality, space planning, user attitudes and behavior, energy use, and building management, to name just a few areas of competence.

Diagnostic assessment includes a range of disciplinary tests and methods: occupancy analysis, including behavior, attitude, and actual use assessment; building enclosure studies, including air leakage quantification and migration; acoustics and vibration; illumination; thermal comfort; electrical systems performance; HVAC systems performance, including air distribution and circulation; air quality; and energy utilization.

Occupancy Analysis

Occupancy analysis is one essential part of a transdisciplinary approach to diagnosing occupied buildings. It provides critical base data and information on occupancy needs, patterns, and misfits to complement, enrich, and focus other tests. It deals with actual occupancy and use conditions in the building at the time of tests.

Occupancy analysis also provides an initial screening functioning in a large study by using key informant interviews and systematic observations which provide a general overview of conditions and levels of satisfaction while focusing upon localized problems or misfits [8]. Through the use of questionnaires distributed to a sample of occupants, a profile of standard conditions and levels of satisfaction and perceived comfort can be prepared for each space and for the building as a whole.

Gathered with concurrent base instrument testing of ambient environmental conditions, occupancy analysis data can be used to focus more detailed testing in specific areas as necessary, thus reducing the enormous costs of blanket instrument testing. Occupancy analysis provides critical data on perceived environmental comfort and effectiveness to compare with the actual measurement of environmental conditions. Occupancy analysis is also concerned with planning for change over time without a loss of environmental quality.

A Case Study

The Context

This transdisciplinary research study project was carried out from 1982 to 1983 by a team of professionals with varied training and expertise in areas ranging from energy analysis, ventilation, air quality, lighting, and acoustics through occupancy analysis and building management. The project aim was to develop new diagnostic techniques for improving the fit between building occupancy and performance. A building located on a downtown site in a major Canadian city was selected for study not because it had problems but because it was a typical general purpose office building. The building had recently achieved full occupancy and was experiencing difficulty in achieving a reasonable energy budget. One of the goals of the project was to provide specific data and recommendations for improved energy performance, while improving or at least maintaining adequate ambient conditions and the quality of the work environment for occupants [9].

The Building

The U-shaped building includes eight stories and a basement, with a total building area of 65 032 m² (700 000 ft²) and an estimated capacity of 2500 occupants. A wide range of federal government departments and agencies began to occupy the building in 1978, and full capacity was reached in 1982 with 42 different lettings. Because of a government restraint program, as of January 1983 there were approximately 1800 employees working in the building with approximately 10 to 12% of the desks vacant. The government services offered in this building attract an estimated average daily visitor population of 3000 to 4000 people, many more than the actual total employee population.

The building's U-shape defines a central interior atrium that starts on the second floor and is two stories high. Main entrances to the building are on the first, or ground, floor. The ground floor is connected to the second floor atrium by escalators and elevators. The ground and second floors include major public spaces and services such as a post office and stores as well as office areas.

The design concept for the office areas was to provide 80% open office space with enclosed spaces provided away from the window walls. The configuration of the building overlaid by the interior circulation patterns and core locations create floor shapes and sizes that differ at almost every level.

Each office area is unique in shape, size, depth, and orientation. Continuous windows on the facade give office spaces generally good access to exterior light and views, especially on the north, east, and west edges. The distance to windows from some workstations on the south side of the building may be as great as 27.4 m (90 ft).

Three mechanical systems service the building. One system services the basement and first and second floors. A second and third system each services half of Floors 3 to 8. The building systems were designed exclusively for open office plan, with air distribution, fluorescent lighting, and fire sprinklers integrated into a suspended coffered ceiling system.

Perimeter heating is provided along the exterior walls. The air handling system is a variable air volume (VAV), with primary air diffusers located in the ceiling coffer grid along the perimeter walls. Return air is carried through a ceiling plenum. Power and communications are provided from the ceiling through power and communication (PAC) poles, even near exterior walls. A Honeywell Delta 1000 computer is used to monitor the mechanical systems and to switch lights on and off. Four building engineers use the information from this central source to adjust the HVAC systems as necessary.

Methodology

Prior to in-depth site investigations by the entire diagnostic team, the occupancy analysis group conducted a brief preliminary survey of the building. Two members of the five-person occupancy analysis group spent a week on site to establish base information about such characteristics as numbers of users and operating procedures, to make contact with each occupant group, and to prepare up-to-date layout plans for use by the larger team.

The occupancy analysis group then developed a stratified random sampling approach that allowed the team to analyze data according to each specific work group as well as by room or work area. To draw the sample, each workstation on the updated layout plans was numbered with a code that included floor, space, and desk references. The sample was first stratified by floor and room. Within each room, a random 25% sample of 464 desks was chosen to receive a long in-depth questionnaire. All other desks received a short summary questionnaire.

From the sample of 464, we randomly selected a subsample of 29 workstations, at each of which thermal comfort, air quality, acoustic, and illumination data were gathered as well as data on occupants' perceptions, attitudes, behaviors, and backgrounds. These data are being compared and contrasted to produce a comprehensive picture of the impacts of the ambient environment on individual occupants. This sampling plan provided the framework that unified all diagnostic testing in the building. It allowed qualitative and quantitative data to be cross-related and analyzed and facilitated communications about work in progress. Prior to arriving in the field, each team member received a workbook with up-to-date layouts and the sample location specially indicated for individual reference and notes.

The entire diagnostic team of 16 individuals was in the field at the same time for approximately 2 weeks. The occupancy analysis group was the first group into every occupied space. This group administered focused interviews with managers and handed out questionnaires to other users pri ,ı to further instrument testing and discussions which otherwise might have biased results. All managers, facilities coordinators, building operators, and other key informants were interviewed, totaling 66 focused interviews. Sample workstations were systematically observed for indications of use and need. This information was shared with members of the entire diagnostic team at daily debriefing sessions, enabling the team to develop hypotheses about, and to anticipate special conditions in, each space before carrying out further measurements. As soon as the interviews were completed and questionnaires distributed in a space, other measurements were taken at the sample workstations.

Communications between disciplines about the various substudies and tests were critical to maintain the transdisciplinarity of the diagnostic work. At the end of each day of field work, the entire team met around plans of the building to discuss work done and to develop joint insights, strategies, and hypotheses about data collected and problems encountered. Team members annotated directly onto plans shared observations, findings, and comments for collective reference and further analysis. As testing proceeded, findings and observations began to reinforce one another and to better define priorities and potential responses.

A common coding scheme was used to enable the team to compare instrument measurements of ambient qualities, occupant perceptions of these qualities, and established standards such as those of ASHRAE. These comparisons are being analyzed for the sample of 29 workstations to probe the actual performance and interactions of the various ambient environmental components on a microscale. Other studies focused on interactive forces on sector and building-wide scales. Computer energy modeling, simulation, and cost benefit analysis have been carried out and are part of final recommendations [10].

General Occupancy Analysis Findings

Unlike previous buildings we have diagnosed, the building was not selected as a study site because of occupant dissatisfaction. Rather, the team was called in to improve energy performance without creating occupant dissatisfaction so often associated with energy savings in tight buildings. The questionnaire data show that employees in this building generally feel it is a slightly above average building in which to work. In the context of this adequate assessment, employees rank some environmental qualities of the building slightly above average, such as electric lighting, and rank others very much lower, such as ventilation. Taking the building as a whole, occupant perceptions can be used to distribute environmental qualities into four problem levels as shown in Table 1.

Perceived occupant rankings of these problems differ between specific areas of the building. Assessments of visual privacy in the workspace are largely determined by whether the workspace has a door or is a screened location in an open area. Similarly, people occupying private offices rank speech privacy and noise quite differently than those in open office areas, although there are other privacy issues within enclosed offices. Relative humidity is ranked low throughout the building, partly due to climate and partly to building operation and maintenance procedures. Employees clearly consider ventilation to be a problem in the building, with a lack of fresh air being the greatest single perceived problem. Odors also are perceived as a problem. In addition, many comments offered in interviews and insights gained from systematic observations raised questions about the interactive effects between the performance of the HVAC systems, and the ventilation, relative humidity, and temperature those systems deliver, with other building systems such as lighting and partitions. Furthermore, the problems which we discovered, such as temperature fluctuations and lack of thermal control, are similar to

TABLE 1—*Levels of building-wide environmental problems perceived by occupants.*

Level	Problems
I[a]	illumination
	workspace arrangements
	layout
II	daylighting
III	temperature
IV[b]	visual privacy
	ventilation
	relative humidity
	speech privacy and noise

[a]The fewest problems were on this level.
[b]The most problems were on this level.

those we have encountered in other buildings and illustrate a lack of coordinated performance fit between systems throughout the building.

Integrated Performance Assessment: Ventilation, Relative Humidity, and Temperature

Data from instrument assessment taken individually of temperature, relative humidity, and ventilation indicate minor problems with performance in each discrete area. More complex problems emerge, however, when these assessments are linked to occupancy use patterns and concerns, all of which can be the result of cumulative deficiencies in design, fit-up, operation, maintenance, and use. An integrated assessment of the actual performance of the HVAC system links data on mechanical systems with occupancy and other data. Such integrated analysis explains many of the problems that occupants perceive with ventilation, temperature, and relative humidity, which stem in part from a lack of attention to component efficiency, management, and occupant well-being in air quality, distribution, and circulation. As in most buildings, air supply is controlled by monitoring temperature and humidity, not by monitoring the quality of air circulation at people level. The team developed insights into the closely related issues of air quality, distribution, and circulation based on initial analysis of occupants and their activities.

Major decisions impacting air quality include design and operation decisions about the degree of fresh air intake versus recirculated air. Actual operation modes can reduce system design performance. System operation procedures, which are inappropriate to occupant needs, can decrease the energy effectiveness of systems throughout the building and diminish the quality of work conditions. Interviews with building engineers revealed this in our case study. Each engineer had a different perception of how the building systems operate. None had a clear picture of building energy costs, nor did they, as a group, consciously employ coordinated energy conserving procedures. Furthermore, each engineer used personal performance criteria when operating the building systems. Such practices result in occupants being exposed to changes in temperature, humidity, and ventilation as engineer work shifts change, and energy is not conserved.

Innumerable occupant complaints about intermittent strange odors were traced back to one humidification system, which was seldom run despite frequently low relative humidities (20% or less). When humidifiers are intermittently used, the water supply is subject to stagnation and calcification, emitting an odor to supply air, which generates complaints from occupants. Cleaning this particular system is complicated by the lack of an appropriate drain and by the apparent frequency with which it must be done.

Assessment of ventilation requirements has been at only a gross level. A unique aspect of this particular building is the extremely high flow of visitor traffic. The majority of visitor traffic ends up in seven major waiting rooms throughout the building. For instance, the Job Bank has an average of 800 visitors per day, and Immigration has 300 to 500 people per day. Although the density of people in the waiting areas is often considerably higher than in adjacent office areas, both the waiting and office spaces are usually on the same ventilation zones and controls, so that air conditioning cannot respond uniquely to the increased and variable loads of the waiting areas. Smoking and other odors are also particular problems, and carbon dioxide (CO_2) measurements were high (900 ppm versus an ASHREA comfort standard of 325 ppm). The buildup of CO_2, or oxygen depletion, appears to influence users' perception of air quality. As CO_2 and heat build up, occupants feel that the air is stuffy. These conditions are not only offensive but often are stressful for waiting clients as well as for staff who work in or near these waiting areas.

The HVAC systems are centrally controlled and are operated on an assumed 9:00 a.m. to 5:00 p.m., Monday through Friday, maximum and continuous occupancy condition. In this building, 25% of the occupants are normally at work before 7:15 a.m., well before systems are ready to cope with these loads. Seven percent of all occupants with assigned desks in the building regularly work out of the building, and are *in* the building the equivalent of only 1 day per week. An additional 11% work out of the building at least half time. Yet prior to this study, all space in which these employees worked was continuously lit and conditioned to standard levels whether occupied or not during "occupancy hours." Such an operation pattern is neither efficient nor effective.

More serious problems can arise when the operating pattern does not fit actual use. The building contains a print shop without special ventilation zones or controls. A print shop employee working overtime on the weekend on a rush job became ill after working with standard print room supplies without adequate ventilation, since conditioning of space is minimal during off-hours in order to conserve energy.

Copiers also often negatively affect employees' perception of air quality and ventilation. Most copiers generate some degree of heat and particulate or other pollution, yet a majority of copiers are located in office areas with little or no special venting or ventilation. One high volume copier was installed in a separate room that appeared to be vented. During an interview, the manager of that area reported that excessive temperatures from this copier had been the source of a staff grievance. He later incidentally observed that absenteeism had trebled since move in. The temperature in the copier room never dropped below 32.2°C (90°F) during working hours, and in the adjacent open office area we observed a large number of fans and air ecologizers. Closer inspection of the copier vent revealed that the exhaust air was being dumped into the open plenum above the suspended ceiling, raising the temperature in surrounding office areas. In another situation, a vent dumped warm copier exhaust air into an external wall, raising the possibility of material degradation on the building enclosure.

The introduction of data and word processing workstations also has been inadequately planned and has created problems. In one installation, a room 6.7 by 12.8 m was enclosed on the south perimeter of the building to accommodate twelve word processing workstations. Heat from the machines together with solar gain became so excessive in the space that staff walked off the job. When a unit air conditioner and humidifier were installed, heat was reduced, but the air conditioner was noisy and did not provide uniform cooling throughout the room.

Air distribution decisions, such as the size of ducts, the layout of zones including the length of runs, the location of diffusers and controls, and the type of return plenum also influence effective temperature and ventilation. In this building, performance of the systems was diminished by the lack of appropriate mechanical and electrical fit-up. After the design and installation of the ventilation system, partitions were built without adjustments to the ventilation system and controls. Many office areas have some or all of their thermostats in a separate, adjacent space. Often two such thermostatically linked spaces have inconsistent uses, different solar orientation, and are dissimilar in size. Over half of the departments in this building report thermostatic zone problems. For example, a thermostat located in a meeting room controls both the meeting room and the adjacent open office areas. When the meeting room is in use, heat builds up and the thermostat calls for cool air. The result is that energy is expended to cool the open office area, which does not need cooling, as well as the meeting room which does. Occupants in the open office experience discomfort and may turn on space heaters.

The converse also occurs. Some thermostats located in a surrounding open office area control the temperature and ventilation for a small meeting room. The meeting room becomes hot and stuffy when in use because there is no thermostat in the space to respond to changed conditions. Side effects include: people avoid using the meeting rooms, holding meetings/discussions at their desks, thus distracting others in the open area; when the meeting room is in use the door is left open, reducing confidentiality and increasing distractions for workstations located near the door; fans are used in the meeting room, increasing energy consumption and generally not improving conditions. In sum, occupants suffer, meetings may be less effective, and energy is wasted.

Another problem of inappropriate mechanical fit-up relates to the design of a return air plenum between the suspended ceiling and the slab. As fit-up proceeded, many partitions were built and other interruptions introduced into the plenum space. One result is that, through large areas of the building, the return air streams through occupied spaces rather than through the plenum. Some occupants in the paths of these streams experience drafts and temperature fluctuations and are exposed to odors and other pollutants. Other occupants work in areas with minimal effective air return.

Team members, following up occupant complaints about lack of ventilation, found instances where diffusers, probably disconnected while lighting fixtures were being installed, spilled air into the plenum. In other cases, reduced performance stemmed from a lack of building systems maintenance and testing procedures. For example, some variable air volume boxes were malfunctioning due to lack of maintenance, allowing boxes to shut entirely if heat is called for, supplying little or no ventilation during perimeter heating cycles. Sensors throughout the building were not regularly calibrated so that the systems they control often did not respond to actual conditions. For example, additional cool air may be supplied to an already cool space. Energy is not efficiently utilized and occupants suffer discomfort.

Finally, the circulation of air within occupied areas is greatly affected by the selection and placement of furniture, equipment, and screens within spaces. The selection of screens in open offices is a good example of decision conflict. Screens are selected to increase privacy, both visual and acoustic, and to enhance decor. However, their selection affects the performance of several systems. High screens which sit on the floor are selected because they are believed to provide greater acoustical privacy. Tests, conducted with tracer gases and thermographic imagery, in workstations enclosed by high screens which extend to the floor demonstrate that air from the diffusers flows along the ceiling and never penetrates down into the screened areas to reach occupant nose level. The result is little effective ventilation. This situation could be greatly improved if screens were raised off the floor several inches. In addition, high screens block light from ceiling fixtures and greatly reduce effective illumination at the work surface. The choice of dark or deep-colored screens may further negate illumination effectiveness.

Office layouts have significant impact on how people use space and how effectively energy used for lighting, temperature, and ventilation is in promoting occupant well-being and productivity. Even when initial layout designs respond effectively to occupancy, office layouts are continuously modified over time by official actions planned by the tenant department and by independent actions of individual occupants, such as rearranging screens and reorienting desks. Both types of changes often are uninformed and do not take into account the trade-offs inherent in layout alternatives between performance of thermal comfort, air circulation and quality, illumination, and visual and acoustic privacy.

To compound problems of temperature and ventilation, occupants often have little or no understanding of how the building systems work—how to make their spaces warmer or cooler, control air flow, get enough light, or achieve acoustic privacy. Without information, occupants develop personal theories about how systems work and use these theories in controlling or adjusting their environments to achieve what they believe to be improved performance. This results in actions such as bringing in fans and heaters, blocking heat registers, taping over air diffusers, and tampering with thermostats (even the tamper-proof ones), actions that often increase energy expenditure, unbalance systems, and reduce intended performance.

Summary

This approach to diagnosing total building performance demonstrates that occupants can be reliable informants on the performance adequacy of a building's environment and systems. Interview, observation, and questionnaire data indentify many problems which would be more time-consuming and costly to identify by other test methods.

Even in an "energy conserving" building design, inadvertent energy drains and cumulative reduced systems performance can be considerable when occupancy and use patterns are neither anticipated nor responded to and when occupants do not know the consequences of their actions. Diagnostic studies demonstrate that the degree of environmental quality and energy effectiveness achieved in a building is highly dependent on how well design, occupancy, and facility management are integrated. To keep buildings effective requires a better understanding of the delicate balance between decisions made during design, fit-up, occupancy, operation, and maintenance. It also requires assessments of the actual performance of building systems under the dynamic conditions of occupancy.

References

[1] Mill, Peter A. D., "Fundamental Considerations Prior to Diagnosing Total Building Performance," in *Energy Conservation in the Built Environment*, 1982, pp. 2.387–2.410.
[2] Sterling, E., Sterling, T., and McIntyre, D. "New Health Hazards in Sealed Buildings," *AIA Journal*, April 1983.
[3] Moramarco, S. S., "Does Your Office Make You Sick?," *American Health*, March, 1982.
[4] Stewart, T. F. M., "Practical Experiences in Solving VDU Ergonomic Problems," in *Ergonomic Aspects of Visual Display Terminals*, E. Granjean and E. Vigliani, Eds., Taylor and Francis, London, 1980.
[5] National Research Council, Committee on Vision, *Video Displays, Work, and Vision*, National Academy Press, Washington, DC, 1983.
[6] Duffy, F. et al, *The ORBIT Study: Information Technology and Office Design*, London, England, April 1983.
[7] Architectural Diagnostics, "Impact Assessment on Office Environments of the DOC Office Communications Systems Field Trial," Department of Communications, Ottawa, Sept. 1985.
[8] Drake, P., "Building Diagnostics: The Canadian Experience," in *A Report from the Workshop on Building Diagnostics*, Advisory Board on the Built Environment, National Academy Press, Washington, DC, 1983.
[9] Building Diagnostics, Inc., and Architectural and Building Sciences, Public Works Canada, "Energy and Occupancy," report to Public Works Canada, Ottawa, March 1983.
[10] "Architectural and Building Sciences, Public Works Canada," Vol. 1: "Summary Report, Stage 1 in the Development of Total Building Performance," Public Works Canada, Ottawa, 1983.

Jay D. Farbstein,[1] *John Archea,*[2] *Min Kantrowitz,*[3]
Robert G. Shibley,[4] *Jean Wineman,*[2]
and Craig M. Zimring[2]

Designing and Building with Rehabilitation in Mind

REFERENCE: Farbstein, J. D., Archea, J., Kantrowitz, M., Shibley, R. G., Wineman, J., and Zimring, C. M., **"Designing and Building with Rehabilitation in Mind,"** *Building Performance: Function, Preservation, and Rehabilitation, ASTM STP 901,* G. Davis, Ed., American Society for Testing and Materials, Philadelphia, 1986, pp. 39-45.

ABSTRACT: Rehabilitation is viewed as a series of modifications that enhance a building. In this sense, rehabilitation can occur at any point in the building's life, even during construction. These modifications will inevitably occur as total building performance is better understood and as the performance objectives for a building change over its useful life. Design and construction should, therefore, provide for this inevitable rehabilitation. However, it is rare that a client requests a study of total building performance before the building is built.

The state of Florida has recently commissioned a diverse team to investigate its building delivery process. The study is focused upon Florida A & M University's new school of architecture, with less detailed examinations of five other new buildings of varied functions.

The key features of our study include a number of tasks: first, tracking the construction process of the six buildings (analysis of program and design decisions, modeling of the state's building delivery process, assessing change orders); second, monitoring the move-in process and premove adaptations; third, carrying out postoccupancy evaluations of the six buildings. These will be comprehensive evaluations, looking at user response to the designed environment as well as technical performance in terms of energy, maintenance, and repairs. This paper describes in more detail the methods used for each task.

The significance of the study lies in its comprehensive, integrative approach, where information from each task will be weighed in light of the concerns and findings from the other tasks. We will try to answer questions about the appropriateness of the programming, design, construction, and management processes used. Technical and functional performance also will be compared. Overall performance will be judged in the light of the multifaceted points of view of the various interested parties. It is hoped that, as a result of

[1]President, Jay Farbstein & Associates, San Luis Obispo, CA 93406.
[2]Associate Professor, College of Architecture, Georgia Institute of Technology, Atlanta, GA 30332.
[3]President, Min Kantrowitz and Associates, Albuquerque, NM 87102.
[4]Head, Department of Architecture, School of Architecture and Environmental Design, State University of New York at Buffalo, Buffalo, NY 14214.

this study, rehabilitative modifications during initial construction will be reduced on future projects.

KEY WORDS: total building performance, performance monitoring, postoccupancy evaluation

The project that provides the context for this paper is just getting under way. It is of interest to ASTM because of the opportunity it gives to discuss issues concerning the achievement and maintenance of environmental quality (that is, how to make buildings whose performance responds well to the social, functional, and technical requirements of their occupants and owners).

One of the major concerns facing those involved with facility development is how to organize a project development and management system that can deliver required performance at acceptable costs of money and effort. This problem is compounded by the multifaceted nature of governmental building clients and users, where several agencies may be responsible for funding decisions, another may own the building, yet another may manage it, and still others may occupy and use the space with nonofficial users and neighbors.

We postulate that the match between the performance required of a building and that actually provided is accommodated through a gradual process of adaptation. Different elements of the process are accomplished at each phase of facility development, construction, and use. Therefore, there is a need for an integrated program, design, build, evaluate, modify sequence.

There is a much greater ability to affect functional and technical performances—and at a much lower cost—at the early stages of program development and design [1]. If required performance can be established and responded to at these stages, modifications at later stages can be limited in scope and cost. Thus, the adjustments or "rehabilitations" can be better controlled.

A Model of "Rehabilitation" Throughout Facility Development and Occupation

"Rehabilitation" can be viewed as those actions that allow a building to be returned to a state of usefulness. Presuming that a facility was originally useful, rehabilitation restores it to acceptable (or better) levels of functional and technical performance. This implies that programming and design are processes of "habilitation," the making of facilities that are habitable.

In fact, the facility development and occupancy process involves planning for, and successively moving nearer and farther from, a state where satisfactory accommodation is provided. In the early stages, required performance is defined. As design progresses, a physical solution which is expected to give satisfactory performance at an acceptable cost is proposed and developed for construction. Many trade-offs and modifications occur during design as the solution moves closer and closer toward a satisfactory one. During construction, further decisions are made, and deviations from the design almost always occur. These deviations involve design modifications and, sometimes, changes to work already in place. They are intended to achieve cost savings, to make the building conform better to the design (where it deviated incorrectly from it), or to respond to newly emerging or changing occupant needs.

By the time occupants move into the building, many changes may have occurred which would modify the program requirements as well as the design. During occupancy, many more changes occur. The latter range from fine-tuning the building to minor repairs to major modification or reconstruction.

Table 1 shows how building modifications respond to performance requirements as they are developed, are tested, and change through the phases of facility development and occupancy.

It is the hypothesis of this paper that these modifications should be understood as a process of feedback/feedforward working to create and maintain an environment which is at least presumably satisfactory in supporting its occupants' needs. Understood in this way, the planning, construction, and modification process implies an explicit set of monitoring functions which are needed to steer the facility towards performance in the range of acceptability. While these monitoring functions are becoming accepted in the practice of construction management and value engineering for technical and cost performance, they are less common for functional performance. Yet, function can be compromised by technical changes. Therefore, the monitoring needs

TABLE 1—*Building modifications in response to changing performance requirements.*

Phase	Performance Requirements	Building Modifications
Programming	Initial specification of performance requirements (easy to change)	None required, only change program
Design	Translates program into design which responds (more or less) to performance specification (not time-consuming to change)	None required, only change design
Construction	Translates design documents into physical product (some aspects relatively easy to change, others harder and more expensive)	By change order: may involve alteration in designed or specified items; may involve tearing out work already in place
Initial occupancy	Performance begins to be tested in use (minor adaptations easy, major ones harder/more expensive)	Minor changes by users' maintenance staff; major changes will be required if mission changes or functions change in ways that were not anticipated in program or design
Ongoing occupancy	Performance may be formally evaluated by a POE; performance requirements may change (building may be capable of easy response or not; can be very expensive)	Ongoing maintenance and repair; building will begin to deteriorate, requiring more maintenance and more functional modifications

to be of an integrated nature, balancing the technical and functional implications of any proposed design solution or building modification. The remainder of this paper describes such an integrated process that is currently being applied in Florida.

Monitoring Performance for Continual Rehabilitation

To provide a broad-based approach to the monitoring and evaluation of the Florida facilities, a systematic research procedure has been developed involving four methodological approaches. These approaches will be carried out by a team of researchers with expertise in each area. The team will be assisted by an advisory task force representing the interests of people who have been involved in project planning and funding and who will be involved in the operation of the buildings.

The considerable lead time for the project will allow the team to explore a wide range of important interrelationships between user satisfaction, behavior, and physical building performance that are seldom addressed. The collection of premove-in data allows comparison of user satisfaction and behavior before and after occupancy; it also allows programmatic and design predictions to be compared to actual behavior. Moreover, the collection of data at six sites allows comparisons between multiple buildings and the creation of norms for technical and functional performance.

Monitoring the design and construction management process not only allows lessons to be learned about reducing time and cost problems in design delivery but also helps clarify the impact of these phases on building performance and user satisfaction. (For example, it may emerge that problems in use or physical comfort are due to changes during construction rather than to programmatic or design solutions.)

Finally, the planned ongoing postoccupancy evaluation affords an opportunity to evaluate the facility's capability to respond to changes in use and performance requirements. Explicit performance requirements and quantitative criteria will be developed for each of the six buildings. This will be done in the areas of user satisfaction, productivity, energy utilization, comfort, security, and so forth. In evaluating the performance of building systems, criteria developed from prior projects will be compared to data gathered during the construction phase and to instrument measures taken of each subsystem during the occupancy period. The next section describes methods to be used for the postoccupancy evaluation.

Methodological Strategies for Postoccupancy Evaluation

Four methodological strategies appear to be appropriate to assess the interrelationships between building performance and behavior. These strategies include evaluation of user satisfaction, attitudes, and behavioral responses to the buildings; analysis of patterns and intensity of use of the buildings; assessment of physical conditions in the buildings; and monitoring and evaluation of the design and construction management process.

User Satisfaction Analysis—This analysis will involve obtaining primary data directly from building users through the use of questionnaires and interviews to assess users' perceptions, attitudes, and satisfaction with the buildings. In addition to administrative personnel, staff, and client groups, this analysis will include students, faculty, support personnel (technical, clerical, maintenance), visitors, and other interested persons (such as alumni). The analysis of user satisfaction will focus on major interior and exterior spaces and will address at least four issues:

1. Satisfaction with and perceptions of: building use and environmental conditions, including space utilization (intensity of use); the fit between activities and the physical setting; energy-conscious design; and other special features.

2. The image of the building interior, exterior, and setting, including scale, form, materials, and finishes.

3. Safety of persons and property (health, safety, and security), including 24-hour use of the building, theft and vandalism, accidents, and crimes against persons.

4. Communication and social interaction, including intrafaculty and staff, faculty-student, and student-student communication; the accommodation of small, moderate, and large groups; and the ability to achieve solitary and small-group privacy.

Building Use Analysis—Observational analysis and behavioral mapping will be used to assess space utilization and behavioral responses to the buildings. The analysis will focus on such issues as levels of space utilization, efficiency of use, and the fit between activities and the physical setting. In the case of the new architecture building, for example, these issues would include use of design labs, accommodation of specialized activities such as juries and charettes, adequacy of faculty offices, and use of exterior spaces.

Building Performance Analysis—This analysis will involve the use of observational techniques and instrumentation to evaluate building performance and to document how the building responds to demands made upon it (including weathering, wear and tear, vandalism, etc.). Remote sensing by permanently and temporarily installed instruments will provide data on physical conditions in the buildings during different times of the day and year and will be used in an energy analysis. Monitoring by "behavioral trace" analysis will be used to assess building response.

Design and Construction Management Analysis—We will monitor design and construction management to determine patterns of change orders and to provide a comparative analysis of the speed and efficiency of the construction processes used on the six buildings. Due to the orientation of the ASTM audience, more detail is offered here concerning the assessment of construction processes and the monitoring of technical performance.

Tracking Construction

Time and cost problems in the construction phase of a building are not necessarily the result of design or drafting errors. Often, problems are a result of construction management, of conflicts between design concept and the limits of physical structure, of a lack of clarity in the program or design, or even of a client's initial lack of interest in the program or design and his/her sudden involvement once construction has begun. In each of these instances, an attempt is made to solve problems at a point in the process when it is very difficult and expensive to make modifications.

In the present project, several aspects of the building delivery process will be addressed.

First, the key steps in the university's and state's design delivery process will be researched and a systems model developed through interviews and review of documents. The process will be evaluated with respect to adequacy of information flow, effectiveness of decision making, and so forth. Any innovations in the building delivery process will be recorded and examined for their immediate and long-term impacts on building costs, building quality (as defined by both building performance and suitability for users), and construction scheduling. The process also will be compared to other systems such as those of the state of Illinois, U.S. National Park Service, U.S. Army Corps of Engineers, and the government of New Zealand.

Second, we will document and analyze program and design intentions to help establish performance expectations for the six buildings. These intentions will serve to guide the subsequent evaluations. For example, change orders are often the result of changes in programmatic requirements which affect scheduling and cost.

Third, we will attend weekly construction meetings to document the construction process and record any changes in strategy. A team member will attend all meetings of the construction management group and record discussions, decisions, and reasons for changes in strategy, sequence, materials, etc.

Fourth, change orders will be recorded and analyzed. Change orders are a common measure of efficiency in construction management. Minimizing change usually minimizes cost and time overruns. The examination of changes ordered during construction and the reasons for them can lead to procedural and technical insights into the problems outlined in previous paragraphs. This examination will enable the research team to describe what changes are most frequently requested, why they are requested, when they occur and with what time/cost penalities, and how they are processed.

We do not necessarily assume that change orders are bad; they can be solutions for saving time or money or improving quality. Nonetheless, they are an acknowledgment that something new was learned during the building process which the owner, architect, and contractor all agree should be addressed. This issue is rooted in the question, "Could that learning have occurred earlier in the process of building delivery (program development or design) and, therefore, have been more easily addressed?"

Monitoring Technical Performance

In addition to monitoring the success of the building functionally and in terms of user satisfaction, our team also will assess its technical performance. This is relatively unusual for a study whose origins defined it as a postoccupancy evaluation (POE), since POE's only rarely have looked at the building as a whole social/technical system. However, this broad point of view is essential if the interactions among parts of the system are to be understood.

Our efforts in this area will include advice to the owners on "instrumentation" of the building for automatic remote sensing of energy/climatic performance (and, perhaps, space use). Such instrumentation will generate data allowing assessment of solar design, showing whether or not conditions within the building approximate design criteria. They also will give a baseline from which to understand user response to interior climatic conditions and comfort. Analysis of utility bills will provide added insight into the building's energy performance.

In addition, we will monitor the physical condition of the building over its first few years of use. This will include on-site observation of vandalism, natural wear and tear, and weathering. We also will track maintenance and repair orders to identify areas where building systems or materials fail or where programmatic changes necessitate building modifications.

Conclusion

In conclusion, we are embarking upon a study that will be rather unique in examining the total delivery system—the functional and technical performance of a set of buildings. This will place us in a position to assess the ability of delivery, planning, design, and management systems to create and maintain facilities which may need less frequent or extensive rehabilitation—since needs should have been anticipated, problems avoided, and changes allowed for in advance.

It will be several years, however, before we are able to report on results and to judge whether or not this promising approach has been successful.

Reference

[1] "Life Cycle Cost Analysis: A Guide for Architects," American Institute of Architects, Washington, DC, 1977.

John M. Gray,[1] *John R. Daish,*[1] *and David Q. Kernohan*[1]

A Touring-Interview Method of Building Evaluation; the Place of Evaluation in Building Rehabilitation

REFERENCE: Gray, J. M., Daish, J. R., and Kernohan, D. Q., **"A Touring-Interview Method of Building Evaluation; the Place of Evaluation in Building Rehabilitation,"** *Building Performance: Function, Preservation, and Rehabilitation, ASTM STP 901,* G. Davis, Ed., American Society for Testing and Materials, Philadelphia, 1986, pp. 46–68.

ABSTRACT: Accommodation options are to purpose build, to use ready-made, or to rehabilitate. The paper argues that rehabilitation is the option most likely to provide for good fit between organization and building. The procurement process must be one which allows management to link decisions about the organization with decisions about the building, taking account of differing interest groups. It is suggested that a participatory form of postoccupancy evaluation is a managable basis for initiating environment/behavior change. The paper gives a step-by-step description of a touring interview method of evaluation in current use in New Zealand and summarizes the lessons learned from efforts to institutionalize postoccupancy evaluation as a normal part of building procurement. The paper concludes with the suggestion that participatory evaluation has utility as a way to involve different interest groups in reaching negotiated agreement in programming for rehabilitation and as a basis for improved overall performance of buildings.

KEY WORDS: building performance, rehabilitation, habitability, organization, participation, postoccupancy evaluation, touring interview

Organizations select, build, or adapt their physical surroundings to satisfy various requirements. But whose requirements? Whose values count in the accommodations stakes? By what processes can management in an organization, faced with the prospect of changing accommodations, come to understand and reconcile the different values and requirements of all groups with an interest in their building?

This paper describes a participatory form of postoccupancy evaluation

[1]Senior lecturers, School of Architecture, Victoria University, Wellington, New Zealand.

from which it has been found that various interest groups can benefit either in terms of the existing facility or in terms of future facilities.

Postoccupancy evaluation (POE) is, of course, ordinarily a process which occurs *after* occupation of a facility. The proposition here is that the participatory "touring interview" method of building evaluation could have considerable utility as a *pre*occupancy planning tool through which management can establish the requirements of different interest groups, obtain a large number of positive ideas about accommodation problems, and gain widespread support for their final accommodation decisions. Participatory POE processes empower various individuals or groups with interests in a building. Groups which otherwise might have little or no say in how a building is designed or operated are able to influence change to the building (or to a building program) to suit their requirements.

When an organization moves to purpose-built, ready-made, or rehabilitated accommodations, it presumably expects to eliminate many of the problems associated with the previous accommodations. But how sure can we be that the accommodations will be better? Who can say that the new accommodations will not throw up a new and unexpected set of technical and functional problems? How can the organization avoid taking with it, like unwanted baggage, existing unresolved social, political, and organizational problems? Traditionally, the technical issues in "building" and the social/political issues in "organization" have been thought of as separate domains operated on by separate professional institutions. This is a fatal separation. Some state-of-the-art practitioners/authors [1-3] provide convincing argument and evidence for treating organizational behavior and the built environment as inseparable dimensions in programming and ongoing operations.

To shift from thinking "building plus organization" as separate entities, to thinking "organization/building" as a unity requires a shift towards joint work on the part of those who traditionally play separate roles. It is extremely unlikely that one person or even a small team could satisfactorily encompass all the knowledge and experience required to tackle change to organization/building as distinct from change to building *or* organization. Some kind of meeting ground is needed—a situation, different players, an agenda, and a process for working together.

Predicting Organizational "Fit" with Respect to Accommodation Options

It is not a simple matter to look at an organization and an existing or proposed building and say how well they "fit." Some design professionals and managers with long experience may understand these matters, but such expert individuals may not be present or available when critical planning decisions are made. How can those in an organization who are not experts in the relationships between buildings and human requirements, and who may not even be aware of the complexities of such relationships, nevertheless make sensible choices when faced with accommodation alternatives? Accommodation decisions without expert intervention or guidance are an ongoing feature of the commercial and industrial world. What are the best chances in this context for a good fit between organization and building?

Some key elements in these questions are:

1. Understanding the organization in such terms as individual, group, and corporate values, goals, operations, and so on.

2. Understanding the building in such terms as structures and services that cannot be altered easily, parts that can be altered or moved easily, layout, equipment, finishes, air quality, normal operation, and so on.

3. Finding a process by which people with various interests can, with or without expert outside help, relate their organizational, group, and individual requirements to the physical constraints and opportunities.

The likelihood that an organization will be able to forecast the degree to which it fits with a building on move-in day and in the future relates to how well the building and the organization are understood. Most people without expert knowledge of buildings find it difficult to understand abstract plans and specifications of buildings but can quite readily make useful judgments about a building if they can see it and experience it directly. This is analogous to choosing clothes. When deciding on tailored clothes, it can be quite difficult to imagine the final article from the sketches, patterns, and verbal descriptions of the tailor. It is helpful to try on a similar article by the same tailor and by inspecting the cloth. Ready-made clothes, on the other hand, can be directly experienced. They can be tried on in the store and assessed for fit.

It is also difficult to know about an organization by simply reading or talking about it, even for experts in management. It is far more real if it can be seen in operation, if the organization can be "toured." It is then that the individual, group, and corporate operations and values may be understood best and with the most certainty. If knowledge of the organization is combined with knowledge of the building, we have the best possible situation for assessing their compatibility (Fig. 1).

The basic accommodations options open to any organization are to purpose-build, to use ready-made, or to rehabilitate. In planning stages, it is clear that the client enjoys (or fears?) the greatest range of possibilities if building from a bare site and the least range of possibilities if moving into ready-made accommodations. The rehabilitation option lies somewhere between these two poles. For designers and clients, rehabilitation means significant opportunities for making meaningful changes to a building to fit with corporate and individual requirements. Rehabilitation, in this respect, is similar to purpose-built in that there is opportunity for major change to the physical environment—the rehabilitated building is, in effect, to the client/occupants, a new building. Rehabilitation also has elements of the ready-made

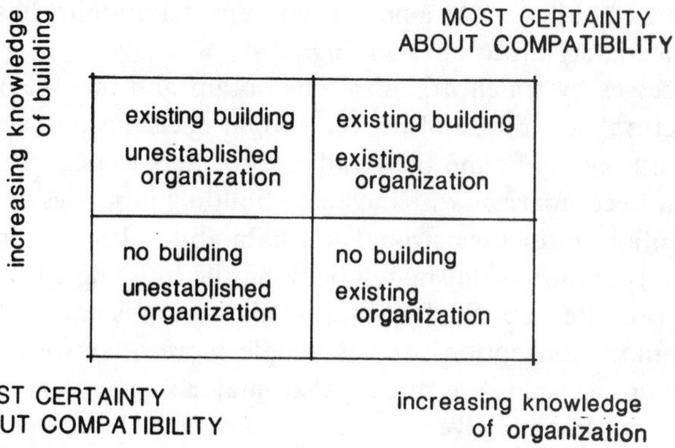

FIG. 1—*Assessing compatibility: a function of combining knowledge about the organization and the building.*

option in that there is a substantial part of the final building to view *before* rehabilitation starts and thereby a better chance for people who are not trained in architecture/building to imagine the end product and make judgments as to its suitability. To return to the clothes-buying analogy, rehabilitation is like buying or inheriting a sound but old-fashioned garment and having it substantially altered to fit a different body for a different occcasion. In short, rehabilitation is an accommodation option which is attractive because it combines some of the predictability and certainty of a ready-made building with the open-ended possibilities of purpose-built premises (Fig. 2).

The Concept of Habitability: Linking Organization and Building through Process

Habitability can be thought of as the degree to which a building can be made agreeable and functional for (or by) the occupants. Conceptually, and more powerfully, it is a dimension which seems allied to Irwin Altman's use of the term "dialectic" to describe an environment/behavior unity [4].

Habitability would be difficult to measure in terms of a building's influence on organizational behavior or in terms of a reciprocal relationship between

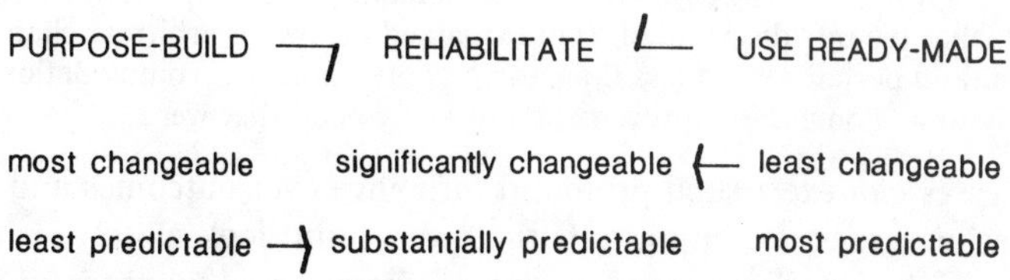

FIG. 2—*Combining the goals of "predictability" and "changeability."*

organization and building. As a holistic concept, habitability has more to do with the dialectic organization/building.

Most processes by which organizations obtain and inhabit buildings involve a structural separation of organizational decisions and building decisions. The building users and the building providers work separately and at arm's length. In comparison with most new building processes or with finding space, rehabilitation focuses strongly on habitability because there is more likely to be recognition of mismatch between the building environment and the organization. Perhaps the fact that rehabilitation is not yet as routine as other accommodation options makes people more attentive to the way in which planning decisions are made. Also, major segments of the puzzle of architecture are already "givens;" some of the major building decisions are made already, leaving room for attention to matters of detail which are important but frequently overlooked. *Process* means more than simply the way something gets done. Process may strongly influence outcome. The process by which various interest groups relate and work towards accommodating an organization is likely to have an influence on habitability.

Process and Product—a Management Dilemma

Processes that are efficient at face value are not necessarily effective in producing results which are satisfactory to the various interests represented in a building. Johnson [5] has cited cases of rehabilitation in Scottish housing areas in which one process resulted in protracted periods of negotiations with disgruntled occupants and eventual complete restructuring of the social makeup of the locality over a period of 7 years.

> The final cost of the exercise is not known, but, even if it is deemed a success on economic grounds, it must be adjudged a failure on social ones. The disruption in the neighborhood would have been no worse if the block had been demolished and redeveloped.

By way of contrast, one success story involved rehabilitation work on housing in Liverpool, England, in which the architects installed a liaison person in a show house in the area to advise and inform tenants about the changes going on and to coordinate the process of "decanting" and rehousing the original families in the same area. The architects in this case [5]

> ... recognized that the *process* of improvement was as important as the end *product*, that tenants disgruntled by unexplained delays, or arbitrary changes in program, and perhaps given less than adequate temporary accommodation were not likely to welcome the improvements, however good they were ....

If processes can exert such profound influence over outcomes and the accommodation issues are important, then we should look closely at the processes by which accommodation options can be assessed by different interest groups, and we should seek processes by which different interest groups in an organization can participate in establishing requirements.

POE as a Manageable Form of Participation in Environment/Behavior-Related Change

Evaluation is a process which can be used to gain information on the two content elements in accommodation—the building and the organization. One form of evaluation called the "touring-interview" is a participatory process which provides a link between different interest groups in a building. It is conceptually an interview in that the participants consist of two groups, one a task group (analogous with the neutral interviewer) and the other an interest group (analogous with the interviewee). This is similar to Fred Steele's use of the touring interview in which an expert consultant walks around a facility with a client [Ref 6, p. 100].

> The touring interview is really a combination of observations and interviews. I ask a client to walk around his spaces with me and free associate about what he sees and feels. I also ask specific questions from time to time, if he has not mentioned an element that I think is significant. However, I try to wait until the client has mentioned whatever is relevant to him, since I do not want my own set of significant elements fed back to me. The aim is to get inside the world of the user . . . .

As with one-person interviews, the group-touring interview is conducted one interest group at a time. To complete a building evaluation, a number of interviews are conducted, each with a different interest group. The interest groups are only brought face-to-face at the discretion of the task group. Whether or not there is face-to-face contact between all interest groups, the POE task group is bound to publish the recommendations and observations of the various interest groups in the wording and form agreed to during the interviews. In this way differences and agreements between interest groups are clarified and shared. Then, at the discretion of the interested parties and management, there may start a round of negotiations to resolve issues.

The Touring Interview Method of Evaluation Developed in New Zealand

The POE program in current use at the Ministry of Works and Development in New Zealand is based on three levels of evaluation. One, the Investigative level of evaluation, has the participatory group touring interview process as its central feature. Other levels of evaluation are adopted in the program (Table 1), but it is the investigative level of POE that has been developed, tested, and implemented over the last 3 years. Its development and place within a POE program is reported elsewhere [7].

The decision to adopt a participatory approach in investigative evaluations is based on the belief that most buildings must satisfy a range of personal and corporate values and different requirements. Any attempt to make an overall evaluation must take into account such diversity. This thinking has led to the development of the idea of evaluating a building by systematically walking through it with representatives from groups of people with distinctly different interests in the facility.

TABLE 1—*Levels of POE in the Ministry of Works and Development (MWD) evaluation program.*

Evaluation Levels	Characteristics of Levels
INDICATIVE	short duration; in the order of 2 person-days; based on short interviews and document reviews; checks attainment of main goals; indicates obvious successes or failures; uses conventional management methods
INVESTIGATIVE	medium duration; in the order of 20 person-days for task group and 1/2 person-day for each "participant"; based on multiple open-ended small-group interview while touring a facility; addresses individual and corporate values/requirements in relation to building and operations; combines social science and management methods
DIAGNOSTIC	medium or long duration; in the order of 15 person-days; focused, expert diagnosis of one facet of a facility or operation; uses quantifiable methods; statistical; analytical

Touring interviews involve two sets of people with distinct roles: various participant groups and one task group (Fig. 3).

The task of a participant group is to evaluate the building from their point of view and as representatives of an "interest group." Where an interest group is small in number, such as a design group of architects and consultants, all may be represented. When the number is large, such as is typically the case with the occupants of a building, then a sample is drawn.

The role of the task group is to facilitate the participant groups in making their evaluations. The task group plans and manages the evaluation tasks, records the evaluation data and its subsequent review, and arranges publication of whatever documents are used to communicate the outcomes. The touring interview involves the participant group and the task group in three connected activities: an introductory meeting, the touring interview itself, and a review meeting. The complete investigative POE process has eight steps, all of

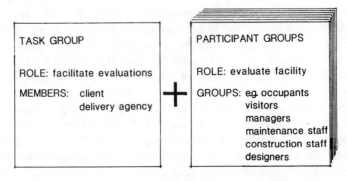

FIG. 3—*Roles in an investigative evaluation.*

which involve the task group and one of which (Step 5) involves the various participant groups:

1. Plan program.
2. Invite participants.
3. Study documents.
4. Prepare for touring interviews.
5. Facilitate touring interviews.
6. Collate and analyze data.
7. Report.

The remainder of this paper is a description, with comment, of the activities within these steps which are necessary to conduct a postoccupancy evaluation, followed by a conclusion which argues that the process has utility as a preoccupancy evaluation tool in rehabilitation.

Step 1: Planning the Evaluation Program

An evaluation may be initiated by any individual or group with a "stake" in the facility; ordinarily, the client or the design agency will propose a POE. In any event, it is crucial that the idea has wide support and the necessary mandates. If information is not asked for, it will not be welcomed, particularly if a part of the findings are negative.

To begin, a task group is formed. The task group has two to four members. It is advisable to draw the personnel from different organizations with a major involvement in the facility to be evaluated. For example, one member could come from the design/delivery agency and one from the funding agency and one from the occupying organization/department.

The task group has a number of preparatory tasks, one of which is to decide who should be involved in the evaluation. The aim is to have a reasonable cross section and sample of those with clearly different principal interests in the building to be evaluated. The choice of whom to invite is obviously influenced by the type of facility and the concerns of those that initiated the evaluation. Ideally, all major interest groups should be represented in an evaluation. For instance, a program may call for evaluations by these groups: occupants, managers, visitors, owner, designers, builders, consultants, maintenance personnel, cleaners, and local residents. In planning the evaluation, six to ten touring interviews are usually scheduled, each with a group of two to six participants who represent a particular interest in the building. The task group should check "what's in it" for each of the participant groups that they would like to invite. If there is no obvious benefit to a group from taking part in an evaluation, then they should probably not take part. Another "rule" for the task group at this stage is to be sure that there is "money in the back pocket"—there must be the mandate and money for something significant and obvious to happen as a result of the evaluation effort.

The task group then programs the POE in more detail, taking resources and constraints into account and planning the tasks in a way that feels most comfortable to them. At the end of this step, the task group will have a list of participant groups to take part in the evaluation, a draft of the touring interview program, and a management plan for the remainder of the POE project. Experience shows that the task group can accomplish most if not all of this first step in a single work session of about 3 hours.

Step 2: Invite Individuals Representing Different Interest Groups to Become Members of Participant Groups in the POE

The total number of people in each group and the number of groups needed to represent a particular interest will depend on the size and diversity of the interest group population. A relatively large population of occupants may call for two or three participant groups of about six members to provide a reasonable cross section of variables such as workplace, job, knowledge, experience, age, gender, and culture. On the other hand, a participant group of three maintenance personnel may represent almost the entire population of maintenance staff for the facility.

The composition of a participant group is usually a matter for considerable debate. The desire for scientific rigor in sampling very often conflicts with practical needs. For instance, it may be extremely difficult socially to say "no" to an individual manager who wants to take part in an evaluation but who has not been "selected" in a random sample. Or the task group may realize that one person proposed as a participant has a forceful personality or by virtue of position is perceived to "have the say" and is therefore likely to dominate other members of the participant group. In one POE in New Zealand, the task group decided to reduce the number of touring interviews by combining two interest groups, senior management, and junior management in one touring interview. In this case, the junior personnel were reluctant to express their opinions in front of their seniors.

Participants should individually receive invitations to attend the evaluation. The invitations are accompanied or followed by a brief explanation of the purpose of the POE and the part participants play in the evaluation. It is important to hear from all participants so that alternative arrangements can be made in the event that someone cannot attend. The invitation step in the process is complete when all participants are confirmed and the program is finalized.

Step 3: Study the Project Documents to Understand the Project Background

This step involves selecting and scanning files and other documents about the building. The purpose is to understand enough background of the building—why it is the way it is now—to be able to prepare a factual summary of its main points. The summary of background is included in the final report on the POE and is used by readers to "flesh out" their knowledge of the building. This helps place the evaluation comments and recommendations in perspective. It begins to explain causes for situations found at the time of an evaluation. For example, in one POE in New Zealand several participant groups were critical of the siting and internal layout of a group of buildings with respect to the views. On the face of it, this appeared to be a design mistake, but the background summary described the circumstances in which the site was developed under instruction from the client, in haste and using plans from a previous project.

A summary description of a project may typically contain the following information:

1. A summary of the "background" of the project, with major events, dates, decisions, costs, and people involved.

2. Diagrammatic plans/layout of the building and site.

3. Brief written description of the facility in terms of the physical provisions and the operations.

Step 4: Prepare for Touring Interviews with Participant Groups

In preparing for the evaluation events "in the field," the task group must allocate tasks to each member and assemble the equipment, documents, and pro formas which will be needed. In essence, the mission of the task group is to manage the process by which the various participant groups evaluate the facility. The task group is not itself judgmental.

There are three main roles for task group members:

1. The facilitator, who guides the participant groups through the process of evaluating the facility and preparing recommendations.

2. The notetaker or "memory," who notes the content of participant observations made during each touring interview and recalls these topics during the review meeting in which the participant group prepares recommendations.

3. The recorder, who transcribes recommendations onto record sheets and takes measurements and makes photographs to quantify and illustrate the participants' observations.

These roles may be shared, swapped, or combined by task group members, depending on individual preferences and abilities and the number of people in the group. The facilitation role is undoubtedly the most demanding and risk-prone of the three task group functions, for which probably the best preparation is experience. In some instances in New Zealand, task groups have gained experience before their first POE by playing out their roles with a group of colleagues who take on the role of participant evaluators. Another training method is to join a task group as an observer. The task group must arrange for a room to be set aside in the building to be evaluated, which is the base from which they work and is the room used to hold meetings with each participant group during the touring interviews. The specific requirements of this room will become clearer in the following section of this paper, in which the touring interviews are described in detail. Naturally, before the POE, the building management must be alerted to the plans to conduct an evaluation. It is advisable to warn middle management—group managers, supervisors, security staff, secretaries, etc. in all occupied parts of the building—so that they and their support staff are not surprised when groups walk through their territories. In one POE in New Zealand, the task group arranged an on-site meeting of eight managers from occupying departments in the building to be evaluated. This took place about 2 months before the POE. At this meeting-cum-workshop, the task group introduced themselves to the managers, outlined the POE process and procedures, and then conducted a mock-up touring interview in which they and the managers participated.

Step 5: Facilitate the Touring Interview Process by which the Participant Groups Evaluate the Facility

Each touring interview involves the participant group and the task group in three connected activities: a briefing, a touring interview or "walkthrough," and a review meeting. In addition to these activities, the task group makes a physical check (measurement) and photographic record of the occupied building. As this step is the central and least familiar part of the participatory POE process, it will be described in detail. Readers with no wish for such detail may gain an overview by reading the subheadings and the first paragraph under each subheading.

Meet Building Management

On arrival at the facility, members of the task group introduce themselves to the management and check that the program arrangements are in order. It is also a good idea to ask management if they would like to meet the task group at the end of the program of touring interviews to review the main findings and recommendations. If the task group is unfamiliar with the building, they should at this stage take a tour to familiarize themselves with the layout.

Set Up the Meeting Room

The meeting room must be set up, and, if necessary, rearranged as a working place in which no single person, with the possible exception of the facilitator, is the focus of attention.

The participatory POE process requires a room in which there is: (1) a white-board or blackboard or large flip chart in easy view of the participant group members with wall space for up to ten large sheets of paper; (2) comfortable chairs arranged in a semicircle so that people can see each other; (3) a round table or low rectangular table in front of the participants, or else no table at all; and (4) shelves or table(s) to one side to hold materials and equipment used by the task group. The room should be secured when left unattended during the walkthroughs and should be well-lit without glare, well-ventilated, and reasonably quiet (Fig. 4).

The Briefing Session

In the briefing session, members of the task group introduce themselves, talk about the purpose of the study, and outline the touring interview procedure. They also explain the roles of the task group and the participant group. The participants are asked to introduce themselves individually, outline their "interests" in the facility, and what they do or have done in pursuit of those interests.

The facilitator starts the session by welcoming the participants and making a personal introduction. In a few minutes the facilitator outlines the purpose of POE, referring particularly to the benefits which the participants can expect, the procedure or "agenda" for each touring interview, and the part the participants are expected to play in the touring interview that follows. The facilitator's role is described, as is the part which the task group will play. The other task group members then introduce themselves and outline, very briefly, their roles.

Next, the facilitator asks the participants to introduce themselves, encouraging each person to talk about their involvement in the building in terms of how long they have been using it, what they do there, what experience they have regarding similar facilities or similar organizations, and so on. Then the facilitator goes over the touring interview and review session procedures in more detail, explaining what will happen, answering questions as they arise,

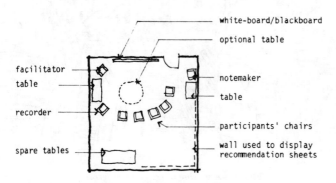

FIG. 4—*A suitable room layout.*

and showing the participant group examples of outcomes from other touring interviews. Before starting on the tour, the route to be taken is discussed. The task group usually will suggest a route and invite the participant group to make alterations. The task group makes it clear that the tour belongs to the participant group and that they should take the tour wherever they think it should go to point out or illustrate good and bad features of the facility or its operation. The facilitator may need to emphasize that the POE process seeks to find out what is good as well as what is not so good. The briefing session typically takes 20 to 30 minutes.

The Touring Interview

Participants and the task group then walk through the building, visiting a representative sample of exterior and interior spaces. In each space, participants notice and comment on what they perceive to be important about the building and its operation and use. The procedure is facilitated by open-ended questions from the task group. Comments are recorded by the task group notetaker on record sheets prepared beforehand (Fig. 5).

The participants talk about whatever they perceive to be important from a position of close knowledge and experience of at least one aspect of the facil-

FIG. 5—*A touring interview in progress.*

ity, while the building itself serves to jog their memories. The task group avoids asking leading or loaded questions such as, "Do you like the color scheme?" or even, "What do you think of the decor?," but instead prompt from time to time with questions like, "What happens here?" and (as a follow-up), "Does that work well?" or "Would you say there are problems?"

The notetaker records keywords and phrases as a "memory bank" to be brought forward to the review meeting immediately after the tour. It is reasonably important, but not vital, that the notetaker hears and notes down all topics raised by the participants, so the facilitator must work to keep the group together and limit concurrent subgroup discussions. On the other hand, it is more important that the participants warm to the event and use the tour as a way of focusing attention on the facility, remembering or rekindling associations with places, people, things, operations, or events. The tour is not primarily a data-gathering exercise, but a kind of memory-jogging process in preparation for the review meeting, which is treated as the main information-seeking (evaluation) part of the touring interview program. The task group's job in the walkthrough is to prompt and guide the participant group to begin uncovering what is most significant to them.

The Review Meeting

When the tour is over both groups return to the room in which the briefing session was held. While the facilitator runs through the review procedure and allows time for the participant group to talk about the tour and the facility in general, the notemaker writes up the keywords or phrases for the topics which were raised by the group. This list of comment topics is a menu to which the group can add as they see fit and from which they select topics on which to make recommendations.

To begin the process of writing recommendations, the facilitator asks the group to select one topic which they agree is very important to them. The facilitator then helps the group formulate a concise statement which sums up their observation on the matter, followed by recommendations they may wish to make. These statements are written on a blackboard or white board so that the wording can be progressively adjusted until the participant group reaches consensus. When the group is satisfied, they move to another topic while the task group member who is the recorder writes up the agreed observation and recommendations on a large sheet of paper, about flip-chart size, in large, clear lettering. This procedure is repeated until the participant group is content that they have dealt with the main points in their evaluation. It is usual for the first few topics to take a relatively long time to complete as the participants learn to reach consensus and make their recommendations explicit. If the group begins to run short of time, the facilitator may suggest that the participants work individually on the remaining topics from the menu. In this event the individual recommendations are posted on the walls of the room with the other flip-chart sheets and amalgamated as appropriate, with the help of the task group (Fig. 6).

It is common for a participant group to generate about 15 recommendations in about 1 to 1½ hours. One useful refinement is to divide the recommendations, as they are documented, into two classes: those to do with "this building" and those to do with "future buildings."

An optional task in the review meeting is to elect the priority or relative importance of each recommendation. There are several ways to manage this. One such way is to "give" each participant an equal number of A, B, and C rankings and ask them to assign all their rankings to the complete set of recommendations. These rankings are recorded directly on the large recommendation sheets which are posted on the walls of the meeting room.

To wind up the review meeting, the facilitator thanks the participant group for contributing to the evaluation and reiterates the agreed procedures for communicating the recommendations to management.

Make Photographic Records and Take Measurements

Either during or on completion of the touring interviews, the task group recorder photographs and measures specific aspects of the facility which have been the subject of recommendations by the participant groups. The purpose of this is to provide graphic illustration and quantitative data to supplement the judgments of the participants. The recorder may wish to make photographs of various stages in the evaluation process for reporting or educational purposes. This needs to be done without fuss—it is best to use a high-speed film to avoid the need for flash equipment indoors. If parts of the evaluation process are to be photographed, the facilitator should explain the purpose and use of the photographs and check that none of the participants object.

FIG. 6—*Building the "wall of recommendations" in a review meeting.*

The physical inspection by the task group or the recorder measures criteria noted in the original building program. The inspection typically includes space dimensions, environmental measures, and provision of fittings and equipment.

Report to the Building Managers on Completion of the Field Work

As a courtesy, the task group informs management that the evaluation tasks have been completed. The task group must expect that management in the building which has been evaluated will be very interested to hear a summary of the principal recommendations made by the participant groups and be alerted to any serious conflicts or issues that have been brought to light, as well as aspects of the facility which have been praised.

Step 6: Collate the Recommendations, Observations, Facility Description, Photographs, etc. and Analyze the Data in Preparation for Reporting

This step mainly involves organizing and sorting the participant groups' observations and recommendations and is the step most likely to take more of the task group's time than they expect or plan. The least demanding procedure and the one taking least time is to photo-reduce the recommendation sheets directly from the touring interviews and publish them in a report together with a brief factual summary of the building and the evaluation program. A more ambitious exercise involves classifying the recommendations in various ways to serve different audiences and different storage/retrieval procedures.

The nature of the work done by the task group in this step is therefore dependent on such factors as personal preference, expected audiences, the classification systems used by organizations with an interest in the evaluation information, the time available, and so on. In POEs conducted in New Zealand, various classifications of evaluation information have been tried in different combinations. Using keywords as a basis, they include:

This building/future buildings.
Sorting by source of information, that is, by participant group.
Sorting by receiver of information, that is, by expected audiences such as client, designer, and management.
Building elements, for example, floors, walls, windows.
Behavioral issues, for example, use of recreation spaces, privacy at telephone.
Room or space type, for example, conference room, kitchen, foyer.
Policy or procurement matters, for example, reuse of plans, contractual procedures, programming processes.
Level of action, for example, fine tune, major change, policy review.

Step 7: Report or Otherwise Communicate Findings

Three levels of reporting are now operating in the Ministry of Works and Development (MWD) evaluations in New Zealand. They are:

1. A single page poster announcing that a POE has been completed. The poster is published at International Size A4 and A2 for distribution throughout the MWD and relevant client department. The smaller A4 poster is suitable for mailing or as a desk drop to individuals who are expected to have an interest in the specific building or in the building type. The larger A2 poster is intended for notice boards.

2. A summary report, stating participant group recommendations transcribed or photo-reduced from flip charts and supported by plans, photographs, and background material. To preserve visual continuity, the cover of the summary report is similar to the poster. Several copies of summary reports are made available to all offices of the client and the delivery agency.

3. The POE file which contains all the data collected by the task group about the evaluation. This usually remains in the MWD office which managed the building evaluation, with copies made for the head offices of MWD and participating client department.

Each level of report provides details on where to obtain further information, if desired. For instance, the poster draws attention to the existence of more detailed information in the other two levels of reporting and to the individual members of the task group. Thus, someone whose interest is aroused by the poster can seek the summary report for more detail and can go further to the POE file, if necessary. This may in turn lead to direct contact with task group or even participant group members for discussion or clarification of issues raised. On the other hand, the poster may be filed, displayed, or discarded.

Step 8: Check Actions Taken and Sign Off

People, especially building occupants, who take part in an evaluation expect positive action to result from their involvement. As previously mentioned, one of the "rules" of POE is that there should be "money in the back pocket" for taking action on the recommendations. The most important tasks to complete are to make sure that communication has occurred, that decisions are remade or issues resolved, and that some reasonable short-term results have occurred.

In one POE in New Zealand, the task group decided to call a meeting of all participant groups, including management, some three months after the touring interviews. At this meeting they reviewed the recommendations, highlighting those that were most frequently mentioned and given high priority. Then management summarized the actions to occur over the next fiscal year which arose out of the evaluations, and in discussion other interest groups talked of the lessons learned from the evaluation experience.

There are, to date, no satisfactory ways to quantify the benefits of POE. The costs, we know, are miniscule in comparison with the capital or operating costs of buildings, and, since the benefits are shared, so are the direct costs. However, those who take part in POE very often report that the benefits exceed their expectations. A typical comment is, "Why haven't we done this before?"

Lessons Learned from the New Zealand Experience

Near the end of the 3½-year research contract with the MWD, the research team from Victoria University of Wellington, which developed the touring interview POE method, sat down with Robert Shibley,[2] who has had a close association with the research from its beginnings, to ask, "What have we learned so far?" From the ensuing discussions, there emerged four principles underlying the development of the POE method and its introduction as a normal ongoing service of the MWD Architectural Directorate.

Participation

The principle of encouraging widely based participation is based on the belief that participation promotes commitment to each evaluation and to the overall program. It is, in fact, the key to ownership of the POE program by the MWD and client personnel. It is they, rather than outsiders or "experts," who will initiate, plan, conduct, and report evaluations at the investigative level. The principle also encompasses the idea that participation promotes face-to-face contact, improving communication and relations within the MWD and between the MWD and its clients. Feedback from evaluations already carried out shows that the evaluation process enhances the quality of communication within a client organization, and it is valuable in offering MWD staff opportunities to meet building users from whom they are often remote. The MWD is beginning to enjoy the public relations benefits which flow from all these contacts.

Participation in POE also helps develop individual and corporate understanding of the relationships between environment and behavior. This understanding is broadly based and within the organization so that as change occurs over time the organization knows how to respond without resorting to periodic upheaval and intervention from outside experts.

Robustness

The principle of robustness suggests that only a flexible and open-ended approach can maximize opportunities for success with POE. Robustness

[2]Principal consultant to the research team; employed by the State University of New York at Buffalo.

should ensure that the evaluation process can remain a straightforward and adaptable working tool which can be used for different purposes by a wide range of MWD and client personnel. Versatility also can ensure that, as well as conferring immediate benefits to occupants through fine-tuning the evaluated building, the learning benefits can be spread among those involved in briefing, designing, operating, and maintaining other buildings.

Robustness implies a degree of adaptability and choice in most aspects of planning an evaluation. For instance, the method must be robust enough to withstand different answers to:

1. What is the purpose?
2. How is it initiated?
3. Who pays for it?
4. Who will take part?
5. How will outcomes be communicated? Simplicity of method, format, and tasks assists robustness by ensuring that the evaluation can be carried out with the minimum of preparation and training. Guidelines need to be written in direct language and suggest rather than dictate methods. Similarly, redundancy built into the evaluation process can assist robustness by allowing for mistakes or gaps in its conduct. For instance, having more than the minimum number of two people in the task group may ensure that the inexperience of some members is compensated for by others.

Facilitation

The principle of facilitation affects individual attitudes towards each evaluation and to the on-going POE program. One strength of the New Zealand POE program is that its support and impetus comes from middle management personnel of the MWD and client departments. This is not a top-down operation with directives from the head office and a set of inviolable procedures to follow. Motivation is derived from the participants' awareness of the direct benefits of conducting evaluations. The executive task is to offer a framework of promotion, financial support, education events and workshops, and program assistance through guideline documentation to provide a "curriculum" within which personnel can initiate POEs and where they can maximize benefits.

Utility

The principle of utility refers to the extent to which POE can demonstrate benefits to those involved against the costs incurred in its operation. Until a POE program is firmly established and widely accepted, it may be necessary to emphasize short-term benefits which can be clearly perceived by individuals in the MWD and in client departments, which will attract government support.

When the program has been operating for some years, the MWD will have available a system of reviewing its own performance with respect to design, construction and management services, the quality of the advice it gives its client departments, and the quality of the buildings delivered. The client departments will be in a position to manage and modify their own buildings better, provide better programs for future buildings, and use the evaluation process as a way to improve communication links within their organizations. Longer term benefits to both MWD and clients will be derived from the joint learning associated with POE. Long-term benefits to the government system as a whole will result from the enhancement of the MWD's role as advisor to government. We hope over the years to build a data base from which academic researchers can synthesize general truths.

If POE is to survive as a normal ongoing operation in the building game, it must first and foremost provide a quick and useful return for the effort expended. This need not mean an academic/scientific sellout to the pragmatic interests of practicing professionals and clients, but it does call for a cooperative form of action-based research-in-practice which is not the norm in either academia or practice.

Adapting the Participatory Touring Interview POE for Use in Rehabilitation

Let us now return to the proposition in the first few pages of this paper, that an adapted form of participatory POE has utility as preoccupancy planning tool in rehabilitation. What adaptations are needed? How could rehabilitation be better as a consequence of undertaking this kind of preoccupancy evaluation?

Earlier in the paper we argued that rehabilitation is an attractive accommodation option compared with purpose-built or ready-made because it strikes a balance between knowledge of the organization and the building and the opportunity to make significant change.

The POE method described is a process which works best with a knowable, observable building and a significant opportunity and openness to organizational change. Thus, at a fundamental level the participatory group touring interview method of POE can be readily applied to rehabilitation.

To illustrate: Suppose a city council (that is, the municipal office) is planning to move to rehabilitated premises in a nearby street. The building that they will alter was occupied by a company which assembled and distributed electrical components, so the premises consist of offices and clean factory and warehouse spaces. The council offices have a known staff establishment, and almost all will move with the organization to the "new" accommodation when it is ready. The two premises are comparable in many respects but different in some. With this scenario, *pre*occupancy evaluations (that is, programming evaluations) could be conducted almost exactly as described, first in the existing city chambers and then with the same interest groups in the new location before rehabilitation starts. Suppose, on the other hand, that the company making electrical components is moving their operation to another city to be closer to their markets, and they have decided to buy and rehabilitate an existing building which is ideally located but very different from the one they are vacating. With this scenario, only a few people on the payroll will move with the organization, and the building requires such substantial change that it is difficult to imagine and assess the effects of the changes. Preoccupancy evaluation is still important, but to use the participatory POE method would need a number of adaptations.

Firstly, the building would have to be brought to a stage in alteration at which its final form is more easily imagined by the various interest groups but still capable of significant change. One way to do this is to "clean out" the unwanted or unusable parts of the building and then conduct touring interviews before the final design stages. Yet another way to understand the building requirements would be to evaluate a surrogate facility if a similar building or operation could be found.

Secondly, with this scenario, people would have to be brought in to represent various interests in the operation. One possibility is to invite surrogates to evaluate the facility. This has the difficulty that surrogates are unlikely to have any personal stake in the outcome of the evaluation. Another possibility is to agree to hire people in advance of starting work and pay them to evaluate the building before rehabilitation is well underway. Failing these techniques, it may be necessary to accept that some interest groups are not represented in the evaluation/planning phases, or that they are "represented" by management or outside experts.

Concluding Comment

For some years professional facility programmers have used evaluation as a technique for gaining essential insights and information which help them establish requirements for facilities. What, then, is different or special about the method of evaluation which has been outlined in this paper, and, specifically, what claims can be made for its place in programming for rehabilitation?

Perhaps the feature of this evaluation method that sets it apart from most is that it is "participatory," whereas others tend to be "expert" operations. This method deliberately seeks diverse opinion from a wide range of people with an interest in a facility, whereas most evaluation techniques rely on expert judgments by an individual or small group with or without consultation. The participatory touring interview approach takes the philosophical stance that there are many experts; those with the closest involvements in a facility are the experts in their areas of involvement because they have the knowledge and experience that is of most value in establishing facility requirements. Thus, the evaluation is made by those with a stake in the facility. They have something to gain from the evaluation effort. True, they also are biased toward their own interests and concerns, with the result that the method does not always satisfy conventional academic criteria. There may be losses in scientific reliability but gains in social and political arenas that are not normally addressed in more vigorous scientific evaluations. For instance, the participatory approach brings together conflicting interests and requirements, setting the scene for negotiations and consensus before conflict is built into a facility.

We see this form of POE as a suitable basis for establishing the overall performance of buildings. If management is considering rehabilitation as a possibility, then the participatory POE is a controllable, adaptable, and robust way to gain information on the range of values held by various interest groups. It is a process by which management can uncover social, cultural, and technical benefits and costs inherent in the accommodation options open to an organization. The participatory touring interview method has a special place in programming because the process draws attention to both the organization and the building as a unity, not as separate entities. It is possibly the best tool available to management in choosing between accommodation options, programming for rehabilitation, and assessing the fit between organization and building.

Acknowledgments

The research referred to in this paper was conducted under contract between Victoria University of Wellington and the New Zealand Ministry of Works and Development between October 1979 and March 1983. Evaluations have been conducted during and since the contract, first by the research team and later by the MWD and their client departments.

The principal researchers are John Daish, John Gray, and David Kernohan of the School of Architecture at Victoria University. Professor Robert G. Shibley, State University of New York at Buffalo, has been principal consultant to the research team since late 1979.

References

[1] Becker, F. D., *Workspace: Creating Environments in Organizations,* Praeger Publishers, New York, 1981.
[2] Davis, G., "The Relationship of Evaluation to Facilities Programming," paper presented at a symposium on Evaluation of Occupied Designed Environments, Georgia Technical Institute, Atlanta, GA, Feb. 1982.
[3] Duffy, F., "Briefing and Initial Design," paper presented to a symposium on briefing sponsored by the Building Research Establishment, Garston, England, 1981.

[4] Altman, I., paper presented at an invitational seminar on planning the office work environment, sponsored by the Canada Employment and Immigration Commission, Ottawa, Canada, 1981.

[5] Johnson, J., "Housing Rehabilitation," T. A., Markus, Ed., in *Building Conversion and Rehabilitation*, Newnes Butterworth, London, 1979.

[6] Steele, F., *Physical Settings and Organizational Development*, Addison-Wesley Publishing Co., Reading, Mass. 1973.

[7] Daish, J., Gray, J., Kernohan, D., and Salmond, A., "Incorporating POE as a 'Normal' Activity," in *Proceedings*, Thirteenth International Conference of the Environmental Design Research Association, College Park, Maryland, 1981, pp. 201–209.

Peter Jockusch

Developmental History of Institutions—Life History of Their Buildings

REFERENCE: Jockusch, P., "Developmental History of Institutions—Life History of Their Buildings," *Building Performance: Function, Preservation, and Rehabilitation, ASTM STP 901*, G. Davis, Ed., American Society for Testing and Materials, Philadelphia, 1986, pp. 69–85.

ABSTRACT: This paper attempts to discuss mutual influences of the organizational development of institutions and their buildings. This is done in a dynamic approach in that the process of birth, growth, maturity, aging, and decay of institutions is described in its mutual impact on the life history of buildings from the briefing and design through realization, utilization, alteration, and rehabilitation to the physical decay and demolition or rebirth.

Building performance is not only a characteristic of the building itself but is highly determined by the dynamic process of development and transition which an institution undergoes during its existence.

So, even flexible and adaptable buildings show a deterministic, static character, and their total building performance must be permanently readjusted during the history of their use.

Building rehabilitation and preservation is seen as a means to support the organizational development of institutions in certain critical phases of their existence. The appreciation or condemnation of old buildings—as seen from institutional expectations and needs, from policy and value concepts, and from strategic and economic aspects—stems by no means only from functional or technological reasons.

KEY WORDS: organizational development; life history of buildings; building performance; revitalization (rehabilitation) of buildings; dynamics of supply and demand of buildings maintenance policy; life spans of buildings, offices, schools, research institutions, and communal buildings

My contribution to this conference is an extract from ongoing research in the dynamics of organizational change and its impact on building needs and building use. In Europe, rehabilitation and the upgrading of existing buildings seems to have become one of the main tasks of architects and engineers.

[1]Professor, Department of Architecture, Kassel University, Kassel, Germany D 3500.

In an area of shrinking population, this task seems more important than the conception, design, and realization of new accommodations on virgin sites. This paper analyzes the impact on each other of developing organizations and of the buildings in which those organizations are housed. This approach requires a look at *organizational* problems to assess, describe, and evaluate the development (for example, the birth, expansion, maturity, decay, and redundancy) of organizations. I seek the reasons for changing building needs, for fit or misfit of the demand for and supply of facilities and for changes in the value and importance of the buildings as physical resources of such institutions. My approach also requires that I look at the buildings to assess, describe, and evaluate the life span of buildings. I do this from the initial intentions of the conceivers (for example, the designers and the clients of a new building), through all alterations and changes of users and functions, to the obsolescence, decay, and, finally, the demolition or the rebirth of the building. In contrast to other papers presented at this conference, I will not continue to ask *how* we can assess overall buildings performance. I want to enlarge our views on the forces that determine overall building performance by asking some *what's*, *who's* and *why's* in a transdisciplinary way.

My methods are descriptive and evaluative rather than quantitative. My observations and evaluations are interpretive. They are close to architectural history and anthropology. I seek a sympathetic understanding and assessment by being descriptive and holistic. The work is done by analyzing written and drawn material and in field studies using interviews, building performance assessments, postoccupancy evaluations, and organizational analyses.

My conclusions are based on observations over many years, although I mostly will use only one single case study to illustrate these conclusions.

Each section starts with a series of statements, supported by case material. This sounds deductive, but it is presented this way to sharpen the issues. In fact, I worked from the cases through evaluation towards conclusions which form the basis for the issues identified in following paragraphs.

The intent of this paper is not to identify a set of methods that can be used to produce better and cheaper building rehabilitation in the future. The purpose, instead, is to provide insight into and to increase awareness of how the mechanics and dynamics of a building's occupant organization could help to guide future decisions about the selection of methods for building assessment and performance studies.

For me, this research in the organizational analysis of buildings is part of my attempt to overcome the gap between organizers' and managers' activities in the planning and operational control of organizations, on one side, and architects', engineers', producers', and suppliers' work of designing, realizing, and delivering buildings, on the other. The architects and producers of buildings do not sufficiently understand organizational and managerial tasks, and managers have only a vague idea about the design and production of buildings. Both groups are not well enough informed to exploit the organizational potential of the physical resources that buildings and their equipment represent. My interest is historical and analytical because I see an evolutionary process underlying all sorts of transitional dynamics related to conceiving, producing, and running buildings that are keeping an institution alive. I only can understand the future of an organization if I know about its past and future development trends.

Buildings as Physical Resources for Institutions in Transition

Let me start with a statement of three key issues which my paper attempts to illustrate and highlight in some detail:

1. Building performance is not only a characteristic of the building itself but also is highly determined by the dynamics of development and transition which an institution undergoes during its existence.

2. Building rehabilitation is seen as a means of supporting the organizational development of institutions in certain critical phases of their existence.

3. The appreciation or contempt of old buildings is by no means restricted to functional or technological reasons. It also is influenced by the expectations and needs, policies, values, and strategic and economic aspects of an institution.

I now will focus on the evaluation of some life events in the developmental history of institutions. I will concentrate on the birth and growth of institutions as well as on their aging and decay, rather than on their maturity and midlife crises. Each of the following sections begins with a statement which summarizes my case study findings, followed by relevant case material.

The Importance of the Beginning

A new institution needs freedom to develop in the inception phase. Therefore:

1. Create definitive, permanent conditions at the latest possible moment in the history of a new institution.

2. Enjoy the delights of transitional and improvised status.

My case study for this is a nonprofit research institute. A senior scientist received a commission to establish a solid state physics research institute. Forty young scientists were brought together to work with minimum restrictions. They were able to recruit staff, procure all the necessary equipment, tools, and working aids, organize themselves physically and socially, and develop their own rules of behavior, decision making, and conflict avoidance.

The first working environment was in a transition space in a run-down administration and spare-parts production building of a car factory. Despite the poor environmental standards and the relatively high population density, there was euphoria, inventiveness, and high social and scientific creativity. In this starting phase, much environmental stress was accepted. This situation seemed to stimulate the talent of the physicists for improvisation. Space and services were arranged in unusual layouts and performed well.

Despite inadequate and substandard environmental conditions, an extremely positive and friendly social atmosphere evolved. Everybody wanted to make the enterprise a success. They were successful as a result of considerable effort, their high scientific caliber, the opportunity for and the encouraging of socializing among the scientists, and a lot of luck.

In terms of Herzberg's motivation-hygiene theory, [1], the institute showed low hygiene and high motivation factors. This is just the opposite from what I have criticized in most of the new high-technology office buildings: too much emphasis on comfort and hygiene and too much denial of motivational issues [2].

Five years later this institute had left its starter home and had moved into a new permanent purpose-built building that was extremely spacious, pretty, and comfortable. Everyone was equipped with individual, autonomous laboratories which demanded a low degree of sharing and a low social density. Growing staff numbers produced more anonymity, and competition developed among those who in the initial phase had cooperated. Some of the staff became professors and left the institute. Others had to leave because contracts were not continued. The initial egalitarian atmosphere among colleagues became more hierarchical and functionally differentiated. The social coherence of the institute suffered internally, and, as the new building is on a virgin site far from the city, people began to feel isolated.

There was a deterministic environment-and-behavior causality; here two dynamic phenomena impacted people's behavior. Certainly the new building with its higher standard, unusual layout, and isolated site caused problems for the social and individual behavior of staff, but also the institutional and operational dynamics of a maturing institution changed the tasks and performance of the staff as well as the social culture in the institute.

The presence of what might be called "wealthy dissatisfiers" in the new building brings me to my next message:

> Poor accommodation in the inception phase of an enterprise is accepted more than improved standards in "permanent" buildings.

Five years later the institute had changed its scientific concept. Many new faces can be seen. The pioneers of the inception phase are almost all gone. The building has been altered in parts and looks messy now. Space per person has decreased due to an increase in number of staff. The building and the institution have undergone changes that make the fit of demand and supply better today than in the first year of use. The worst phase was the first years in the new permanent building, when the young institution was in a critical state. Staff fell into a mood of grief and frustration when they compared their new space to the physically inadequate but socially positive transition space they previously occupied.

People who had been happy in the temporary accommodation showed a decreasing tolerance for environmental inadequacies in the new building despite the fact that hygiene and comfort standards in the new building were considerably higher than they had been in the transition space. I have been told that the scientific productivity decreased for a while at the same time as the conditions for such work were improved. Apparently the overcrowding in the last four years in the transition space (despite high loads of mutual disturbance and permanent invasion into personal territories) created a social entity which most of the staff remembered liking very much. They were not aware of this as long as they were in the old building. Those in the high-energy, start-up phase simply did not care about or were indifferent to their surroundings, that is, they would have worked as well in better environments but were willing to tolerate and to accept low environmental standards.

Summing this up and repeating my key statement, I would say:

> People in transient conditions, in a state of uncertainty and tension, are more likely to accept poor physical accommodations and may perform better than in the self-confident luxury of a highly refined ultimate physical environment where tension is removed and physical comfort maximized.
>
> Therefore, in planning facilities for new institutions in their inception phase, I would suggest occupying an interim accommodation which allows members of the new organization to learn to work together, to develop rules and standards which evolve into design requirements. In other words, let them rehearse in a temporary building. The ultimate building will be better value in use for money if its design requirements have slowly emerged.
>
> Finite conditions should be developed as late as possible and the delights of transitional, improvised space enjoyed as long as possible.

In Praise of the Provisorium

While the research institute began in a temporarily removed, run-down old factory building, there is another approach for beginners: bypassing unwanted building consequences of organizational change by reducing the life span of buildings to the life expectancy of a certain organizational setup. Some new universities have started in something like barracks or huts which provided collapsible, single-story, provisional accommodation. Little time or effort was needed to begin use. Physical standards were low, but there was complete freedom to add, change, demolish, or rebuild the facilities. Those in new institutions in the pioneer stage need to learn to work together and to identify their design needs through use of existing facilities. From this very positive experience, planning and organizational details of the final buildings can be tested. By doing so, one could reduce the high rate of change which normally occurs in the inception phase of a permanent building. This would avoid unwanted changes caused by the lack of understanding of original requirements and would allow management to focus on planned changes in response to new technologies, new forms of work arrangements, changing project teams, etc. (For details of new British universities, see Ref 3).

We have been working with some of these institutions in their inception stage in order to discuss with them the kinds of long-term facilities they want. In a participative briefing process, we like to make the temporary facility a test case for the more permanent working situation.

Some people want to go even further by trying to create temporary or transitional accommodation as the permanent solution for organizations and institutions which experience a high and unpredictable rate of change.

In some cases, temporary accommodation is provided on a permanent basis as a buffer or umbrella space which can help to balance at short notice unforseeable demands. Military structures and traveling circuses have this kind of spontaneity and ad hocness, although they are organized extremely well.

One does not care much about the building itself and its history. One just uses it as a shelter and tool and not as an end in itself. Some people may feel free only if they can maintain a transitional state. In Central Europe this attitude hardly is known anymore, but we have the history of nomads, of tribal societies, and of gypsies who become anxious if asked to settle themselves.

Change by Growth

Looking at any growing institution from a long-term continuous perspective brings me to my next message:

> The fit of people and space in a growing institution is never perfect either in size or quality. Both are subject to dynamic alterations over time and can go up *and* down.

Over the life of an institution there are periods of space undersupply and also of oversupply. Oversupply occurs shortly after new facilities have been occupied or in times after great recessions. If the growth of space demand is almost continuous and the provision of facilities takes place stepwise and in good time, then the space/person ratio graphs as a stepwise, jagged curve. A quickly growing institution with an exponential growth like the Dutch Insurance Company Centraal Beheer illustrates this phenomenon (Figs. 1 and 2).

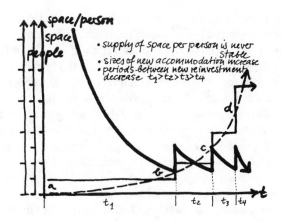

FIG. 1—*Space provision over time.*

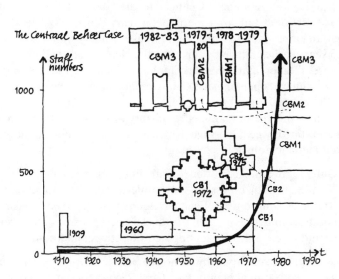

FIG. 2—*Space provision for increasing staff numbers: the Centraal Beheer case.*

At Centraal Beheer the period for doubling of staff was 40 years originally and is 5 years at present. This tremendous growth may be part of the concentration and expansion process that happened in the sixties and early seventies in the insurance business.

Phase 1 started as early as 1909 in one of the old 17th-century *Grachtenhouses* which were built as a *Cantoor* (office) building for one of the ancestors of the founder of Centraal Beheer. This converted old building was good and was large enough for 51 years. In 1960 the company moved into Phase 2, a five-story cell office building which was purpose-built, owner-occupied, and new. But only 12 years later, the firm had increased in size and now was restricted in its development by inadequacies of the old building in size, layout, and communication technology. Centraal Beheer also suffered from the general congestion in Amsterdam. Therefore, in 1972 the firm moved into Phase 3, its famous new headquarters built by Hermann Hertzberger at Apeldoorn.

At the time it was a developmental milestone in European office buildings. The firm could experience all the virtues of the time: egalitarian attitude, self-determination of work flow, decentralization of decision making, humanization of the work process, openness to the general public, and integration of "nonfunctional" and social elements. Only one third of the staff moved from Amsterdam 200 km east to Apeldoorn. At that time, to find enough qualified staff in Apeldoorn, one had to make the workplaces particularly attractive. The firm was very successful indeed. Only 5 years later, in 1977, they had increased to a point where an annex building to house another 360 people had to be built as Phase 4 at an adjacent site. The architecture there was more rigid, cheaper, and less open. Changes in the labor market made it much easier to attract new staff. In just another 4 years Centraal Beheer decided to take over an empty factory which could house as many staff as they had employed 5 years earlier. Since by this time the Netherlands had changed from an employees' labor market to an employers' market, Phase 5 was a very rigid, low standard, open plan which abandoned many of the objectives of the famous 1972 Hertzberger building [4].

Let me now put the developmental history of Centraal Beheer in a wider context and state my next message, which expresses my belief in the virtues of disjointed incrementalism in planning:

> Quickly growing institutions should not pursue a long-term development plan unless it is dynamic in terms of objectives, strategies, and context. Each developmental step should incorporate as much as possible from the previous steps and also should be capable of adopting new objectives and knowledge.

The accommodations used by Centraal Beheer reflect the philosophy or ideology of organizational planning and architectural design in the time when the buildings were first occupied. The insurance company started in the age of individual or small group offices and went on through rationalization, mechanization, high technology, humanization, and, again, banalization of office work environment. Changes in the social culture, in working conditions, and in organizational patterns at Centraal Beheer are thus part of the developmental history of the workplace in the office. This history has been dramatically described by Fritz [5] as a sequence of suffering by staff under the burden and strain of work, supervision, and control as well as under constantly increasing claims for efficiency and exploitation of the workforce.

Over time, accommodation and environmental standards change in both directions. There may be periods where more advanced levels of user demand (forced by economic growth) drive environmental standards up. At other times, the opposite occurs. Changes in the labor market may allow employers to reduce standards of office environments because the retention of jobs becomes a more important issue for staff (see Ref 2 for more details).

From Tailormade to Straightjacket

My next message describes the owner-occupier's dilemma:

> Procuring a new building is an historic and unique event in the developmental history of an institution. Planning and setting objectives causes in-house turbulances in the power structure which intensify as the building comes closer to move-in.

In Germany many administrative and industrial firms invest much of their capital in their own real estate property. Purpose- or custom-built accommodation has the virtue of better meeting the owner-occupiers' needs and of communicating to their own staff, to competitors in the market, and to the general public the image of that firm. Such buildings become trademarks and part of the publicity strategy.

These buildings can become an obstacle to the development of a firm if the planning and design process for the new building causes a stormy discussion among executives and changes the power balance entirely. The occasion of the procurement of a new building is historic and unique for a firm. The introduction of new technologies and new institutional and management patterns can destabilize the whole firm. In my country, the mandatory rights of staff participation come in here as well, especially if it leads to redefining the quality of working conditions. The debate over objectives and requirements accelerates as more of the building is realized and as one comes closer to occupancy. It continues during the first years of use.

Users' judgments about building performance and environmental quality vary greatly during the different stages of this debate. Strong architectural personalities use all their persuasive powers to convince their client that the building is a good one. Masterpieces of modern architecture may become straightjackets. Users blame buildings for troubles and frustration that in fact are managerial rather than environmental. Also, economically wealthy firms can suffer from the tailormade, owner-occupied building. Some of these firms collapsed and became bankrupt by tying up too much money. Sometimes the building was built only to hold up the decay of an existing institution and to stabilize the morale and team spirit of that institution. It also may be that the big boss of a firm in financial trouble allows a new building to be built primarily to show his competitors on the market that he is still alive.

These phenomena can be observed in many large mature institutions, especially insurance companies, public administration facilities [6], and facilities for higher education. We have studied lately the history of the German branch of an office machine company which commissioned a very fine and rather prestigeous building in 1972. The firm experienced several serious crises in the years 1972 through 1976 due to turbulences in the information technology market. It is now stable again after tremendous internal changes both in management and products. Internal changes include the introduction of new data processing and filing systems, new patterns of share-in-use of costly equipment, new division of labor among staff, and new departmental organization. Furthermore, the building, which initially housed only administrative and sales promotion departments, now also had to house departments for repair and maintenance as well as hardware storage and handling as part of the primary functions.

In only 10 years the building had undergone serious internal physical changes. Its all-embracing aesthetic unity has been severely destroyed. One can observe the complete misfit of third-generation office machines on second-generation furniture in first-generation office layout and finishes. The original architect's firm has not been commissioned again to work on the re-adaptation of the building (for ongoing research see Ref 6a).

Architects have a strange desire to harmonize all items of the working environment through design, despite the fact that building components have different life expectations. From the concept of the shell, the scenery, the furniture, and the equipment through the selection of table cloth, crockery and cutlery in the refectory, flower decoration, the uniform of doormen, receptionists, and hostesses, lettering at doors and signposts, choice of pieces of art to the graphics design of advertisements, the ambitious architect tries to aesthetisize everything and anything in the building. Practicing the right of the originator, architects jealously watch any changes made by the corporation and ask to be involved in order to maintain the original aesthetic balance. (The most famous showpiece of that kind is the Scandanavian Airlines Systems (SAS) Hotel at Copenhagen designed by Arne Jacobsen.) Owner-occupants of famous office buildings also employ special staff members from the estates management department who are trained architects and who originally were appointed during the briefing and design stage to act as the client's liaison staff with the architect. Their role is to monitor any alterations that might occur after occupancy. Having been involved with the architect from the beginning, these people feel so enthusiastic about the architect's concept that they now act as his watch guard to report on any "crimes of change" that deviate from the architect's original conception. When the librarian of the law library in such an office placed a handwritten note on a very expensive and precious wooden piece of furniture, saying, "Will users please leave books on the tables and not try to remove them into the shelves," our facility guide became very upset and was worried about such "signs of use and life." This anecdote suggests how the development of inhouse rules are driven by concerns for aesthetics.

Political Versus Functional Arguments for Grading Down and Grading Up of Historic Buildings

The next set of issues concerns facilities in their midlife crisis. They show the dominance of political forces both in organizational changes and in attitudes towards the appreciation or contempt of existing buildings:

> Historic buildings may be graded up (or down) for political reasons. This may be antifunctional and may deny current building performance. Politicians may want to exploit the visual dominance and prestige of a historic building monument to enhance their own reputations. Politicians often think of buildings in terms of grandios and long-term ideal concepts. They may devaluate and destroy remaining use values of historic buildings and create investment ruins in their place.

My paradigmatic case for these issues is the county-level regional administration, which has been experiencing a long-term organizational transition. In the last 50 years the small towns and villages have permanently lost decision-making power and administrative duties. In the Gifhorn region, for example, smaller towns and villages have had to close their administration offices. The county administration has taken over these responsibilities. The trend towards concentrating administrative responsibility at the county rather than at the village level was stimulated by a larger constituency and the dedication of more administrative duties at county level. The institutional organization of the administration also has changed. Formerly, different functions were administered by lower ranks of staff who were headed by only one general director of the county (*Oberkreisdirektor*). Now the different administrative functions are located in separate departments, all of which are headed by their own department heads (*Dezernenten*). This increased the autonomy and political power of the departments and challenged the power of the general director of the county. Concentrating and centralizing all the administrative functions under one roof became a way of coordinating the different functions and reasserting the power of the county administrators.

The trend toward centralization came at a time when the functional need for it already was diminishing. In the early seventies an increasing number of documents and people moved between the different departments (which made centralization appropriate). In the last decade, centralized electronic files and terminals have been introduced, and cashless money transfer for all taxes, fees, rates, and excise duties came into operation. Social welfare and annuity payments are also now handled electronically without cash. As a result, both the information handling within the administration and contact with the private customers has diminished, making centralization less appropriate and meaningful.

Prior to the move to centralize all administrative offices in one building, the administration was accommodated in historic houses comprising over 13 buildings. Each department could be identified with one or two of these existing buildings. Thus the administration was "among the people." Although staff and county population liked this, there was a strong claim from the regional politicians for a single new building. To provide a rationale for that, the old buildings were deliberately called inadequate in environmental standard and inappropriate for modern information technology, and their location was criticized for being too dispersed and difficult to find.

The concentration in one new building has meant the loss of individuality for different departments whose identity used to be supported by their location in many little individual buildings dispersed throughout the town. The concentration has increased the internal functionality of the administration but has made worse the approachability and transparency of administration for the customer.

Now I turn to political arguments for the upgrading of historic buildings and start with the statement that:

> It is a facet of German regional parliamentary life that the more the role of regional politicians is reduced (in relationship to legislative and political work done on the level of the federal states or on the national level), the more these politicians demand buildings for representation.

The example of the county administration, Gifhorn, shows that hearings and political debates used to be organized using the "traveling circus principle"; that is, meetings were held in schools, big pubs, or festival halls in different villages and small towns of the county. This is not good enough for many politicians. Therefore, they pressed for what we call "the parliamentary opera": centralized, self-expressing, and more distant from the people. The decision was made by the county politicians to put the parliamentary functions in a nearby old moated castle as a means of enhancing their status and importance.

The castle is a registered monument of the Middle Ages and has a high reputation among the public. Now, the castle houses only a small prison, a little regional museum, and minor parts of the county administration. It is seriously run down. However, the castle is the biggest, prettiest, and—apart from the church—the oldest existing building of the little town. The politicians liked the idea of putting their parliamentary and representative functions in the old castle in order to use its visual dominance and prestige to express their own importance. For this reason, among others, they upgraded the ruined castle and found reasons to justify a tremendous expenditure to restore it.

When we were asked to develop the functional space program for the castle renovation, one of the first things we did was to ask the public about the image of the county administration and parliament and the image of the castle and about the fit of both. We found (*a*) that the importance of the building for the people is independent of its physical conditions and its present function and (*b*) that the image of the castle is for historic and traditional reasons associated with just the counterimage of an open, transparent, nonimposing, friendly, and fearlessly approachable administration people wanted. This gave us many good ideas about which administrative functions should be put into the castle and which should be put into the new annex building. This information also helped us decide not to make the new building part of the castle but rather to locate it at a nearby site. To attain support for the project, additional functions such as the local museum and a café and restaurant were introduced into the brief. This helped to win public support and justify the extravagant cost of renovation. It also may help to overcome the emotional distances of people to the former feudal establishment. The only genuine traditional and historic function of the castle as a museum had not justified saving the building from physical decay. The cost of restoration and rehabilitation of the castle could be raised and justified only by locating representative and administrative functions in it.

When we began to allocate new uses in the old building, we realized how important the structure of the building is for functional planning. Although we tried our very best not to transform the building to the program but rather vice versa, the rigid application of functional and technological norms for public administration to an historic monument necessarily destroyed some of the monument's identity.

Some functions now suffer a misfit of plus or minus 20% (which is a tolerable margin), yet people now accept the inconvenience of having to walk downstairs and across the courtyard to reach another department, even though they originally wanted to be in close proximity. If the building constraints in a beautiful historic building are important, functional requirements—at least in an institution like our county administration—seem to be flexible to a certain extent. The main loss of functionality is compensated for by the new individualization of smaller user groups and organizational units within such an expressive architecture. (For details, see project documentation by Gifhorn [7].)

Institutional Decay and Rebirth—the Case of the School House

One of the most dramatic examples of institutional decay and its impact on changing building needs are primary and secondary schools. The demographic influence of falling birth rates in almost all the Western European countries has created a growing redundancy of school spaces, to the extent that, since the peak of the midseventies for primary schools and the early eighties for secondary schools, school enrollments have dropped down to something like 50%. Thus, many schools are considerably underused or must be closed down [8].

Here I would like to raise a town planning issue:

> The importance and performance of an old building must be seen from its contextual qualities both in its contribution to the ensemble of surrounding buildings and in its sociofunctional setting. The assessment of total building performance must include contextual criteria.

In areas of low population density, closing schools because of reduced enrollment and organizational concentration means an increase in traveling time, distance, and cost for the school population. Furthermore, as the school is a sociocultural focus for the community, closing the school building means to deprive a community of many opportunities for educational, social, and cultural activities. For these activities, no special accommodation can be provided, and they owe their existence to the fact that in off-peak hours the school house can be shared. In my country, the official attempt is to avoid closures of existing schools and to run those schools even for very small pupil numbers. This allows the more effective use of the existing schoolhouse for other functions.

We see that the schoolhouse changes its purpose from just being a school to a multipurpose and multiinstitutional building. One likes to keep the importance of the schoolhouse for the community by extending the functions to socioeducational and social function. In some cases the building houses fewer school functions than other activities and some schools are converted to become store building, dwellings, old people's social meeting places, or a mix of all these functions. For further information see Ref 8 and a forthcoming Organization for Economic Cooperation and Development (OECD) publication by the same authors.

Old school buildings as physical objects and resources are mostly rundown in technical standards, especially if enrollment figures constantly drop, some of them to a serious state because no money is available to keep these buildings alive. In some cases they are filtering down to rubbish. Once they reach this status, they can be afforded by poor social groups and upgraded by restimulating the remaining value in use with rather primitive self-help means. School buildings as a sociocultural symbol signalize a social focus of the community and add to the self-respect of such communities. This then may counteract the serious consequences of decay of importance and political power of the small communities.

So I would like to summarize in saying:

> Redundant school buildings provide chances for the have-nots and their social needs. Keep schools alive—they might become a sociocultural focus.

Conclusion: What to Do With the Building Stock?

In conclusion, I would like to ask how we are managing our building stock. I said at the beginning of my paper that our future task as architects will be concerned more with upgrading and rehabilitating existing facilities than with the conception and realization of new ones. "The value you give to things depends on the way you look at them," said Michael Thompson [9] in his rubbish theory, in which he talks about the creation and destruction of value. I have tried in this paper to show with case histories that I selected from our much larger collection of life histories of institutions and their buildings, that the decisions taken to rehabilitate or to condemn an old building are far from being based only on technical or economical or functional reasons. The real motives of people for such decisions can better be explained in terms taken from the language of the social sciences.

The esteem of a building to an organization, to opinion leaders, or to the general public as well as the social and emotional values attributed to a building seem to guide people more than anything else in their decisions.

I will now discuss five different approaches to monuments preservation (as in Germany) because these concepts reflect some of the differing value systems of people who decide upon the future use of existing buildings and the chances for their rehabilitation. Since we have opened up the notion of monuments (from the architecture of the feudal classes and the church to all sorts of important architectural landmarks and relics of human ingenuity rediscovered by industrial archaelogists; we also now include built documents of the social history, such as workers' homes of the early urbanization and industrialization period), we can no longer draw a clear distinction between monuments and other old buildings.

The positive effect of this comprehensive understanding of monuments certainly is that no one can easily destroy existing buildings simply because they are old and worn. The negative consequence of it may be that public opinion is against demolition of almost everything simply because it all may belong to our national heritage.

I see five concepts of restoring historic buildings:

1. The first is a conservative attitude in the pure sense of conserving buildings as they were with the technical means, materials, and craftmanship of the time of erection of such buildings. Even the future use of the building should continue past uses or at least show sociocultural continuity. This attitude might turn our whole built environment into a museum and the users into players of historic roles.

2. Other extreme positions treat monument preservation as part of social politics [10], saying that most upgrading drives existing people out and destroys an inherited social structure that needs support, especially if, as usually happens, it is people of lower classes who still live there. These people ask for upgrading in a participative way, keeping speculators out and allowing mon-

ument preservation only for improving the living conditions for todays' residents. This denies mobility and market mechanism. It has a long tradition, especially in decaying cultures.

3. More moderate concepts of monument preservation say that monuments can be rehabilitated and physically upgraded only if new uses justify it, that new uses cannot always completely fit with the existing spaces and usability. Therefore, minor building changes and extensions certainly may be allowed. New interpretations of existing building structures for changed uses will be necessary. This approach implies the right for cautious appropriation. It demands from the future user that one is aware of the historic importance of the building and that the future use adds to the continuity in the building history.

4. There is another way of looking at historic buildings which grades down the remaining usability potential and grades up architectural symbols and forms, using them as marketing vehicles for improved market values. This approach keeps only facades and exterior appearance and behind them builds any new speculative accommodation that money can buy. Some authorities would allow higher plot ratios in rehabilitated old buildings of that kind than they would allow on the same side for new buildings. Therefore, to dismantle an existing building down to the facade and to rebuild something new behind it may have an advantage in some cases.

5. Some ironically minded students lately presented a paper to me urging the abolishment of monument preservation because they think that neoformalist architecture makes more monuments quicker and cheaper than any restoration and rehabilitation of really old buildings can offer [11].

Let me close with a pessimistic late-European statement—I fear that after some generations nobody will notice the difference any more, and our growing cultural-historic illiteracy may help us that way.

Acknowledgment

The presentation of this paper at Bal Harbour was enabled by a travel grant from the German Research Association (DFG), Bonn-Bad Godesberg. The author gratefully acknowledges the time consuming efforts taken by Franklin D. Becker to review this paper.

References

[1] Herzberg, F., *The Motivation-Hygiene Theory. Work and the Nature of Man*, World Publishing Co., 1966. (Reprinted in *Organization Theory*, Pugh, Ed., Penguin, New York, 1975.)
[2] Jockusch, P., "Towards a Redefinition of Standards for the Quality of Working Life," paper presented at the 20th Congress of the International Association for Applied Psychology, Edinburgh, Scotland, available from authors.

[3] Jockusch, P., "Development Planning of British Universities," in *Proceedings*, Central Archives for University Planning, Vol. 5, Werner Publishing Co., Dusseldorf, 1967.

[4] Duffy, F., "Hertzberger's Legacy," *Architect's Journal*, 28 July 1982, pp. 34 ff.

[5] Fritz, H.-J., "People in Office Environments. On Long-Term Changes in Spatial Working Conditions in Offices, with a Comparison of Cell and Open-Plan Offices," Heinz Moos Publishing Co., Munich, Germany, 1982.

[6] Jockusch, P., "Conflicts in Office Design," paper presented at the 4th Conference of the International Association for the Study of People and Their Physical Surroundings at the Universite Catholique de Louvain-la-Neuve, 1979, available from the author.

[7] Becker, Duffy, Ellis, Ettinger-Brinckmann, Jockusch, Wilson, "Achieving Office Quality," a report of cross-cultural research on the nature of office quality and its relation to the processes of development, design, procurement, and management, Anglo-German Foundation, London, in press.

[8] "Preparatory Feasibility Study for the Realization-Competition for the District Authority of Gifhorn," city of Gifhorn, Germany, Ed., 1980.

[9] Hegger, M. and Kennedy, M., "Empty Schools—Problems or Chances?", *Bauwelt*, No. 3, 1981.

[10] Thompson, M., *Rubbish Theory. The Creation and Destruction of Value*, Oxford University Press, New York, 1979.

[11] Burckhardt, L., "Monument Preservation as Social Politics," *Congress Proceedings*, Department of Town Planning, University of Kassel, Kassel, Germany, 1977.

[12] Beier, W. and Caster, B., "Monument Protection in the Year 2000," thesis, Department of Architecture, University of Kassel, Kassel, Germany.

Bibliography

Hegger, M., Hegger-Luhnen, D., Jockusch, P., Krietsch, H.-J., "Future Use of Redundant School Buildings," monograph, National Institute of School Buildings, Berlin, Germany, 1977.

Jockusch, P. and Hegger, M., "Operational Analysis and Utilization Investigations as Means for User Needs Assessments—Examples from Natural Sciences and Nonclinical Medicine," monograph, Central Archives for University Planning, Stuttgart, Germany, 1977.

Jockusch, P., "User Attitudes Towards Facilities Management," paper presented at the Professional Seminar on Facilities Management in Institutions of Higher Education, CERI/IMHE/GC/77, OECD, Paris, Sept. 1977.

E. George Stern[1]

Planning Standard Guidelines for Inspection and Evaluation of the Structural Condition of Existing Buildings

REFERENCE: Stern, E. G., **"Planning Standard Guidelines for Inspection and Evaluation of the Structural Condition of Existing Buildings,"** *Building Performance: Function, Preservation, and Rehabilitation, ASTM STP 901,* G. Davis, Ed., American Society for Testing and Materials, Philadelphia, 1985, pp. 86–89.

ABSTRACT: The guidelines for the inspection and evaluation of the structural condition of existing buildings provide information on how to approach the inspection and evaluation, what to look for during such an inspection, how to evaluate observations, and how to determine what actions should be taken and what procedures should be followed in improving a given situation in which the building is found. The guidelines are both material- and system-oriented, thus covering the materials commonly used in building construction and repair as well as the systems involved in the design and construction of the structural members, components, subassemblies, and unfinished as well as completed buildings.

KEY WORDS: buildings, building construction, evaluation, inspection, reconditioning, rehabilitation, repair, upgrading

Purpose

The guidelines are designed to assist building owners, designers, builders, building officials, and regulatory bodies in making technical decisions to evaluate the structural condition of buildings when consideration is given to repair, reconditioning, rehabilitation, and upgrading of existing buildings to meet specific use requirements and to fulfill given performance criteria. Thus, it is envisaged that these guidelines will serve as tools for the structural assessment of buildings in line with existing or anticipated occupancy and use requirements or both.

[1]Chairman, ASTM E06.14.01 Task Group, and Earle B. Norris Research Professor Emeritus of Wood Construction, Virginia Polytechnic Institute and State University, Blacksburg, VA 24060.

Introduction

As recently as 1979, more than $42 billion was spent in the United States on the upkeep and improvement of residential buildings, while $77 billion was spent on new housing, according to the U.S. Department of Commerce. In addition, an estimated $425 billion is being spent annually in the nonresidential rehabilitation field, with this amount continuously increasing from year to year. It is assumed that the renovation industry has grown approximately 12% annually during the past few years. Indications are that this trend will increase, particularly during difficult economic times in order to fill existing pent-up demand when construction is restrained because of a lack of funding.

Renovation of existing buildings and the repair of damaged buildings are important activities. How, when, and what to renovate and repair are usually based on somewhat haphazard personal or committee approaches and decisions and not necessarily on systematic and detailed studies in line with standard procedures prepared by experts in given fields.

Many fundamental decisions need to be made when giving consideration to the renovation and repair of buildings. They include, in addition to the structural aspects dealt with here, those concerning humanitarian, social, cultural, environmental, transportation and traffic, architectural, management, construction, performance, maintainability and maintenance, use flexibility economic, energy, material, and human resource requirements and considerations. From the technical viewpoint, they need to cover not only the structural but also the mechanical aspects, which are described in the governing documents issued by code and regulatory authorities. In most instances, these documents have been issued to be applicable to new construction and are, therefore, not necessarily applicable to the renovation and repair of existing buildings.

Because renovation and repair have reached an ever increasing importance in our times, many studies have been performed and have been proposed recently in this field to cover some of the aspects listed. However, little thought appears to have been given by the experts to the systematic evaluation of the structural condition of existing buildings. Therefore, a demand seems to exist for systematic guidelines for the inspection and evaluation of the structural condition of existing buildings which can be of assistance to building owners, designers, builders, and building officials in making structural evaluation decisions. Such guidelines could be included by reference in the documents which are issued by code and regulatory authorities and, therefore, could be applicable whenever the structural condition of existing buildings is under investigation for decision-making purposes under given conditions.

The guidelines have to be based on precise rating and classification standards to be established with respect to inspection and evaluation of the structural condition of existing buildings. These standards have to serve as the basis of measuring the structural condition and of indicating, for example, what is an acceptable and nonacceptable structural condition.

Guideline Subject Matters

The proposed guidelines are expected to cover:

1. *Materials*
   (a) concrete and reinforced concrete
   (b) stone and masonry
   (c) wood and wood-base products
   (d) ferrous metals
   (e) nonferrous metals
   (f) gypsum and gypsum products
   (g) glass
   (h) plastics and composites
   (i) paper and paper products
2. *Systems*
   (a) foundations
   (b) structural framing
   (c) floors
   (d) walls and partitions
   (e) ceilings
   (f) roofs
   (g) ramps and stairs
   (h) chimneys and fire places
   (i) building environment

Program

The various chapters which are to cover these aspects are to be written by volunteers who have the specific expertise in the particular field under scrutiny. Each author or group of authors is to be responsible for his special contribution. On the other hand, like most other ASTM publications, each guideline chapter will be reviewed and will pass through the ASTM consensus route in order to assure that all viewpoints—that is, those of the producers, users, and specialists—have been given due consideration.

The proposed standard guidelines should be representative of the overall thinking of all involved directly or indirectly in the subject matter.

The inspection is to include: (1) periodic inspection as a part of the routine maintenance program; and (2) nontechnical inspection (a) to assure continued performance where problems may or may not be anticipated, (b) to follow a cataclysmic natural or man-made event, (c) to follow failure of a structural member, component, subassembly, or building, and (d) to determine the structural condition on behalf of an existing or anticipated occupancy or in the light of an anticipated use change or an addition, whether planned or not.

The evaluation may be based on: (1) a preliminary inspection to look for obvious problems or areas requiring detailed inspection and a summary condition report, (2) a detailed inspection which may be nondestructive in nature, (3) observation evaluation, and (4) field sampling. Such evaluation and diagnosis may culminate in recommendations of procedures for corrective actions, including repair, reinforcement, rehabilitation, and other forms of modification, if required, not considered a part of this standard.

Such recommendations would recognize that it is frequently not economically feasible or justified to bring an existing structure up to currently acceptable governing code requirements and regulations. The recommended procedure must be cost-effective for the anticipated service life of the building without knowingly compromising the occupant's safety. Whenever repairs and reinforcement work are required and to be undertaken, other forms of upgrading the building also may be desirable and requested at that time.

The structural condition is to be described in the structural assessment of the building as found during its inspection and evaluation and should include such statements which can lead to justified and economically feasible rehabilitation, reconditioning, and possible upgrading.

Existing buildings include old (including historic) and new, conventional and exotic, structurally simple and designed, inspector-approved and condemned buildings, be they residential or nonresidential, which are used or can be made useful in such a way as is anticipated. Such buildings may have been erected using a variety of construction materials and construction techniques and may be in any performance condition which may range from excellent to poor to condemned.

Publication

It is presently anticipated that the completed chapters of the proposed guidelines be presented at appropriate meetings and conferences. They should be published as soon as a consensus has been reached as to their contents. Such publication may take place in the "grey section" of the appropriate ASTM Book of Standards in order for such material to become generally available as soon as feasible. Finally, publication of all chapters is expected in an ASTM standard guideline separate or in book form.

In the light of the billions of dollars expended in this and other countries annually in renovation and rehabilitation of existing buildings, guidelines for the inspection and evaluation of the structural condition of existing buildings, properly prepared by experts in the field involved, might become a best-seller among ASTM-sponsored publications.

Chapter Authors

Anybody with expertise in the fields involved and who is willing to contribute to the proposed guidelines should contact the author of this paper for such details as will be needed prior to the drafting of the guideline chapters.

Building Preservation and Rehabilitation for Historical Buildings and Building Materials

Volker H. Hartkopf[1] and Vivian E. Loftness[1]

Promoting Energy-Efficient Rehabilitation and New Infill Construction in the Inner City

REFERENCE: Hartkopf, V. H. and Loftness, V. E., **"Promoting Energy-Efficient Rehabilitation and New Infill Construction in the Inner City,"** *Building Performance: Function, Preservation, and Rehabilitation, ASTM STP 901*, G. Davis, Ed., American Society for Testing and Materials, Philadelphia, 1986, pp. 93–110.

ABSTRACT: During the past decade, major technical advances were made in energy conservation and in the use of alternate energy sources for residential construction. At the same time, the problem of rising energy costs has increased for large segments of the population, offering an unprecedented stimulus for energy-efficient construction practices. Nonetheless, the actual introduction of the new energy technologies into the planning, design, construction, and use of housing today still remains surprisingly unsophisticated and often is localized to new middle-class suburbs. This paper introduces an inner-city case study and demonstration project in Pittsburgh, Pennsylvania, that has attempted to penetrate these problem areas by demonstrating the political, economic, social, and technical reality of major energy savings afforded by inner-city rehabilitation and infill construction. To promote the introduction of the available new materials and energy technologies into the existing housing development process, the project team has developed workbooks of relevant guidelines, targeted at key decision-making groups: politicians and community officials; financiers, appraisers, and developers; designers and builders; and owners and renters.

KEY WORDS: inner-city revitalization, urban redevelopment, energy-conscious urban infill, rehabilitation, retrofit, energy-efficient housing

Project History

The Manchester inner-city case study and demonstration project deals with the needs of a typical declining inner-city neighborhood with a dwindling population of low to moderate income residents. As with many nongentrified urban neighborhoods, rising energy and housing costs combined with stagnant incomes have resulted in greatly reduced disposable incomes for the resi-

[1] Associate professor and adjunct associate professor, respectively, Institute of Building Sciences, Department of Architecture, Carnegie-Mellon University, Pittsburgh, PA 15213.

dents, leading in many cases to the necessity of fuel subsidies. In fact, the approximately 1000 households in Manchester spent $1 million for gas and electricity in 1980. By 1985, this in all likelihood will rise to 2 to $3 million, absorbing up to 100% of the disposable income of many of today's residents. Despite the $40 million of fuel subsidies in Philadelphia in 1980, the $150 million in Pennsylvania, and the $1.5 billion per annum in the nation, few active programs have been developed for the energy-efficient rehabilitation and infill of inner-city neighborhoods.

Conceived by Carnegie-Mellon University's Institute of Building Science with the Manchester Citizens' Corp. and supported by the U.S. Department of Energy, the Pittsburgh Urban Redevelopment Authority, and the Department of Housing and Urban Development, the Manchester project was founded on the premise that both national and community political, economic, and social goals could be met through inner-city revitalization. For the nation, this translates into a significant decrease in imported energy dependency, a measurable improvement in environmental quality, and a partial alternative to fuel subsidy (and eventual housing subsidy) for low income residents through decreased energy demand. For the community, this effort translates into improved housing conditions both physically and thermally, the arrested decline of the neighborhood, and the potential for continuously affordable housing through stable or reduced energy outlays.

The Manchester project (Fig. 1) is successfully demonstrating the advantages of inner-city revitalization through the energy-efficient rehabilitation of abandoned housing (12 units by Carl Detweiler and Associates), the energy retrofit of existing housing (10 units by Richard Glance and Associates), and the infill of new energy-efficient construction on vacant land (15 units by Urban Design Associates). As an alternative to continuing urban sprawl, the repetition of this form of inner-city revitalization has the following energy and related advantages:

1. Significant reduction of transportation costs (energy and other) by reducing distances from home to work, home to entertainment, and home to services and the renewed viability of urban public transportation by increasing density.

2. Improved use of urban infrastructure and the significant embodied energy therein (easily measured against the creation of new infrastructure for equal numbers of dwelling units in the suburbs) and a corresponding improved tax base for the city.

3. Reduced need for fuel subsidy and potentially associated housing subsidies in the future.

4. Decreased individual heating consumption through such energy conservation measures as increased densities, shared walls, improved construction materials and standards, more efficient appliances, and energy use guidelines; this provides a corresponding improvement in thermal comfort.

Although the technologies are available, the market is ready, and the advantages of energy-efficient revitalization of the inner city are undisputed, the method for promoting these changes within the existing housing development process still is not clear. As will be described, the Manchester project has developed a four-prong method aimed at critical decisionmakers—politicians, financiers, designers/builders, and users—for promoting the energy-efficient rehabilitation and infill of housing in the inner city.

Promoting Inner-City Energy-Efficient Revitalization

Today, promoting the integration and use of the multitude of new materials, components, techniques, and designs already available for significant energy conservation in housing is a far more significant problem than the refinement and development of new energy technologies. In effect, the ultimate test of the existing innovations must be their acceptance and integration within the present building development process. Innovation must work within existing political, social, economic, and technical contexts. To achieve this in the case of the energy-efficient revitalization of Manchester, four conditions were taken as givens:

1. *Technical*—No radical departure from the existing construction process would be undertaken, such as the introduction of "high-tech" wall constructions relying on industrial processes. Instead, the project would demonstrate the potential of incremental improvement of existing materials, technologies, and construction processes.

2. *Economic*—Economic viability and affordability must be assured, implying that additional capital costs must be offset by the monetary savings of energy dollars within first-year mortgage and energy costs of comparable housing.

3. *Social-Cultural*—Building types, materials, and images must be suitable to the existing community and the historic context, enhancing neighborhood viability and acceptability within the city.

4. *Political*—The mix of housing approaches—rehabilitation, renovation, and new infill construction—must improve the city tax base, reduce the threat and reality of subsidies, and improve the image of the urban core. This improvement must outweigh the normal political alternative of continued commercial and warehouse development.

Based on the successful introduction of highly energy-efficient infill housing and energy-efficient rehabilitated and renovated housing in Manchester, four workbooks were written [1–4]. These workbooks are intended to illustrate and quantify the costs and benefits of the revitalization project to their respective audiences: politicians, financiers, designers/builders, and users. Most importantly, these workbooks are intended to promote a wider spread continuation of energy-efficient inner-city revitalization.

FIG. 1(a)—*Manchester project—Sheffield Street.*

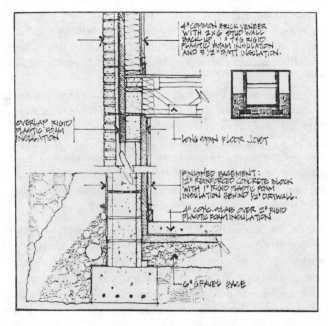

FIG. 1(b)—*Manchester project—foundation details.*

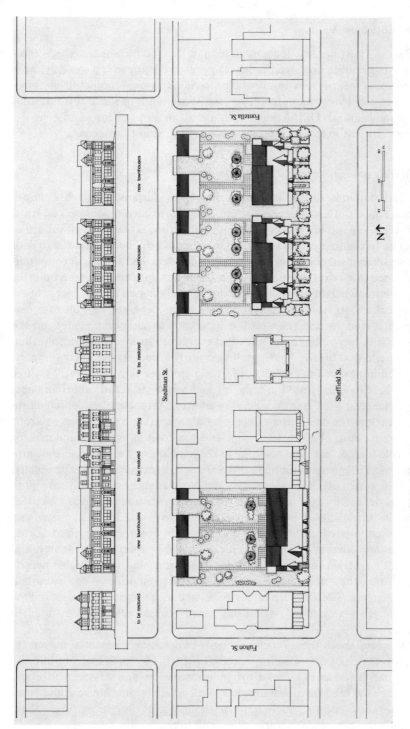

FIG. 1(c)—Manchester project—site plan and street elevation.

The Politicians' Vantage

Over the past decade, federal, state, and local politicians have been challenged to generate and enact policies to conserve nonrenewable energy, be it for national security, environmental protection, regional competitiveness (reduced cost of living, manufacturing, transportation), or social rest (affordable home heating). Of the range of solutions, in terms of costs and benefits, energy-efficient urban revitalization is one of the most promising.

Urban Revitalization or Suburban Sprawl?

There should be no doubt that housing that is clustered to increase density within a mixed-use urban area, offering close proximity of jobs and services, will create vastly more energy-efficient neighborhoods than present suburban models. In the first place, the urban townhouse neighborhood saves 70% of the site-embodied energy needed by standard detached suburban communities, since this infrastructure exists in the urban core and must be built for new suburban neighborhoods. Secondly, the building-embodied energy in existing urban structures provides a 50% savings per dwelling unit over new suburban construction (new infill construction in the urban center, on the other hand, has no building-embodied energy advantage over new suburban construction). Thirdly, housing clustering (row houses and low-rise apartment buildings) at a net density of 15 to 35 units per acre can save 20 to 30% of the heating energy used in today's single family detached suburban housing designed at 5 to 7 units per acre. In addition, promoting residential movement back to the cities offers the potential to weatherize and energy retrofit existing buildings and to set design and construction energy standards for new construction with the potential of reducing present residential consumption up to 85% in new buildings and 50 to 80% in existing buildings. Finally, the close proximity of jobs, services, and entertainment can easily save 30 to 50% of the energy used in daily personal transportation, as well as make feasible the efficiencies of public transportation systems. Indeed, the facts and figures assimilated in the urban-suburban comparison completed at Carnegie-Mellon University [5] clearly indicate that the opportunity to achieve significant long-term energy savings is far more promising within higher density mixed-use urban neighborhoods than in existing suburbs or new suburban developments. The absolute values associated with these percentages and the graphic ten-year impact on housing energy consumption is illustrated in Fig. 2.

Over and above these inherent energy efficiencies, residential movement back to the cities offers an unparalleled potential for politicians to improve the urban tax base, to increase urban infrastructure and services utilization, to reduce the need for alternative low to moderate income housing and housing subsidies, and to greatly improve the image of the "increasingly abandoned" city as a place to work, shop, and live.

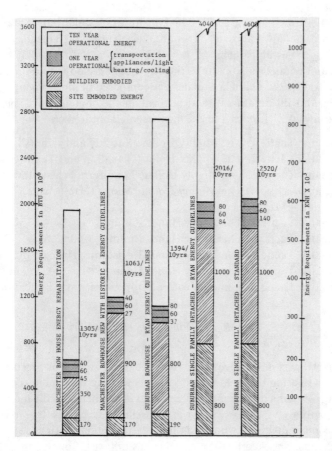

FIG. 2—*Initial and ten-year energy requirements for various urban and suburban housing types.*

The Political Approach to Energy-Efficient Urban Revitalization

Significant energy-conserving residential and mixed-use urban revitalization will not be realized without political intervention. Market forces alone will encourage only those who have the power and ability to realize private profits without paying attention to balancing overall city image and welfare. Adopting a "laissez-faire" attitude under present conditions will favor continued suburban sprawl, urban residential abandonment replaced with parking lots, warehouses, and vacancy, continued tax-base deterioration; and increased fuel subsidies, and ultimately will increase separation of upper and lower income groups as the rising energy costs must be absorbed by those least able to afford them. Consequently, the city and region must set goals for the functional, social, economic, and visual mix desired. In "The Politicians' Workbook [1]," the fundamentals of a healthy, vibrant urban redevelopment have been described in case studies, looking at successful urban revitalization in Baltimore, Salem, Lancaster, Toronto, New York, and Toledo.

Following the establishment of the fundamentals and rules that will help make urban revitalization possible, the city must develop tactics for their realization. Today, the politicians' palette is composed of nine major financial, legislative, and informational tactics, forming the contents of "The Politicians' Workbook." Tactics 4 and 5 have been elaborated on.

"Politicians' Tactic 1. The Mighty Dollar: Subsidy and Grants"
"Politicians' Tactic 2. The Mighty Dollar: Taxation and Tax Incentives"
"Politicians' Tactic 3. The Mighty Dollar: Long-term Private Investment"
"Politicians' Tactic 4. The Mighty Dollar: Short-Term Private"
   (Speculative) Investment"
"Politicians' Tactic 5. The Heavy Hand: Zoning"
"Politicians' Tactic 6. The Heavy Hand: Building Codes"
"Politicians' Tactic 7. The Heavy Hand: Registering Historic Buildings"
"Politicians' Tactic 8. The Heavy Hand: Giving Power to Communities"
"Politicians' Tactic 9. Communication: Opportunity and Education"

Politicians' Tactic 4. The Mighty Dollar: Short-Term Private
(Speculative) Investment

Many Northeast cities have made their greatest catches for speculative investment by floating bonds to provide lenders with tax-free interest earnings, making investments in the inner city equal to investments on the money market. Unfortunately, abuses also were possible, especially by well-versed higher income individuals who used these tax-free bonds to finance their own neighborhoods. Shocked by substantial losses in taxes, Congress hastily shut down the entire building bond-writing program, leaving the struggling inner-city neighborhoods without investors. The second major short-term investors in revitalization are those who see a clear promise of return on investment, either through setting up businesses that could ostensibly survive anywhere or by the advertisement value of their "good neighbor" actions. The third major speculative investor group is composed of enlightened developers with an undying faith in urban centers or a continuing social conscience. John Portman of Atlanta, the Rouse Corp., the National Housing Partnership, among others, have demonstrated this faith in the rebuilding of some of the most exciting urban centers.

The politicians' role in these speculative investments, however, is critical. The city's image, its tax incentives, its infrastructure, and its services must be sound. Salesmanship and an enlightened picture of the city's best future must be continually portrayed and supported. Legislation must be in place to ensure that these speculative investments will help build the city in the best possible way, from zoning densities, mixed use, setbacks, and parks to setting building codes for scale, detail, quality, and energy efficiency. Without these

guidelines and the opportunities for a real return on investment in the revitalization of inner cities, many urban neighborhoods will be displaced by profit-
able (at low land values) parking garages and warehouses. The Manchester
neighborhood redevelopment has succeeded because of all three short-term
tactics—bonds, enlightened developers, and a growing potential for real return on investment—supported by a long-standing political commitment.

Politicians' Tactic 5. The Heavy Hand: Zoning

Trends in city and town zoning practices have been to differentiate land
use, building type, and density. Taken to its extreme, the separation of "in-
compatible land uses" created sterile downtown areas, isolating activities
from each other and destroying the mixture and vitality of neighborhoods.
Eventually, high land values in the central city became principle obstacles to
making cities attractive places to live. Even if builders were able to assemble a
sufficient plot of this land with great difficulty, they would be forced because
of its cost to develop it at a density and quality that would ensure exclusivity.
The remaining old neighborhoods, isolated from urban vitality by both
cheap-and-simple land uses (for parking lots) and central business districts,
have little chance of attracting new residents. New approaches to zoning,
however, can encourage a better relationship between housing, work, entertainment, services, and transportation, with a fuller understanding of the pedestrian scale and mixed-use density needed for successful residential neighborhoods.

Incentive zoning offers the developer a benefit of additional density or
larger coverage in exchange for such public amenities as pocket parks, pedes-
trians arcades, etc. Special district zoning, pioneered in New York City, identifies the theme of an area—its physical mix of activities and its social and
cultural texture—and then ensures its preservation through zoning. This type
of zoning can maintain significant historic buildings as cornerstones or cata-
lysts for neighborhood development, waterfront views, unique scale and
building detail, theatre districts, or existing boutique or craft areas. Zoning
for street amenities can include regulations for tree planting and maintenance
(even by private building owners), regulations for public open spaces, cano-
pies, balconies, benches, historic district lighting, etc. The critical factor is
maintaining a continuous pedestrian access and a favorable mix of activities,
avoiding the "broken teeth" of parking lots, loading docks, and faceless commercial building walls.

All tactics must be analyzed one by one, looking for known successes and
failures, workable combinations, and promising possibilities. The debate between free enterprise and political intervention also must be addressed, realizing that there is no completely "free" market system where no government-
sponsored incentives and subsidies and hidden social costs cannot be found.
In the interest of social integration, energy efficiency, and quality of life, poli-

ticians must understand the costs and benefits of all regional, urban, and neighborhood programs and reinforce those tactics or combination of tactics that create the best conditions for urban revitalization. Throughout the selection and implementation of these tactics for urban renewal, however, it should be remembered that energy conservation offers a key to lasting residential urban revitalization.

The Designers' and Builders' Vantage

With land, construction, and energy costs outpacing personal income increases in the past decade by a factor of two to one, the affordability (and subsequent purchases) of median-priced housing has greatly reduced. Today, the depleted housing market potential can be increased only by more economically designed, constructed, and maintained housing. To this end, higher density housing in the inner city, especially in partially abandoned neighborhoods, has the greatest potential for cost savings in land purchase, site preparation, maintenance, and related personal transportation costs. New building forms such as terraced housing, maisonette configurations, and developments in traditional rowhousing have demonstrated that higher density housing does not spell the loss of privacy or identity. Indeed, the minimum-side-yard, insensitively windowed, detached homes now being built in the suburbs often result in greater loss of privacy, identity, and image than urban townhousing.

Consequently, the energy advantages of shared walls, reduced exposure, and favorable orientation can now be promoted as a viable if not preferable way of providing new housing. Given the cost and energy savings offered by this design step alone and the addition of major energy-conserving technologies and components, designers and builders now can provide a greater number of dwelling units affordable to a greater number of people. As calculated and now demonstrated in the Manchester energy-efficient revitalization project, the critical design and construction steps necessary for providing affordable energy-efficient housing in the inner city include the following.

Designer/Builder Tactic 1: Build Urban Densities

Medium-density housing should be the focus of urban revitalization, aiming at 25 to 35 dwelling units per net residential acre. In Manchester, this was achieved through a combination of 15 to 20 units per acre of infill housing on vacant land and 35 units per acre of rehabilitated shared housing. In comparison to the 7 units per residential acre typical of dense single-family housing, the decision to go to shared walls saves 2500 to $3000 per unit for construction ($300 per year in mortgage costs) and 20 to 25% of the heating energy required (approximately $140 per year), not to mention the savings on land costs.

Designer/Builder Tactic 2: Significantly Improve Building Insulation and Tightness

Additional insulation, improved detailing to reduce air infiltration including an exterior wind (not vapor) barrier and a continuous interior vapor barrier, well-oriented, high-quality windows and doors, and a sun-space porch have been calculated to reduce heating energy demand of medium-density town house units by an additional 50 to 55%. Specifically, the guidelines call for an approximate doubling of thermal-resistance values from R11 in standard construction to R25–27 for walls and from R19 to R35–37 for ceilings/roofs, in conjunction with reducing window area to 25% of exposed wall and cutting air infiltration to less than 0.7 air changes per hour.

This savings of approximately $230 per year was offered at an additional construction cost of $6500 per unit. Although this additional expenditure would not provide a cost-effective alternative alone (adding $675 to the annual mortgage), in combination with the first- and long-term cost savings offered by the increased density step, the design/construction package is already cost-effective in the first year. As a welcome alternative to the suburban single family home, the designer and builder now can offer a new inner-city home at equal carrying costs in the first year, including mortgage and fuel, with steadily improving financial conditions for the urban dweller as fuel costs continue to rise.

Designer/Builder Tactic 3: Optimize Responsiveness to Climate for Energy Conservation, Passive Heating, and Cooling

Arriving at a dwelling design, specification, and construction based on Tactic 1 and Tactic 2 alone most likely would result in an unpleasantly dark dwelling isolated from its surroundings. In order to mitigate the climatic liabilities and to utilize climatic assets (view, light, outdoor living), the following guidelines [6–8] also were enacted in the Manchester project. Use landscaping to provide protection from the harsh winter winds, to provide shade from the harsh summer sun, and allow the winter sun to strike the building surfaces. Orient the building so that at least one major face of the building sees the winter sun, so that winter winds are not head on, and so that summer winds can be felt. Configure the home so that self-shading is provided on the southern facade (and east and west if they are exposed) and introduce extensions to capture winter sunshine (sun-space porch) and buffer winter winds (air lock entry). Size and design openings to maximize solar gain, providing 10% glass area on the north while allocating 30% glass area on the south; provide controls such as air locks at all major doors and night insulation at windows to reduce heat loss while optimizing solar gain. As seen in Table 1, these climate guidelines for urban infill design and construction can offer an estimated additional 25 to 30% savings (5000 Btu/ft^2/year for the already conserving row house).

TABLE 1—*Long-term energy impact attributed to various decisionmakers.*
X = direct; O = indirect, through, for example, legislation.

Choices	Energy Impact per Equivalent Unit Size				Politicians	Communities	Lenders	Developers	Appraisers	Real Estate	Designers	Builders	Owners	Renters
	1 year	30 years	1 year	30 years										
	Inner-City Revitalization		Suburban New											
Location (embodied energy & transport)	460	1620	1880	2600	X	X		X	O				X	X
	Rowhouse		Detached											
Building type (exposed surface)	70	2100	100	3000	O			X			X	X		
	Energy Efficient		Standard											
Energy conserving design/construction quality	20	600	70	2100	O	O	X	X	O	X	X	X	O	
	Conserving		Nonconserving											
Appliance quality	30	900	60	1800	O	O		X				X	X	
User impact (moderate)	50	500	130	1300	O								X	X
30-year total, moderate user	5720 million btu		10 800 million btu											

The Homeowners' and Renters' Vantage

Since rising energy costs are becoming a more and more significant contribution to our annual cost-of-living increases, homeowners and renters (especially at low to moderate incomes) must protect disposable income through energy conservation or thermal discomfort or both. Presently, living in a standard-construction, single-family home in the suburbs with standard appliances, moderate energy-operating practices, and commuting to work requires about $230 per month in total energy use (heating, electricity, car travel). By contrast, an energy-conserving row house in the inner city with efficient appliances, improved energy-operating practices, and minor commutes to work requires only $100 per month in total energy use. For a family with a combined income of $20,000, this can mean the difference between 26 and 7% of their disposable income for energy (Table 2). With a doubling of present energy prices, this difference will grow to 40 and 11% of disposable income. By

TABLE 2—*Percentage of disposable[a] income needed for energy.*

Family of 4: Gross Annual Income	Suburban Home, 20 Miles from Work, Standard Construction, Single Family Unit		Inner-City Home, Bus or Walking Distance from Work and Shops, Energy Conserving Rowhouse	
	Percentage of Disposable Income for Energy		Percentage of Disposable Income for Energy	
	Normal Energy Users	Extreme Savers	Normal Energy Users	Extreme Savers
$30 000	14%	11%	7%	4%
$20 000	26%	20%	14%	7%
$10 000	70%	54%	36%	18%

[a] Income *after* taxes, social security, insurance, health. Income *before* food, clothing, entertainment, education.

this time, the $10 000-income family has no discretionary income left and is, in fact, living in poverty.

To counteract this growing plight, today's homeowner and renter have five responsible steps to take: selection of appropriate location; selection of appropriate building type; selection of appropriate building design and construction quality; selection of energy-efficient appliances and decorations; and, finally, energy-efficient home caretaking including daily, monthly, and annual activities. In combination, these five steps can promise the homeowner or renter up to 85% energy savings or as much as $1600 a year as compared to traditional energy costs.

Homeowner Tactic 1. Select the Most Energy-Efficient Location

Even a zero-energy house in the suburbs would still demand a 40-mile round-trip car commute to work. Housing that is located within walking or short bus commute to work could save the homeowner over $600 a year (including busing costs) in gas, maintenance, and repairs. In addition, there is the energy embodied in the site and services to be considered, a cost indirectly charged to the homeowner.

Homeowner Tactic 2. Select the Most Energy-Efficient Building Type

Confronted with a choice between purchasing or renting an apartment, an attached town house, or a single-family detached home, the homeowner or renter should be aware of the heating energy associated with the various building types. To this end, the critical factor is the square footage of shared walls, exposed walls, and heated floor area. Row houses with identical floor area, insulation levels, and construction detailing will require 25% less heat-

ing energy than the comparable detached home (assuming identical user behavior). In general, "middle" apartments of equivalent floor area and construction will consume 50% less heating energy than the detached home.

Homeowner Tactic 3. Select for Energy-Efficient Design and Construction Quality

As previously described, the siting, landscaping, orientation, configuration, opening design, and overall construction quality contributes to more
than 80% savings in heating energy requirements compared to present standard construction practices. The lion's share of this savings is contributed by:
compact forms (just stated); well-insulated outside wall, roof, and even floor
with careful design and construction to ensure air tightness; as well as air-lock
entries and double-glazed windows orientated for solar gain. The Manchester
project has demonstrated that these 80% savings can be achie͵ ᴗ economically. It is important, however, that the home buyer or renter look at all
monthly carrying costs (mortgage *and* energy for heating, appliances, transportation) to appreciate the value of the sometimes higher priced, energy-
efficient home.

Homeowner Tactic 4. Look for Energy-Efficient Appliances

Energy requirements for appliances such as refrigerators/freezers, washers, dryers, dishwashers, stoves/ovens, television, and lighting can cost up to
$360 a year (approaching 70 million Btus of energy) in an average home, if the
appliances are used often and energy inefficiently. Different makes of appliances, however, can have significantly varying energy requirements. One re-
frigerator-freezer may cost $55 a year to run while another may cost $85 a
year. These annual costs can make a big economic difference, especially if one
plans to own an appliance for several years. Careful shopping and possibly
small additional cash outlays in appliance purchasing can save the homeowner more than 50% of the annual energy consumption for appliances
(Fig. 3).

Homeowner Tactic 5. Energy-Conserving Home Caretaking

Although the house location, type, construction quality, and appliances
have major impacts on home energy consumption, the occupants can halve or
double the estimated annual operating costs through their home "caretaking." There are basically two kinds of home caretakers: the "energy
waster," who overheats the house and opens the window, leaves on all the
lights, and uses appliances with only partial loads, and the "energy saver." In
a nonenergy-conserving home, the waster may spend $1800 a year in house-
hold energy, compared to the saver who spends $900. In the energy-efficient

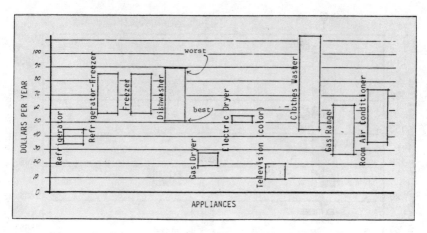

FIG. 3—*Cost of appliance use: range from best to worst in each category, average annual cost.*

home described in Homeowner Tactics 1 to 4, the waster may spend $800 a year in household energy, while the saver spends only $400! (Fig. 4).

"The Homeowners' Workbook" [4] describes the daily, monthly, and annual activities required to save this 400 to $900 (or even $1400!). The caretaking steps range from the energy-efficient use of home heating, home electricity, and home hot water to transportation and home cooling (or summer comfort if cooling systems are not used). As shown in Fig. 5, the home caretaking guidelines describe the actions for heating energy savings possible through managing windows, walls and roofs, outside doors, inside doors, clothing and fabrics; heating system management; heating system maintenance; and the energy-efficient use of sunshine. The caretaking actions for electricity energy savings focus on the efficient use and maintenance of lights, refrigerators-freezers, ovens and stoves, dishwashers, clothes washers, dryers, and television sets. The home caretaking needed for hot water savings (for energy *and* water bills) includes efficiency in clothes washing, showering or bathing, dishwashing, and food and hand washing. Finally, the home caretaking needed for staying cool in summer, and cooling energy savings if fans or air conditioners are used, returns our focus to the management of windows, walls and roofs, clothing and fabrics; cooling system management and maintenance; and in this case the energy-efficient use of wind.

The Financiers' Vantage

The four major groups addressed in the "Financiers' Workbook" [2] are: developers, lenders, appraisers, and real estate brokers. The overall aim of these groups is profit through developing, financing, owning, and selling real estate. Although they play different roles in the pursuit of this goal, each of these real estate financiers is particularly sensitive to the accurate assessment

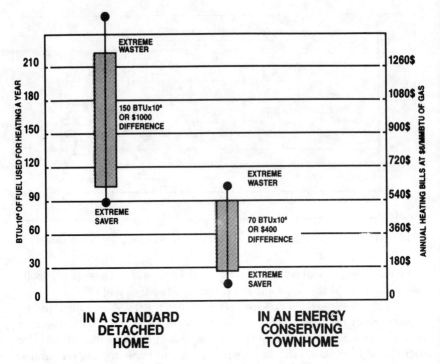

FIG. 4—*Wasters versus savers.*

of the short- and long-term economic effects of political, social, technical, and economic forces.

Major forces in the political context, such as tax laws, civil rights legislation (that is, school desegregation, fair housing), energy pricing and regulation, as well as federal lending practices, all have a strong influence on regional population migration and the relative attractiveness of urban redevelopment or suburban expansion. The forces in the social context also are critical to the financiers since they influence the consumers' choice of location and type of housing. These social forces include the actual or perceived quality of public schools, ethnic relationships, consumer awareness of energy issues, consumer perceptions of urban versus suburban quality of life, and trends in population statistics (household formation, size, and age of households). The technical context encompasses the range and quality of design and construction services, as well as the suitability of technical solutions to issues of building performance, including energy efficiency. The economic context sets the final stage for arbitration between these political, social, and technical forces. Consumer income, availability of capital, cost and availability of existing housing and new construction, as well as energy costs and availability, all set limits of affordability and marketability.

Within these contexts, developers assess housing markets, consumer pref-

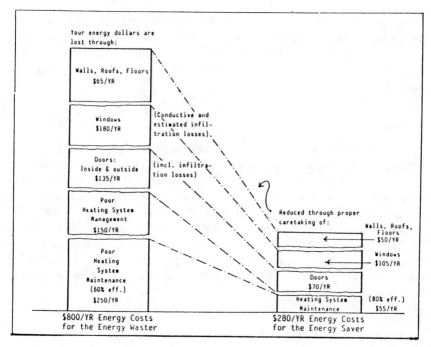

FIG. 5—*Winter heating: home caretaking is critical; the potential differences in annual energy costs in the 1500-ft^2 energy-conserving home.*

erences, and incomes; they determine economic performances of investment alternatives; and they select location and design approaches. Their "bottom line" is high return on investment. Lenders, approached by developers and buyers, must assess the marketability and income potential of a project to determine the amount to be lent and to assess risk appropriately. For this group of financiers, the "bottom line" is secure return on investment. Appraisers in turn assist lenders, buyers, and sellers in the estimation of the economic value of an existing or proposed property through market, income, or cost approaches. Their primary interest is to sell professional services. Brokers sell real estate and steer customers to "preferred" locations.

"The Financiers' Workbook" [2] describes the rationale and method for integrating energy conservation principles into the decision-making processes of these financial players. Energy conservation produces the following advantages. Low operating energy costs improve the affordability of housing. If housing can be supplied at lower *combined* monthly mortgage and operating costs, greater numbers of people can purchase and maintain housing. This increased affordability is particularly valuable to developers. Lower operating energy costs also enable homeowners, in the face of rising fuel costs, to pay their monthly mortgage installments. This reduced risk of foreclosure is particularly valuable to lenders. Similarly, renters can pay their monthly rent, which suits the developer-landlord. With increasing consumer awareness, energy-conserving developments have a considerable competitive advantage over nonconserving ones. Since it is now extremely valuable to assess the energy performance of housing, an additional market also can be opened for appraisers.

Conclusion

The inner-city case study and demonstration project in Pittsburgh, Pa., has attempted to introduce new energy-conserving technologies into existing urban development processes by demonstrating the political, economic, social, and technical viability of these technologies. To encourage replication, the project team has developed workbooks of relevant guidelines for the major decision-making groups. Table 1 quantifies the impact each of these decision-making groups offers to overall energy performance in urban redevelopment. The overwhelming advantages of urban revitalization over continued urban and suburban sprawl should leave little doubt as to the validity of energy-conscious urban revitalization.

References

[1] Loftness, V., Hartkopf, V., and Yoran, N., "The Politicians' Workbook For Energy-Conserving Urban Revitalization," DOE Contract DE-AC02-79CS29287, Carnegie-Mellon University, Pittsburgh, PA, Dec. 1981.

[2] Bartos, S., McGunigle, and Collins, A., "The Financiers' Workbook For Energy Conservation Benefits," DOE Contract DE-AC02-79CS29287, Carnegie-Mellon University, Pittsburgh, PA, Aug. 1982.

[3] Bartos, S. and Collins, A., "The Designers' and Contractors' Workbook For Energy Conserving Design," DOE Contract DE-AC02-79CS29287, Carnegie-Mellon University, Pittsburgh, PA, Aug. 1982.

[4] Loftness, V., Hartkopf, V., and Yoran, N., "The Homeowners' Workbook For Energy Conserving Urban Living," DOE Contract DE-AC02-79CS29287, Carnegie-Mellon University, Pittsburgh, PA, Sept. 1982.

[5] Woodbury, R., Hartkopf, V., and Onaka, J., "Housing Rehabilitation and Construction—an Urban-Suburban Comparison," Proceedings, Third International Conference on Energy Use Management, Pergamon Press, Elmsford, NY, 1982.

[6] Hartkopf, V., "Energy Conservation Guidelines for the Sheffield Block Development, Vol. 1: New Construction," Institute of Building Sciences, Carnegie-Mellon University, Pittsburgh, PA, June 1981.

[7] Hartkopf, V., "Energy Conservation Guidelines for the Sheffield Block Development, Vol. 2: Rehabilitation," Institute of Building Sciences, Carnegie-Mellon University, Pittsburgh, PA, June 1981.

[8] Gaskill, M., "Effect of Occupant Behavior on Energy Use in an Inner City Neighborhood," Institute of Building Sciences, Carnegie-Mellon University, Pittsburgh, PA, Aug. 1981.

Walter S. Chick[1]

Potential Hazards Resulting from the Misapplication of Energy Conservation Measures in Existing Religious Buildings

REFERENCE: Chick, W. S., "Potential Hazards Resulting from the Misapplication of Energy Conservation Measures in Existing Religious Buildings," *Building Performance: Function, Preservation, and Rehabilitation, ASTM STP 901*, G. Davis, Ed., American Society for Testing and Materials, Philadelphia, 1986, pp. 111–120.

ABSTRACT: The development of a practical information data base covering a wide cross section of religious buildings is essential to determine the most effective approach in reducing their demand for energy without creating negative side effects.

Very little information is available on religious building profiles which is of use in determining the potential hazards resulting from the misapplication of various measures.

Applying energy conservation measures to religious buildings presents unique problems. For instance, attempting to apply cost-saving energy conservation measures with an unqualified committee working in its spare time with limited funds often results in structural damage, safety problems, and fire hazards to existing structures; examination of several hundred religious buildings in the province of Ontario has confirmed the existence of many problems.

The most common problem is the improper application of thermal insulation to the roof and walls of buildings. This has resulted in the loss of structural integrity due to dry rot caused by inadequate moisture control. The accelerated deterioration of a building can result in prohibitive maintenance and repair costs to many heritage edifices.

The various effects of insulation on fire safety are also a major concern. For instance, when insulation is applied around heat-producing devices such as lighting fixtures, lack of adequate ventilation can result in dangerous levels of heat accumulation to adjacent combustible materials. Insulation applied to linings under 5 mm (for example, plywood) can accelerate ignition when exposed to an ignition source.

The presence of plastic foam insulating materials is also a major concern due to the potential for vertical spread of fire in cavity walls. Materials such as urea-formaldehyde foam insulation can cause eye and nose irritations in some people and is linked to other health risks.

In geographic areas experiencing heavy snowfalls, the snow loads on roofs can cause failure due to heavy accumulations resulting from the improper use of insulation. Serious

[1]Manager, Commercial Buildings, Conservation Energy Group, Ontario Ministry of Energy, Toronto, Canada.

wetting occurs inside buildings from infiltration of blowing snow where gaps in insulation exist and where moisture barriers are installed in a faulty manner.

Most of these potential hazards can be significantly reduced or entirely eliminated by obtaining competent technical advice and by the adoption of proper installation and construction practices.

Hundreds of questionnaires, in addition to visits to examine a wide variety of religious buildings, have revealed the existence of many of the anticipated problems.

Documentation of these problems should provide a useful resource base of information for those involved in the operation, maintenance, and retrofitting of these important community buildings.

KEY WORDS: religious buildings, energy conservation, hazardous measures, safety

Many potential hazards can result from the misapplication of energy conservation measures in existing religious buildings; utmost care is required to avoid the negative consequences that can result if these hazards are allowed to persist.

A program to provide energy conservation in religious buildings in the province of Ontario came into being as a result of concerns expressed by many religious groups throughout the province. In an attempt to increase the energy awareness level among this highly diverse group, a series of formal presentations were given throughout the province to permit direct contact with those interested in developing energy conservation initiatives within their membership. In addition to providing basic information to the participants, reports prepared for the Ontario Ministry of Energy also were supplied (Refs *1,2*). Direct technical advice also was made available on an on-going basis using technical consultants. This included on-site examination of individual facilities.

With an estimated 10 000 to 12 000 religious buildings in the province of Ontario, the demand and need for this program became self-evident since the majority of congregations do not have direct access to competent technical personnel who are capable of establishing the correct implementation measures and considering the large variety of alternatives that are being offered by a great number of equipment suppliers and installation service organizations.

A considerable number of the existing religious buildings were constructed before the turn of the century. Many are fragile, energy inefficient, and drafty. These buildings lose a lot of energy due to architectural priorities that satisfy various congregational requirements, as well as because of the large variety of different facilities that are usually combined as a single complex. In most cases, religious buildings are operated by more than one person. These individuals share responsibilities for such tasks as operating the heating plant, turning off the lights, selecting the comfort levels, administering the energy budgets, etc.

Very few congregations have available funds to implement costly energy savings measures; for instance, the repair of leaking stained-glass windows can cost between 3000 to $5000, and insulating cathedral roofs can cost many tens of thousands of dollars. In most instances, congregations are forced to accept the cheapest bids since justification to spend money is usually based on a very rapid payback of, say, less than a year. This approach has unfortunately resulted in accepting inferior corrective measures which in many cases are hazardous to the building structure and, more importantly, to the safety of the occupants.

Most potential hazards can be significantly reduced or entirely eliminated by obtaining competent technical advice and by following proper installation and maintenance practices.

Insulation

As a guide to heat loss distribution in a typical religious building, the following features apply:

1. One story (sanctuary).
2. Cathedral ceiling height (average of 10 m).
3. Volume of 3000 to 10 000 m^3.
4. Natural ventilation of approximately 0.5 to 1.5 changes per hour.
5. Little, if any, insulation.
6. Located in a 4000-degree-day climate.

A great deal of heat loss occurs through the uninsulated ceilings (estimates have ranged as high as 50%). It can be appreciated why this area is considered to be the one which most energy committees give top priority to.

Depending on the size of the facilities, energy costs vary between an average of 5000 to over $100 000 per year for large cathedral complexes. Most of this cost is required to heat the building.

A great variety of insulating materials have been applied to religious buildings, covering materials such as cellulose fiber to plastic materials, which include polystyrene, urethane, polyethylene, polyisocyanurates, urea formaldehyde, to name a few.

In general, commercial insulations have two basic structures, namely, a continuous body of gas that contains a dispersion of solid particles or fibers and a continuous matrix of solid materials such as glass, rock, and synthetic plastics insulation, which have gases other than air in their cells and can have a higher thermal resistance value than air; unfortunately, these materials are subject to aging effects due to their escape through the cell walls by diffusion. Also, air and water vapor try to diffuse into these spaces. Large gas molecules take years to diffuse out; however, carbon dioxide (CO_2) can diffuse out in a few days. Urea formaldehyde tends to shrink appreciably, 8 to 10%, over a period of several years, thus reducing the seal quality of the cavities it is intended to fill. It also emits toxic fumes (depending on the additives used) such as dimethyl naphthalene, as well as formaldehyde, which is claimed to be carcinogenic to humans.

Unfortunately, in many instances, spray-on foam-in-place insulation and blown insulation may be the only practical techniques for insulating hard-to-get-at locations. Extreme caution must be exercised in the selection of the appropriate material before it is committed to placement in buildings that are frequently occupied by individuals who have a high degree of sensitivity to them.

It must be fully appreciated that the properties of the wide range of insulations available are extremely sensitive to the method of application as well as to the skill of the applicator in maintaining the level of quality control necessary to provide a safe and long-lasting installation.

Vapor Barriers and Venting

When insulation is applied in and to exterior surfaces, it is essential that moisture not be permitted to remain resident in the insulation or be in contact with wooden structures. Moisture escape from air-conditioned areas can be very serious to the long-term quality of the insulation and to the integrity of the building's wooden structural members. In most instances, vapor barriers are used to provide vapor protection during the heating season. Adequate ventilation paths are required to ensure an escape path for any moisture that enters these areas. As a general rule, at least 150 mm of ventilating space is required above the insulation installed in cathedral ceilings and flat roofs. Ventilation of ceiling and roof cavities must provide for clear air flow from the soffits of a cathedral ceiling to the peak roof vent or continuous flow from side to side of a flat roof.

Unfortunately, many religious buildings examined do not provide moisture protection and control. In the absence of such protection, the likelihood of excessive moisture within the walls, ceilings, and roofs can induce the following conditions:

1. Decay of wooden structures.
2. Destruction of the insulation.
3. Staining of wall and ceiling finishes.
4. Destruction of the ceiling or roof if remedial action is not taken in time.

Several cases have been reported where moisture problems have resulted in the damage of ceiling structures which required complete replacement. In one instance, this repair job was estimated to cost over $40 000.

It also has been found that when insulation thicknesses have been increased, moisture problems become aggravated. Instances have been reported where no problems existed so long as only small amounts of insulation were applied.

This situation is more serious in locations in the northern parts of the province where the climate produces long cold periods—50 to 100 mm of frost can accumulate in the insulated spaces. With the onset of a warm period, this accumulation melts onto the ceiling, resulting in moisture penetrating the ceiling finishes.

John Timusic, Head of the University of Toronto's Building Research Centre, reported in the local press the following explanation for the continuing existence of these serious problems:

> When the energy crisis hit in 1973, we thought we could make buildings more energy efficient just by adding more insulation. But we're dealing with a very very complex science here. . . . We're getting problems we didn't expect because we are dealing with a revolution in how we build things. Now that we've started to install insulation with the polyethylene sheets as an air-vapor barrier, we've got all the extra water concentrating around the electrical outlets or any other break in the barrier, and so we've got spots we can very easily have decay setting in.

An area which has resulted in what appears to be conflicting advice is the situation concerning the recommendation of insulating on the inside of basement walls. In many instances, due to the poor sealing of the outside wall, most of these basement walls, especially those of concrete block construction, have a high amount of moisture permanently resident in them. With the addition of insulation, moisture is entrapped between the chilled wall surface and the insulation, which will cause the rapid deterioration of the wood strapping that is used to retain the insulation to the walls.

Ceiling Fans

One of the most common sights encountered in entering the sanctuary of a religious building today is the presence of a ceiling fan. It appears that product salesmen have done an outstanding job of convincing building committee members that this approach is very cost-effective in reducing the high-temperature stratified air which accumulates at the apex of cathedral ceilings. These units have been used extensively in industrial applications where the following benefits are claimed:

1. Reclaim stratified heat and solar energy absorbed by roof.
2. Use up heat lost from production processes and lighting fixtures.
3. Control humidity.
4. Speed up temperature recovery after loading doors have been opened.
5. Improve comfort and working conditions.

Before installing ceiling fans, a temperature gradient between the floor and ceiling should be at least 7°C. Typical units move about 300 m³ of air per minute. Attractive capital cost recovery is claimed for these units.

The application of ceiling fans to religious buildings appears to meet the need for an improved redistribution of stratified heated air which accumulates at the ceiling.

Unfortunately, many of the basic precautions have not been observed in their application. For instance:

1. Units have been mounted too low or too high to be effective.
2. Insufficient temperature gradients exist between floor and ceiling.
3. Fans have been positioned so as to interfere with the lighting installation, causing a disturbing effect to the congregations.
4. High air velocities have resulted in discomfort to building occupants.

In a number of instances, fan installations have resulted in damage to roof structures where these structures were dependent on the transfer of building heat to prevent an accumulation of ice and snow. In one instance, expensive roof tiles were damaged due to the buildup of ice dams. The replacement of such tile was in the vicinity of $40 each.

In northern regions where the accumulations of snow loads can be very severe, especially during the transitional seasons when wet snow can occur, serious damage can occur to structural members if the shedding of snow is discouraged in any way.

Due to the reduced heat transfer resulting from the redistribution of heated stratified air by ceiling fans, it has been found in a number of instances that the shedding of snow has not occurred and has necessitated its physical removal to avoid overloading the structural members. By not observing the necessary precautions prior to the installation of ceiling fans, expensive corrective measures can be required once damage has taken place.

The improper use of insulation in ceilings and roofs, which prevents the required heat transfer from the inside of the building, can result in similar difficulties being encountered unless other suitable measures are taken to overcome this problem. For instance, a variety of new heating cables are now available that can be applied on all gutter and roof materials, including wood, plastic, and asphalt. These cables can operate effectively to $-40°C$. It should be noted that if mechanical damage occurs during installation of these cables, electrical and fire hazards can result.

Toxic Hazards of Insulating Material Fires

The majority of fire deaths today are due to the inhalation of thermal decomposition products, such as gases, smoke, and toxic vapors. Many new insulating materials release harmful decomposition products very rapidly, and a considerable number are much more toxic than the traditionally used materials.

Due to the increased use of these materials for buildings and furnishings, the problem of toxic products of combustion has resulted in a considerable amount of concern and discussion.

This subject has received the attention of the Canadian National Research Council, Division of Building Research. A summary of the Council's findings is published in Table 1 [Ref 3], which is a list of typical materials along with corresponding harmful products and harmful effects. The authors reported that although considerable effort is being directed towards developing recommended procedures or standard methods of evaluating the fire toxicity of materials, there are as yet no accepted standard methods. Unfortunately, until these standards become available, it is difficult to make definite recommendations concerning the use of materials known to generate significant amounts of toxic decomposition products.

Fire Safety Considerations in the Application of Potentially Hazardous Materials

Many religious building property management committees have been attracted by the low cost of plastic insulations, which are easy to apply to walls, ceilings, and roofs. Few of these committees fully understand the potential hazards to the safety of the occupants that results from misapplying this type of insulation to the fire integrity of their buildings.

Most of the potential hazards can be dramatically reduced and in some instances eliminated by the use of proper protective covers and by proper installation and maintenance practices. Reference 4 discusses various effects of insulation on fire safety, a subject of current interest because of the greatly

TABLE 1—*Main harmful products of materials and general harmful effect.*[a]

Material	Harmful Product	Harmful Effects
Wood and paper	CO	dangerous concentration, 4000 ppm of air (30 min)
Polystyrene	CO; also styrene, but present in smaller quantities	
Polyvinyl chloride (PVC)	HCl; also corrosive	dangerous for even short exposure, 1000 to 2000 ppm
	CO	
Plexiglas or Perspex	CO; also methyl methacrylate, which is as toxic as CO but produced in smaller quantities	
Polyethylene	CO	
Acrylic fibers, wool, nylon	hydrogen cyanide (HCN); CO	120 to 150 ppm

[a]*Canadian Building Digest, No. 197*, National Research Council of Canada, June 1978. For more details, see *Canadian Building Digest*, No. 144.

increased use of insulation to conserve energy in buildings. It is a summary of chapters of the National Fire Protection Association Fire Protection Handbook [5]. The summary provided in Ref 4 is extremely useful for all building committees which are involved in selecting or reviewing recommendations of others that entail the use of potentially hazardous materials; the five points stated are listed below:

1. Insulation can affect the ignition of materials.
   (a) It can increase temperature around heat-producing objects such as light fixtures.
   (b) Applied to the back of thin linings, it increases the potential for more rapid ignition.
   (c) It may be a potential hazard if it ignites easily, particularly in confined spaces such as attics.
2. Insulation can influence the rate at which a fire will grow.
   (a) A well-insulated room will retain heat with resulting potential for faster fire growth.
3. Some insulations are potential hazards as they ignite relatively easily and propagate flame.
   (a) This can increase the rate at which fire propagates as high surface temperatures are attained more quickly.
   (b) Foam plastic in cavity walls with air space has the potential for rapid flame spread.
4. Some insulation products release harmful decomposition products that result in greater production of smoke and toxic gas.
   (a) Smoke and toxic products reduce visibility, impeding evacuation during a fire.
5. Higher temperatures during fires in insulated structures may affect structural strength.
   (a) Exposed structural steel members can lose strength when heated to high temperatures.
   (b) Higher temperatures can cause deflection and buckling of thin walls.

Chimney Condensation Problems

As a highly cost-effective measure, many religious buildings have converted their oil-fired heating units to natural gas units; simple cost paybacks usually take between two to five years.

In a number of instances, chimney condensation problems have been experienced. If this situation is not corrected, damage will result to the chimney, and, under the most adverse conditions, blockages can occur that will prevent the proper venting of combustion gases such as carbon monoxide (CO).

The products of combustions from a natural gas furnace have a lower temperature and a higher moisture content than an oil-fired furnace. Condensation can occur in the chimney if it has three sides exposed, is oversized, unlined, or has leaks through the mortar. To ensure that proper venting of gases is maintained, the chimney base should be inspected through the clean-out door at regular intervals during the heating season.

Other symptoms of a chimney problem are evidence of moisture running down the wall beneath the clean-out door, a white powdery substance appearing on the outside of the chimney brickwork, or broken or deteriorated brick or mortar on the outside of the chimney.

A solution, should this problem occur, is to repair the chimney and, if necessary, to install an approved chimney liner.

Health Considerations in Tightly Sealed Areas

Many groups promoting energy conservation in religious buildings have concentrated on improving the air tightness of their facilities. For instance, many of the small auxiliary areas which form part of these complexes are used as meeting rooms and under certain circumstances will have a high occupancy density.

The operation of air exhaust systems or fuel-burning appliances (including fireplaces and "spot" heaters) removes air from such locations. When too much air is removed, negative pressure can become large enough to reverse the natural flow of combustion gases, and fresh air can be drawn into the chimney. This reverse flow impedes the escape of combustion gases and can result in CO entering the occupied area; needless to say, such a situation must be avoided. When in doubt, occupants who are aware of the potential CO problem can take the simple precautionary measure of opening a window when spot heaters, wood-burning stoves, and fireplaces are in use.

In some cases, incidental ventilation may not provide enough fresh air, and you will have to arrange for additional ventilation. Extra ventilation may be required for one of two purposes: to supply fresh air and reduce the relative humidity or to provide combustion air for a fuel-burning appliance.

Fortunately, there are usually obvious symptoms to indicate that additional ventilation is required. It is important to recognize these indicators and apply corrective measures to avoid such problems. The symptoms of inadequate ventilation are:

1. Condensation on the inner surface of double-paned windows, metal sashes, hinges, and handles.

2. Stuffy atmosphere or lingering odors.

3. Odors from incomplete furnace combustion, back puffing, or poor draft in the furnace chimney.

4. Back drafts and smoking fireplaces.

Open fireplaces are notoriously inefficient. They require vast amounts of air to operate properly and often place an excessive fresh air demand on a tight building. A fireplace may require five to ten times more fresh air than gas or oil furnaces. The result can be poor draft and smoking as the fire gets going.

A good solution is to insulate and seal the fireplace in winter. However, if use is made of the fireplace, consider the other options that follow:

1. Refrain from using the fireplace during very cold weather. This is when it is most inefficient and likely to draw outdoor air down the furnace chimney, preventing furnace fumes from venting to the outside.

2. Bring fresh air directly to the fireplace from outside. A 150-mm insulated duct with a damper can be installed between the outside foundation wall and the floor in front of the fireplace. Install a radiating glass fire screen in the fireplace opening.

3. Open a window in the same room as the fireplace when it is in operation.

Conclusions and Recommendations

Religious organizations that have encountered either one or more of the problems outlined in this paper have gained first-hand knowledge of the implications of inadequate energy conservation measures. These problems have been thrust upon them in a manner they will not soon forget. It is one of the purposes of this review to document the types of negative consequences that can result when inexperienced individuals decide on what they believe is the right course of action without having the benefit of competent technical advice.

It is from situations like these that the building community at large can and must learn if similar occurrences are to be avoided. In looking towards the construction of new facilities, this review underscores the extreme care and attention to detail that designers, builders, and owners must take when applying energy-efficient standards to religious buildings where unique architectural features must be combined with high levels of insulation, air tightness, proper solar orientation, and the installation of an efficient heating and ventilation system to produce structures that can be heated for a fraction of the cost of existing buildings and still provide attractive, comfortable, draft-free, safe facilities for their occupants.

References

[1] "Energy Saving in Religious Buildings," Vol. I, report prepared by the Ontario Ministry of Energy, Toronto, Ontario, Canada, 1982.
[2] "Energy Saving in Religious Buildings," Vol. II: "Putting Practical Ideas to Work," report prepared by the Ontario Ministry of Energy, Toronto, Ontario, Canada, 1984.
[3] Sumi, K. and Tsuchiya, Y. "Evaluating the Toxic Hazards of Fire," *Canadian Building Digest*, No. 197, National Research Council Canada, July 1978.
[4] Lie, T. T., "Effects of Insulation on Fire Safety," *Canadian Building Digest*, No. 218, National Research Council Canada, Aug. 1981.
[5] "Fire Protection Handbook," 15th ed., Section 5, Chapter 5, National Fire Protection Association, Boston, 1981.

Gerald E. Sherwood[1]

Technology of Preserving Wood Structures

REFERENCE: Sherwood, G. E., **"Technology of Preserving Wood Structures,"** *Building Performance: Function, Preservation, and Rehabilitation, ASTM STP 901*, G. Davis, Ed., American Society for Testing and Materials, Philadelphia, 1986, pp. 121-135.

ABSTRACT: For the past 75 years, the Forest Products Laboratory has conducted research on topics ranging from wood anatomy to performance of entire buildings to development of construction guidelines. This paper presents research results applicable to extending the service life of wood structures. It includes information on fundamental properties of wood and on factors that influence serviceability, such as loading, temperature, moisture, chemicals, and weathering. The author summarizes state-of-the-art methods and practices for extending the life of wood structures and includes an extensive list of references.

This overview of technology for preservation and rehabilitation of wood structures should be useful to designers, builders, and regulatory bodies involved in building preservation and rehabilitation.

KEY WORDS: wood structures, preservation, rehabilitation, restoration

Wood is one of the oldest construction materials known to man and has played a significant role in the history of building construction. Even in buildings that are basically of other materials such as masonry, wood often is used for roof framing, doors, and trim. In applications where wood has been protected from deteriorating influences such as decay, it has lasted for centuries. Wood does not lose strength or stiffness due to age alone; however, other factors influence its serviceability.

A knowledge of some of the basic properties of wood is needed to understand what these factors are. This basic information provides the background needed to assess the condition of wood in structures and to take measures to extend the life of wood structures. This paper presents an overview of basic properties of wood, serviceability factors, condition assessment methods, and

[1]Engineer, U.S. Department of Agriculture, Forest Service, Forest Products Laboratory, Madison, WI 53705.

preservation and restoration practices. As such a subject is far too broad for detailed coverage in a paper of this length, the intent here is to point out major concerns and provide an extensive list of references. Thorough coverage of this subject is given in a recent American Society of Civil Engineers (ASCE) publication [1].

Structure and Basic Physical Properties of Wood

Though all wood has the same basic structure, the physical properties that affect its performance vary widely with species and conditions of growth. Complete coverage of properties and how these properties vary for many species is given in Ref 2. Properties of major tropical species of wood throughout the world are given in a three-volume series by Chudnoff [3].

Structure

The basic structural elements of wood are hollow, elongated cells that are mostly arranged parallel with each other and with their long dimension parallel to the axis of the tree trunk. This fiber orientation makes structural properties very dependent on direction. If the fiber direction (or grain) deviates from the axis, strength is considerably reduced. Properties are quite different in the three mutually perpendicular axes of symmetry—longitudinal, radial, and tangential (Fig. 1).

Basic Physical Properties

Knots—Knots are the result of branches growing at an angle to the axis of the tree trunk, and, consequently they show up as defects in a piece of lum-

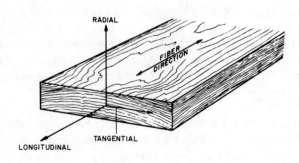

M 140 728

FIG. 1—*The three perpendicular axes of symmetry for wood.*

ber. Because the fibers around the knot deviate from the direction of the major axis, the overall strength in bending and in tension and compression parallel to grain are reduced. The amount of reduction depends on the size of the knot.

Checks and Splits—Wood dries faster on its surface than in its interior. Shrinkage of the surface wood results in tensile stresses across the grain that may cause a fracture along the grain. These fractures on the surface are called *checks*. If the fracture extends completely through the member, it is called a *split*. Both defects reduce the wood's resistance to shear stress.

Density—Density is a measure of the wood substance in a given volume of wood. Low-density woods have a larger percentage of voids than high-density woods. The usual range of density is 320 to 721 kg/m^3 (20 to 45 lb/ft^3). Because the wood substance provides the strength, the more dense woods are generally stronger and stiffer.

Moisture content—Wood contains moisture: up to two thirds of the wood may be water (by weight). Cell walls within the wood fibers are able to absorb moisture equal to about 30% of the wood by weight (fiber saturation point). Any moisture beyond that amount is held in the voids and does not affect the dimensions of the wood. When wood is dried below fiber saturation, the fibers begin to shrink and its dimensions are reduced [4]. It shrinks very little in the longitudinal direction, more in the radial direction, and the most in the tangential direction (Fig. 1). High-density woods shrink more than lower-density wood. As woods dries, it also becomes stronger and stiffer. If wood is not exposed to rain or other direct water sources, it will attain a moisture content in equilibrium with the average relative humidity. This may be as low as 4% in arid locations, as high as 14% in temperate coastal locations, and even higher in tropical locations.

Decay Resistance

Dry wood will not decay. Wood may decay if temperatures are between 4.4 and 37.8°C (40 and 100°F) and oxygen is present. The sapwood, or outer live portion of the tree, deteriorates rapidly regardless of species when exposed to decay conditions. In some species the heartwood, or center portion of the tree, contains fungi toxic extractives that impart good decay resistance (Fig. 2).

Serviceability Factors

Serviceability of wood structures is influenced by a number of factors involving the use of the building, exposure to the elements, and conditions of the structural members. In many cases these factors may be known from the history of the building; in others, it may be necessary to examine the building for clues.

FIG. 2—*Cross section of a log showing the dark heartwood in the center of the tree and lighter sapwood on the outer edge. The heartwood of some species is resistant to decay and insect attack. The sapwood has no resistance regardless of species.*

Loading

Man or nature may load wood structures. Whatever the case, both the amount of load and the duration of application of the load [5,6] affect the performance of structural members. Wood has a resilience that allows it to recover from some short-term loads without permanent set, while the same load applied over a long period of time may produce creep (slow sagging) [7,8] in the structural member, resulting in permanent set. However, sagging of beams does not necessarily indicate a loss of strength. The development of splits may be a more critical indication of loss of strength. Impact loads, such as those produced by wind or earthquake, can weaken structural members by loosening joints, especially if these loads are repeated through several cycles. Settlement of part of the foundation causes a shift in the application of some loads and may overload certain structural members. A similar overload may occur due to failure of an individual member shifting loads to adjacent members. Yielding of one member by creep also can cause a shift of loads to adjacent members.

Temperature

Strength and stiffness of wood generally decrease with increases of temperature, and these decreases can be classified as either temporary or permanent. These properties appear to be fully recoverable up to temperatures of 65.6°C (150°F). Above those temperatures, the wood is permanently damaged. The reduction in strength is directly proportional to the length of time this high temperature is maintained. Time periods with high temperatures that are not continuous are additive. High moisture accentuates the negative effect of heat [9], and this combination accelerates creep [8]. If wood has been exposed to more than occasional short-term conditions above 65.6°C (150°F), the allowable load-carrying capacity should be reduced [10-15].

Moisture

Excessive moisture is the most common factor that reduces serviceability of wood. It has an immediate effect on dimensional and mechanical properties [4], and it also creates conditions suitable for attack by fungi and insects [16-18].

Shrinking and swelling of wood can induce stresses in addition to those resulting from loading. Under certain conditions, wood may warp and twist, producing both structural and esthetic problems. Shrinking and swelling also can loosen joints. Beams often will sag when load is applied before the wood is dried. This sets the wood permanently, so the sag remains even after drying.

Values of the mechanical properties of wood such as bending strength, tensile strength, and modulus of elasticity vary with moisture content (below the fiber saturation point). Thus, allowable design stresses must correspond to in-service moisture conditions.

Free water must be present for the growth of decay fungi. This means moisture content must be above the fiber saturation point; however, experience has shown that at a single reading of 20% moisture content, free water may exist in parts of a wood member. If wood is dried below the 20% level, decay fungi will stop growing and eventually die. However, prolonged high moisture levels will result in total destruction of the wood by decay. Besides fungi, a number of wood-destroying insects also require water to prosper, and some insects are attracted to wood already softened by decay.

Weathering

Wood is durable when exposed to the elements, but the long-term effects of water, light, and heat do cause weathering [19-24]. Initial weathering produces color changes with the darker woods becoming bleached while lighter woods darken. If no microorganisms are present, all wood eventually weathers to a soft silver gray [25,26]. As slight degradation of the surface occurs, rainwater washes out degraded portions and the surface becomes increasingly uneven. Weathering has been cited as causing a loss of about 25 mm (1/4 in.) of thickness per century, but this varies considerably with exposure, weather conditions, and species [27]. Although physical and chemical changes occur on the surface, the remaining wood is unchanged and unaffected.

Fire

During a fire, all types of wood members can be charred (Fig. 3). This char insulates the inner portions of the wood member and prevents high temperatures that might reduce modulus of elasticity of the remaining wood. After the char is removed, stiffness can be calculated based on the remaining cross section. Tensile strength may be reduced on the order of 10 to 15% near the interface of the sound wood and the char, so this must be accounted for in the lower edge of a beam exposed to fire [28]. Structural adhesives used currently

FIG. 3— *Char developed on heavy timber beams in a fire insulates and protects the center part of the beam from damage.*

are phenolic, resorcinol, and melamine formulations, which maintain their integrity during and after fire exposure [29,30]. Older laminated members were sometimes fabricated with casein glue, which is affected within about 25 mm (¼ in.) of the char-wood interface.

Insects

Termites are the most common wood-destroying insects that damage buildings [31]. As mentioned in the section on "Moisture," many insects are attracted to wet wood. While termites prosper in wet wood, they also can provide their own water sources. Subterranean termites build tubes connecting their colonies to the damp soil. Dry wood termites do not require access to soil. Although they are attracted to wet wood, they can establish colonies in wood with only moderate moisture content. Beetles, ants, and bees all require a high moisture content in wood to initiate attack.

Methods of Condition Assessment

In many older buildings, a visual assessment of conditions is all that is required to determine safety. However, where structural members may be highly stressed, more sophisticated methods may be necessary for adequate assessment. Accurate structure evaluation is especially important where building usage is changing and large loads may have to be supported. A critical item of assessment is the location and extent of decay.

Visual Observation

The most obvious indication of structural problems is distortion, such as sloping floors, cracks in walls, sagging roofs, or window and door frames out of square. This could be caused from foundation failure, crushing of wood at bearing points, excessive deflection of wood beams due to creep, or failure of connectors.

Water stains may be harmless, but if a leak has continued for a long time, decay has probably developed. Fruiting bodies of fungi (visible fungal growth on the wood surface) indicate severe moisture problems. Any location where there is a leak could have conditions conducive to growth of fruiting bodies. Any place in the building can leak, but some likely places are around plumbing fixtures and pipes, at roof edges and intersecting roofs, and around chimneys or vents. Other locations to look for decay are on the floor framing in damp crawl spaces and on roof sheathing or framing in poorly ventilated attics. These visual observations of decay require additional inspection methods to determine the extent of damage. Some fruiting bodies may be only the result of initial decay that has not extensively damaged the wood, but they do indicate that conditions are conducive for damage. A clue to decay in advanced stages is localized depression or sunken faces in the wood surface.

Earlier stages of decay are indicated by darkening and loss of luster of the surface or dark streaks in the wood.

Decay Detection

The most common detection method for external decay is the pick test [17]. Any pointed tool can be used to lift a sliver of wood. A splintering break indicates sound wood; a brash break suggests decay (Fig. 4). A knife blade or other sharp tool also can be used to probe the hardness of the wood. Extensive decay causes softening, so the tool easily can be pressed deeply into the wood.

Sounding of wood can be used to detect internal decay, but this requires an experienced person. The wood is simply struck with a hammer. A sharp ring indicates sound wood, whereas a hollow sound or a dull thud may indicate rot. This test only indicates problems, so additional testing of questionable areas is required to establish the existence and extent of decay.

Where decay is suspected, an increment borer is used to remove a plug from the wood, and the entire cross section of the member can be observed and cultured for fungi. Another device is the Shigometer, which measures electrical resistance between two insulated wires inserted at various depths in the wood. A nondestructive device for detecting decay or other voids in wood is the James "V" meter, which measures the time between an ultrasonic pulse generated on one surface and a receiver on another surface of the same mem-

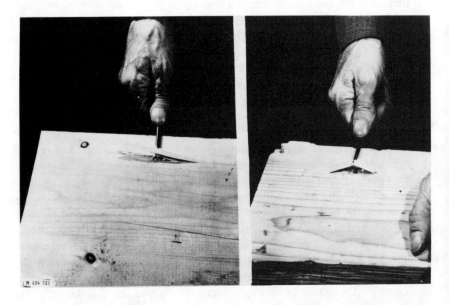

FIG. 4—*The pick test for detecting decay. A splintering break (left) indicates sound wood; a brash break (right) suggests decay.*

ber [32]. These electronic methods require an experienced operator to inter-
pret the results. The increment borer is still required to determine details of
the damage.

Estimating Load-carrying Capacity

If a structural member is in good condition [33–35], its load-carrying capacity can be established. Its species must first be determined and mechanical properties established. If that species is stress rated and grade marked,
the lumber-grading agency can supply allowable stresses. However, it is necessary to know the date the building was designed and constructed because
the allowable design stresses have changed with time. If the species is not
stress rated, the procedures presented in ASTM Method for Establishing
Structural Grades and Related Allowable Properties for Visually Graded
Lumber (D 245-81) can be used to establish allowable stresses based on fundamental properties of the species [ASTM Method for Establishing Clear-
Wood Strength Values (D 2555-81)] and the effect of characteristics such as
knots, slope of grain, etc. [ASTM Method for Establishing Stresses for Structural Glued Laminated Timber (Glulam) (D 3737-83a)].[2] An evaluation of
this type is best accomplished by someone trained in grading lumber. Allowable stresses must be further reduced for wood that has been weakened by
exposure to fire, decay, insect damage, fire retardant treatments [36,37], or
unusually severe loading.

Load-carrying capacity of a structural member also may be reduced by connectors [38–41]. Design values for most connectors are published in the "National Design Specification."[2] General conditions around the existing fastener may reduce the allowable load. Some of these conditions are: (1)
reduction in density due to fungal growth or high temperature; (2) a split in
the area of the connector; (3) wood shrinkage that loosens a connector; (4)
deterioration of a fastener by rust or corrosion which reduces the area of its
cross section.

Practices for Extending the Life of Wood Structures

Excessive water in some form is the main threat to the long life of wood
structures [42–44]. Therefore, it is critical that any moisture problems be corrected and that measures be taken to prevent future moisture problems. This
may involve changes in construction details [44,45], the application of preservatives[3] [46], or replacement of specific wood members with preservatively

---

[2]"National Design Specification," National Forest Products Association, Washington, DC
20036, 1982.
[3]"Manual of Recommended Practice," American Wood-Preservers' Association, Bethesda,
MD 20014.

treated wood. Of course, wood members that have been damaged already require repair or replacement.

Correction of Moisture Problems

Drainage must be provided for all rainwater. Flat surfaces at windows, siding material transitions, porch railings, or similar details must be sloped to prevent water retention [17,45]. This is particularly important where the end grain of wood contacts the horizontal surface because water is very quickly absorbed in the direction of the grain. Any exposed end grain, such as the end of an exposed beam, requires flashing or other type of cover to prevent absorption of rainwater [47]. Flashing is a necessity where a roof intersects a vertical wood surface and at roof edges [44]. A positive drip at the roof edge is required to prevent rainwater from curling back under the roofing or from being absorbed into the joints of the fascia.

Another major source of water is damp soil. If wood is not separated from soil moisture [17], water may condense on floor framing or be wicked up through foundations into wall framing. Good ventilation between the floor and soil should prevent damage [48]. Where a crawl space is especially damp, a vapor retarder material, such as polyethylene film, laid over the soil will greatly reduce the moisture in that space. However, in some cases where the entire soil area had been covered, conditions became so dry that cracks developed between flooring boards. Therefore, it is best to cover only about 50% of the area initially and observe if that reduces the moisture adequately. Some experimentation may be necessary to determine the optimum coverage of soil [44]. Good drainage away from the foundation is always good practice, and it is particularly important to prevent water from flowing under the building after installing a soil cover.

Moisture generated on the interior of the building also can be a problem. This moisture may be from such sources as cooking, bathing, respiration from people or animals, evaporation from plants, or some industrial process [48]. If that moisture vapor is not vented directly to the outdoors and results in high indoor relative humidity, moisture will condense on cold windows or pass through structural spaces such as attics and condense on cold surfaces within the space. The condensation over a long period of time may promote the growth of decay fungi. Condensation on siding may be more of a visual problem with paint peeling and possible buckling. The best preventative for this problem is to lower the indoor humidity by venting moisture to the outdoors at its source. Overall ventilation of the building is an alternative [48,49]. The use of vapor retarders in walls and ceilings to reduce the rate of moisture movement into structural spaces is another preventative [48,50]. The most effective vapor retarders are in the form of films, but some paints provide reasonable resistance to vapor transfer [51]. Double glazing prevents some of the problem of window condensation by raising the temperature of glass. Attic or roof space ventilation reduces the risk of condensation in those areas by venting moist air to the outdoors [52].

Use of Preservative Treatments

Where decayed wood must be replaced, the use of wood treated with pre-servatives is recommended[3] if continued exposure to moisture is expected. This is critical if the wood will be in contact with damp concrete or masonry, near the soil, or constantly exposed to rain. The treatment should be by a pressure process and certified by a recognized quality control agency. Certifi-cation should include the amount of preservative retained and the intended use.

In-place treatment is feasible for protecting wood that is out of ground and exposed to decay hazards but not yet seriously affected by decay. Such treat-ment will add substantially to the service life of out-of-ground wood but is less effective if wood contacts soil. The end grain of wood should be the main target of in-place treatment because here water is most quickly absorbed. Fortunately, the preservative is more readily absorbed here also. Preservative applied to the face of wood does protect the surface, but there is very little penetration [53–58]. Critical joints or exposed ends of wood members should be flooded by applying preservative with a fully loaded brush or by a spray gun adjusted to deliver a fine, solid stream. A caulking gun is sometimes used to apply preservative in the form of a grease. Another type of in-place treat-ment is possible by wicking preservative through a cotton string. The string is tied around a joint, such as at the base of a column supported on a porch floor, and the opposite end is placed in a container of preservative. Over a long time the solution is wicked into the end grain of the column to a greater depth than is possible by a one-time flooding of the joint.

Protection for exposed wood, such as siding and trim, can be provided by brush or spray treatment with a water-repellent preservative [59–61]. The wa-ter repellent causes water to bead up on the surface rather than soak into the wood; the preservative prevents the growth of fungi on the surface. This can be applied to wood that is left natural or as a pretreatment for painting.

Repairing of Structural Members

Structural repairs can take many forms and require complex design proce-dures [2,62–66]. Detailed presentation of numerous repair methods is given in Ref 1. Basic methods are of three major types: (1) increasing the effective cross section, (2) reinforcement of splits, and (3) replacement of portions of wood destroyed by decay.

The area of the cross section of a member is increased by adding material to the member, either at the sides or possibly on the tension face. This may be in the form of more wood or may be metal plates. A critical factor in this type of repair is that the added material be adequately attached to the original member so that the two parts perform structurally as a unit. The usual fasteners for this repair are bolts, but nails, screws, or adhesives also may be used. One method of stiffening light-frame members is to rigidly glue a 25-mm (1-in.) board to the bottom where tensile stresses are high. The result is a "T" section.

The weakening effect of splits parallel to grain depends on their location, length, and whether they are parallel to the axis of the member. Splits at the end of members stressed in compression parallel to grain do not weaken the member if they are not influenced by connectors [67]. In members stressed in tension parallel to grain, splits may not be critical if they are outside the connector area. Where the grain is not parallel to the member axis, splits are a particular hazard. The most common repair of splits is by attaching metal plates on top and bottom and bolting them together or by bolting side plates through the member to form a splice. In some cases where the member is thick enough, a row of bolts can be placed directly through the split. This is referred to as stitch bolting. Variations of these approaches are described in detail in Ref 1.

Epoxy compounds have been used to fill in voids in wood members resulting from decay or other damage [68–71]. If the void is caused by decay, as much of the decayed wood should be removed as possible and a preservative applied before epoxy application. Epoxies are used for wood repair primarily because of their strength and quick-cure rate. They can be injected into the interior of the wood, and, if esthetics are important, the holes can be filled with sealing gel and sanded smooth. In some cases where voids are large, reinforcement bars of steel or fiber glass are placed in the void with ends inserted into the sound wood. Initial curing time is often less than 1 h with final curing accomplished in a few days. Epoxy formulations are available with a wide variety of properties, and the resistance of these repairs to bending and shear forces can vary considerably with epoxy type and quality of application.

Summary

An understanding of the basic properties of wood and of the factors that affect its serviceability is vital background for the preservation of wood structures. This information can be combined with architectural and engineering practice to assess conditions and take measures to extend the life of structures. The references given provide detailed information on specific items, and a complete coverage of rehabilitation and preservation is presented in Ref 1.

References

[1] "Evaluation, Maintenance and Upgrading of Wood Structures-A Guide and Commentary," American Society of Civil Engineers, New York, 1982.

[2] "Wood Handbook: Wood as an Engineering Material," Agricultural Handbook No. 72, U.S. Department of Agriculture, Forest Service, Washington, DC, 1974.

[3] Chudnoff, M., "Tropical Timbers of the World," Agricultural Handbook, No. 607 U.S. Department of Agriculture, Washington, DC, 1984.

[4] Stamm, A. J. and Loughborough, W. K. in *Transactions*, Vol. 64, American Society of Mechanical Engineers, New York, 1942, pp. 379-385.

[5] Madsen, B. and Barrett, J. D., "Time Strength Relationship for Lumber," Structural Research Service Report No. 13, The University of British Columbia, Department of Civil Engineering, Vancouver, British Columbia, 1976.

[6] Wood, L. W., "Relation of Strength of Wood to Duration of Load," Forest Products Laboratory Report No. 1916, U.S. Department of Agriculture, Forest Service, Forest Products Laboratory, Madison, WI, 1951.

[7] Arima, T., "Creep During Temperature Changes, III: Prediction of Creep at Elevated Temperature," *Journal of Japan Wood Research Society*, Vol. 19, No. 2, 1973, pp. 75-79.

[8] Sawabe, O., "Studies on the Thermal Softening of Wood, III: Effects of Temperature on the Bending Creep of Dry Hinoki Wood," *Journal of Japanese Wood Research Society*, Vol. 20, No. 11, 1974, pp. 517-522.

[9] Gerhards, C. C., *Wood and Fiber*, Vol. 14, No. 1, 1982, pp. 4-36.

[10] Beall, F. C., *Structural Use of Wood in Adverse Environments*, Part 1, Chapter 2, Van Nostrand, New York, NY, 1980, pp. 9-19.

[11] MacLean, J. D., "Effect of Heat on the Properties and Serviceability of Wood," U.S. Forest Products Laboratory Report 1471, U.S. Department of Agriculture, Forest Service, Forest Products Laboratory, Madison, WI, 1945.

[12] Millett, M. A., and Gerhards, C. C., *Wood Science*, Vol. 4, No. 4, 1972.

[13] Rattner, F. and Schaffer, E. L., "Determination of Temperature Distribution in Wood With Variable Surface Temperature by Numerical Integration of Duhamel's Integral," Forest Service Research Note FPL-0169, Washington, DC, 1967.

[14] Schaffer, E. L., "Temperature-Time Dependency of Longitudinal Mechanical Behavior of Dry Douglas Fir," *Proceedings*, NSF Workshop on General Construction Relations for Wood and Wood-Based Materials, Minnowbrook, NY, and Syracuse University, Syracuse, NY, July 1978, National Science Foundation, Washington, DC.

[15] Stamm, A. J., *Industrial and Engineering Chemistry*, Vol. 48, 1956, pp. 413-417.

[16] DeGroot, R. C., "Your Wood Can Last for Centuries," U.S. Department of Agriculture, Forest Service, Southern Forest Experimental Station, New Orleans, LA, 1976.

[17] Scheffer, T. C. and Verrall, A. F., "Principles for Protecting Wood Buildings from Decay," Research Paper FPL 190, U.S. Department of Agriculture, Forest Service, Forest Products Laboratory, Madison, WI, 1973.

[18] Wilcox, W. W., *Wood and Fiber*, Vol. 9, No. 4, 1978, pp. 252-257.

[19] Borgin, K., Parameswaran, N., and Liese, W., *Wood Science and Technology*, Vol. 9, No. 2, 1975, pp. 87-98.

[20] Coupe, C. and Watson, R. W., "Fundamental Aspects of Weathering," in *Proceedings*, annual convention of British Wood Preservers Association, London, 1967, pp. 37-49.

[21] Feist, W. C., *Structural Use of Wood in Adverse Environment*, Part 1, Chapter 13, Van Nostrand, New York, 1979, pp. 156-178.

[22] Kleinert, T. N., *Holzforschung und Holzverwertung*, Vol. 22, 1970, pp. 21-24.

[23] Kühne, R., Leukens, U., Sell, J., and Wälchli, O., *Holz als Roh-und Werkstoff*, Vol. 28, No. 6, 1970, pp. 223-229.

[24] Sell, J. and Leukens, U. *Holz als Roh-und Werkstoff*, Vol. 29, No. 1, 1971, pp. 23-31.

[25] Browne, F. L., *Southern Lumberman*, Vol. 207, No. 2517, 1960, pp. 141-143.

[26] U.S. Department of Agriculture, Forest Service, Forest Products Laboratory, "Wood Finishing: Weathering of Wood," Forest Service Research Note FPL-0135, U.S. Department of Agriculture, Forest Products Laboratory, Madison, WI, 1975.

[27] Stamm, A. J., *American Paint Journal*, Vol. 48, No. 25, 1963, pp. 72-88.

[28] Schaffer, E. L., *Journal of Testing and Evaluation*, Vol. 1, No. 4, 1973, pp. 319-329.

[29] Knudsen, R. M. and Schniewind, A. P., *Forest Products Journal*, Vol. 25, No. 2, 1975, pp. 23-32.

[30] Schaffer, E. L., "A Simple Test for Adhesive Behavior in Wood Sections Exposed to Fire," Forest Service Research Note FPL-0175, U.S. Department of Agriculture, Forest Products Laboratory, Madison, WI, 1968.

[31] Johnston, H. R., Smith, V. K., and Beal, R. H., "Subterranean Termites: Their Prevention and Control in Buildings," Home and Garden Bulletin No. 64, U.S. Department of Agriculture, Washington, DC, 1972.

[32] Gerhards, C. C., *Wood Science*, Vol. 11, No. 1, 1979, pp. 13-16.

[33] Agi, J. J., in *AE Concepts in Wood Design*, American Wood Preservers' Institute, McLean, VA, 1976, p. 14-15.

[34] "Inspection Manual," AITC 200-73, American Institute of Timber Construction, Englewood, CO, 1973.

[35] Ifju, G., *Forest Products Journal*, Vol. 14, No. 8, 1964, pp. 366-372.

[36] Adams, E. H., Moore, G. L., and Brazier, J. D., "The Effect of Flame-Retardant Treatments on Some Mechanical Properties of Wood," British Research Establishment Information Paper IP 24/79, Princes Risborough Lab, Aylesbury, Bucks, United Kingdom, 1979.

[37] Gerhards, C. C., "Effect of Fire Retardant Treatment on Bending Strength of Wood," Forest Service Research Paper FPL 145, U.S. Department of Agriculture, Forest Products Laboratory, Madison, WI, 1970.

[38] Ehlbeck, J., "Nailed Joints in Wood Structures," Bulletin No. 166, Wood Research and Construction Laboratory, Virginia Polytechnic Institute and State University, Blacksburg, VA, 1979.

[39] Jessome, A. P. and Kennedy, D. E., *Canadian Consulting Engineer*, Nov. 1960.

[40] Stern, E. G., "Nails—Definitions and Sizes, a Handbook for Nail Users," Bulletin No. 61, Wood Research and Wood Construction Laboratory, Virginia Polytechnic Institute and State University, Blacksburg, VA, 1967.

[41] "Design Manual for Teco Timber Connector Construction," Publication No. 109, Timber Engineering Company, Washington, DC, 1973.

[42] Look, D. W., "Selected Bibliography on Log Structures," U.S. Department of Interior, Heritage Conservation and Recreation Service, Office of Archaeology and Historic Preservation, Washington, DC, 1975.

[43] Rowell, R. J., Black, J. M., Gjovik, L. R., and Feist, W. C., "Protecting Log Cabins from Decay," Forest Service General Technical Report, FPL-11, U.S. Department of Agriculture, Forest Products Laboratory, Madison, WI, 1977.

[44] Sherwood, G. E., "New Life for Old Dwellings—Appraisal and Rehabilitation," Agricultural Handbook No. 481, U.S. Department of Agriculture, Washington, DC, 1975.

[45] "Design of Wood Frame Structures for Performance," National Forest Products Association, Washington, DC, 1980.

[46] Stalker, I. N., *Chemical Industry*, Vol. 50, 1971, pp. 1427-1431.

[47] Oviatt, A. E., "Protecting Exposed Ends of Timber Beams in the Puget Sound Area," U.S. Department of Agriculture, Forest Service, Pacific Northwest Forest and Range Experiment Station, Portland, OR, Nov. 1975.

[48] "ASHRAE Handbook of Fundamentals," Chapter 20, American Society of Heating, Refrigerating, and Air-Conditioning Engineers, New York, 1977.

[49] "Fundamentals of Residential Attic Ventilation," H. C. Products Co., Princeville, IL, 1976.

[50] Sherwood, G. E. and Peters, C. C., "Moisture Conditions in Walls and Ceilings of a Simulated Older Home During Winter," Forest Service Research Paper FPL 290, U.S. Department of Agriculture, Forest Products Laboratory, Madison, WI, 1977.

[51] Sherwood, G. E., "Paint as a Vapor Barrier for Walls of Older Homes," Forest Service Research Paper 319, U.S. Department of Agriculture, Forest Products Laboratory, Madison, WI, 1978.

[52] Baker, M. C. and Hedlin, C. P., "Venting of Flat Roofs," *Canadian Building Digest*, CBD 176, Natural Resource Council of Canada, Ottawa, Canada, 1976.

[53] Black, J. M., "Finishes, Construction Factors, and Design to Compensate for Effects of

Weather on Wood Surfaces," Symposium on World Consultation on the Use of Wood in Housing, Vancouver, B.C., July 5-16, 1971, Vol. 25, Nos. 2-4, Unasylva Publishers, Rome.

[54] "Wood and Wood Finishes in Exterior Use—An Annotated Bibliography of Significant Studies of Coatings, Treatments, and Substrates Modifications," California Redwood Association, San Francisco, 1962.

[55] "A New Trend in Timber Protection—Exterior Wood Stains," Building Research Establishment, Department of the Environment, Aylesbury, Buckinghamshire, England, 1976.

[56] Hess, M., *Paint Film Defects, Their Causes and Cures*, 2nd ed., Chapman and Hall, Ltd., London, 1965.

[57] Hill, R. R., "Effect of Preservative Pretreatment on the Exterior Durability Characteristics of Exterior Stain Finishes Applied to European Redwood and Whitewood," Resource Report WT/RR/14, Timber Resource Development Association, High Wycombe, Buckinghamshire, England, 1975.

[58] Sell, J., *Holz als Roh-und Werkstoff*, Vol. 33, No. 9, 1975, pp. 336-340.

[59] Feist, W. C. and Mraz, E. A., "Wood Finishing: Water Repellents and Water-Repellent Preservatives," Forest Service Research Note FPL-0124, U.S. Department of Agriculture, Forest Products Laboratory, Madison, WI, 1978.

[60] Tarkow, H., Southerland, C. F., and Seborg, R. M., "Surface Characteristics of Wood as They Affect Durability of Finishes. Part I. Surface Stabilization," Forest Service Research Paper FPL 57, U.S. Department of Agriculture, Forest Products Laboratory, Madison, WI, 1966.

[61] "Maintaining Timber Exposed to the Weather," Timber Resource Development Association, High Wycombe, Buckinghamshire, England, 1965.

[62] American Institute of Timber Construction, *Timber Construction Manual*, 2nd ed., Wiley, New York, 1974.

[63] Gurfinkel, G., "Wood Engineering," Southern Forest Products Association, New Orleans, 1973.

[64] Hoyle, R. J., Jr., *Wood Technology in the Design of Structures*, Mountain Press Publishing Co., Missoula, MT, 1973.

[65] Ketchum, V., "Timber Maintenance Methods," *Western Construction News*, Jan. 1945.

[66] Timber Engineering, Co., *Timber Design and Construction Handbook*, 1st ed., McGraw-Hill, New York, 1956.

[67] Ketchum, V., May, T. K., and Hanrahan, F. J., *Emgineering News-Record*, July 27, 1944, pp. 90-93.

[68] Avent, R. R., Emkin, L. Z., Howard, R. H., and Chapman, C. L., *Journal of the Structural Division*, Vol. 102, No. ST4, American Society of Chemical Engineers, April 1976, pp. 821-838.

[69] Avent, R. R., Emkin, L. Z., and Sanders, P. H., *Journal of the Structural Division*, Vol. 104, No. ST6, American Society of Chemical Engineers, June 1978, pp. 933-951.

[70] "Restoring Timber with Plastics," *Building Research and Practice*, May/June 1978.

[71] Phillips, M. W. and Selwyn, J. E., "Epoxies for Wood Repairs in Historic Buildings," Heritage Conservation and Recreation Service Publication No. 1, U.S. Department of Interior, Washington, DC, 1978.

Michael J. Jedrzejewski[1]

A Method for Determining the Allowable Strength of In-Place Wood Structural Members

REFERENCE: Jedrzejewski, M. J., "A Method for Determining the Allowable Strength of In-Place Wood Structural Members," *Building Performance: Function, Preservation, and Rehabilitation, ASTM STP 901*, G. Davis, Ed., American Society for Testing and Materials, Philadelphia, 1986, pp. 136–151.

ABSTRACT: There are numerous older wood-structured buildings in the United States which have great potential for reuse; however, their allowable load capacity is unknown or is not readily calculable due to the lack of grade marks on the wood members which would identify their strength properties.

This paper describes a method by which the allowable strength properties of in-place wood structural members can be determined. The method consists of a series of procedures which utilize current ASTM standards and specific inspection techniques to render the allowable strength properties of the wood members. With the allowable strength properties of the wood members determined, the load capacity of the total structure, of specific members, or of areas of the structure can be determined by the use of common engineering calculations.

KEY WORDS: allowable strength properties, allowable unit stress, clear wood strength, wood structural members, allowable load capacity, in-place structural members, strength ratios

There are numerous older wood-structured buildings in the United States which most likely have great potential for reuse. However, in order to determine whether a wood-structured building can be used to house a specific function, either its allowable load capacity must be known or the allowable strength properties of the wood must be known so that the structure's allowable load capacity can be calculated.

As in the case of most older buildings, the allowable load capacity of an existing wood-structured building is not typically known, since original draw-

[1]Vice-president and Architect, Architectural Investigation and Documentation Services, Chicago, IL.

ings, specifications, or calculations are not available. In addition, grading marks, in most instances, will not be found on the wood members of older buildings. Without these grading marks, the allowable strength properties of the wood members are unknown, and, therefore, the allowable load capacity cannot be calculated.

In some cases, if the allowable load capacity of a structure was not known and the wood members had no grade marks, an assumption would be made by the designer as to their allowable strength properties. From these assumed strength properties, the allowable load capacity of the structure would be then calculated. As one can quickly realize, this procedure could be disastrous if the allowable strength properties of the wood members are actually considerably less than assumed. Alternately, an assumption for the strength properties might be less than actually exists. In this case, the structure would not be used to its full capacity.

This paper presents a method which was developed to determine more accurately the allowable strength properties of in-place wood structural members. This method consists of a series of procedures which utilize ASTM standards as well as microscopic inspection of wood specimens to help determine the allowable strength properties of in-place wood members. Once determined, these strength properties can be used to calculate the allowable load capacity of the structure. The following sections describe each of the necessary procedures of the method in detail.

Procedures

The procedures which make up the method for determining the allowable strength properties of in-place wood members are divided into two categories: field procedures and office procedures. The field category contains those procedures which are carried out in the field at the subject structure, and the office category contains those procedures which are carried out in the office or laboratory. In both the field and office categories, numerous items of data in the form of field measurements, values from ASTM standards, and calculated values must be collected. In order to simplify the collection of these data, forms like those shown in Figs. 1, 2, 3, and Table 1 are used. The forms were developed for simple span joists to determine their allowable bending strength. However, these forms easily can be altered for other types of members (that is, columns, beams, etc.), for other spans (that is, continuous over several supports), and for the determination of other strength properties (that is, horizontal shear, compression parallel to grain, etc.). To help illustrate the procedures required to determine the allowable strength properties of a member, an example has been developed utilizing a simple span joist. Its allowable bending strength will be determined through the procedures discussed in this paper. The following are the descriptions of the procedures in each of the two categories.

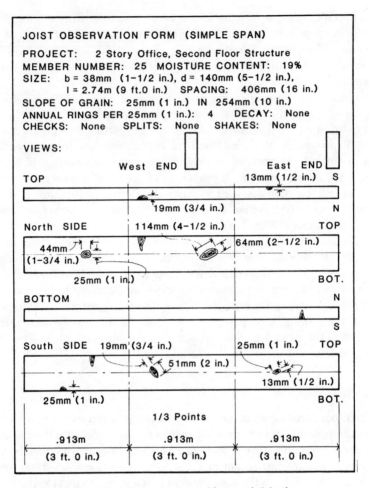

FIG. 1—*Joist observation form with example joist data.*

Field Procedures

Population and Random Sample

Each of the member types (that is, columns, joists, etc.) on a given floor are grouped into populations and are consecutively numbered. As an example, if there are 100 floor joists for the second floor structure of an office building, they should be numbered from 000 to 099. While the members are being numbered, they also should be inspected for visible signs of degradation, including failure, decay, insect attack, or fire damage. Those with signs of degradation should be noted on a plan, since those with decay or insect attack will have to be replaced and those that are fire damaged or have failures will

A STRENGTH PROPERTY: Bending PROJECT: 2 Story Office, 2nd Floor Joists							
*(1) MN	(2) WS	TR (3)	UCWS (5)		AUCWS (6)	AF (7)	AUSCSGW (8)
		DE (4)	AVG $_{(psi)}^{kPa}$	S $_{(psi)}^{kPa}$	kPa (psi)		kPa (psi)
25	Douglas Fir	None	46 774	6260	36 473 (5290)	1/2.1	17 368 (2519)
		None	(6784)	(908)			

* Item Numbers Used In Text

LEGEND

MN	Member Number
WS	Wood Species
TR	Treatment
DE	Decay
UCWS	Unadjusted Clear Wood Strength
AVG	Average
S	Estimated Standard Deviation
AUCWS	Assigned Unadjusted Clear Wood Strength
AF	Adjustment Factor
AUSCSGW	Allowable Unit Stress, Clear Straight Grained Wood

FIG. 2—*Data Collection Form "A" with example joist data.*

B STRENGTH PROPERTY: Bending PROJECT: 2 Story Office, 2nd Floor Joists									
*(9) MN	(10) AUSCSGW kPa (psi)	(11) LSR	(12) SGF	(13) SF	(14) SAF	(15) DLF	(16) TF	(17) MMF	(18) AUS kPa (psi)
25	17 368 (2519)	.37	1.0	.89	1.25	None	None	1.15	8274 (1200)

*Item Numbers Used In Text

LEGEND

MN	Member Number
AUSCSGW	Allowable Unit Stress, Clear Straight Grained Wood
LSR	Limiting Strength Ratio
SGF	Specific Gravity Factor
SF	Size Factor
SAF	Seasoning Adjustment Factor
DLF	Duration of Load Factor
TF	Treatment Factor
MMF	Multiple Member Factor
AUS	Allowable Unit Stress

FIG. 3—*Data Collection Form "B" with example joist data.*

have to be replaced or strengthened. Special attention must be given to look-ing for minute compression failures, especially in bending members, since such defects seriously reduce bending strength properties.

From the population, a random sample of members must be chosen. The sampling is done in conformance with ASTM Recommended Practice for Probability Sampling of Materials [E 105-58 (1975)]. The random sample shall consist of 20% of the population or a minimum of 20 members. With the number of members needed for the random sample determined, the ran-dom sample of members can be picked from the population by the use of a random number table. It should be noted that fire-damaged members should not be included in this random sample. The allowable strength properties of fire-damaged members must be determined by another method which is not discussed in this paper.

Observations of Members in Random Samples

Once the members of the random sample have been picked, each one has to be inspected, and the following forms of information are collected at this time.

Moisture Content—The moisture content for each member of the random sample is determined in accordance with ASTM Methods for Moisture Con-tent of Wood [D 2016-74 (1983)]. One way of measuring this moisture content is with the use of a resistance-type moisture meter. One such meter is shown in Fig 4. The moisture content of each member is then listed on its appropri-ate observation form. In the case of the example joist, the moisture content was determined to be 19%. This value is listed on the Joist Observation Form for Member Number 25 (Fig. 1).

Member Size—The size of each member of the random sample is mea-sured and listed on its observation form (Fig. 1). Their spacing is measured also and listed.

Slope of Grain—The slope of the grain of each member of the random sample is measured in accordance with Section 5.2 of ASTM Method for Es-tablishing Structural Grades and Related Allowable Properties for Visually Graded Lumber (D 245-81). The measured slope of grain is then listed on each member's observation form (Fig. 1).

Shakes, Checks, and Splits—These defects, if present, are measured in conformance with Section 5.4 of ASTM Method D 245-81. Each of these de-fects, if found, is illustrated with measurements on the appropriate view of the member on its observation form (Fig. 1). In the case of the example joist, no shakes, checks, or splits were found.

Decay—If visible decay is present on a member, that should be noted on that member's observation form and located on the appropriate view of the member on its observation form. If visible decay is present, the member will

FIG. 4—*Portable, resistance-type moisture meter.*

have to be replaced, since at this time there is to date no proven method of determining the exact reduction of strength in a wood member due to decay.

Knots—The knots on each face of the members in the random sample are measured in conformance with Section 5.3 of ASTM Method D 245-81. The knots and their sizes are located on the appropriate view of the member on its observation form (Fig. 1). It should be noted that, in most cases, the top face of bending members cannot be inspected due to the presence of decking. In the case of single span bending members, this is not a serious problem, since knots present on the top section will be in compression; however, the knots must be present in their holes. In the case of continuous bending members, knots in the top section can be a serious concern if they occur at or near a support. In this case, the decking must be removed to inspect the top surface.

Wood Specimens—From each member in the random sample, a wood specimen must be taken. The specimen should measure at least 7 by 7 by 7 mm (approximately 1/4 by 1/4 by 1/4 in.). Each specimen should be placed in a sample envelope which is identified by the number of the member from which it was taken. These specimens should be removed only from locations on the member where the removal of the specimen will not cause an overstress condition.

Office Procedures

Species Identification

From each of the wood specimens taken in the field, thin sections approximately 20 μm thick are made from a plane tangential to the annular rings (tangential section), a plane perpendicular to the annular rings (radial section), and a plane perpendicular to the grain (cross section). These thin sections can be made freehand with a razor blade or with the use of a microtome. These sections then are mounted on a microscope slide for inspection with the use of transmitted light microscope. Each microscope slide should be marked so that future identifications are possible. After all the slides are made, they are inspected with the microscope at varying magnifications for specific characteristics which help to identify the species of wood (Fig. 5). It should be noted that the location where a species of wood was grown cannot be determined from a microscopic inspection, and, in the case of some woods such as the southern yellow pines, the various species cannot be separated by microscopic inspection. Once the species of wood is determined, it should be entered under Item 2 on Data Collection Form "A" (Fig. 2). In the case of the example joist, the species was determined to be Douglas fir (*Pseudotsuga menziesii*).

Wood Treatment Determination

Each of the wood specimens must be examined to determine if the wood has been treated with a preservative or fire retardant, since various reductions occur in the strength properties due to the application of such a treatment. Current research at Architectural Investigation and Documentation Services, P.C. indicates that the presence of some treatments can be determined by microscopic inspection of a radial section immediately after it has been mounted on a microscope slide. If the section is viewed at this time, the crystals of the salt types of treatments can be observed, in most cases, before they proceed into solution with the mounting medium. The presence of a wood treatment should be indicated under Item 3 on Data Collection Form "A" (Fig. 2). In the case of the example joist, no form of treatment could be found.

Decay Determination

Even if visual observation of the members indicates no decay, decay still can be present. Microscopic inspection is required again to determine if decay

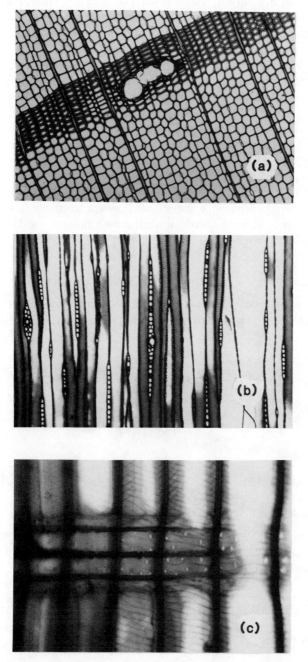

FIG. 5—*Microscopic views of (a) cross section, (b) tangential section, and (c) radial section of Douglas fir (Pseudotsuga menziesii).*

in the form of a wood rot fungus is present. Radial sections are first made from each wood specimen. The radial sections then are stained with two types of stain, one that stains the wood cells and the other that stains the thread-like elements (hyphae) of the wood rot fungus. After staining, each of the radial sections are mounted on microscope slides and inspected with the use of the microscope for the presence of hyphae from a wood rot fungus (Fig. 6). The presence of decay, if found, should be indicated under Item 4 on Data Collection Form "A" (Fig. 2). If decay is present, the member will have to be replaced, since at this time there is no proven method for determining the exact reduction of strength as a result of decay. This member, however, can be used to determine the allowable unit stress for a property to be used in determining the allowable load capacity of the structure. In the case of the example joist, no decay was found.

The preceding microscopic inspections (species, treatment, and decay) can be carried out by either a microscopist who specializes in wood technology or a wood technology specialist.

Average Unadjusted Clear Wood Strength Determination

Once the species of wood is determined, its average unadjusted clear wood strength value for a specific strength property can be found in Table 1, Table

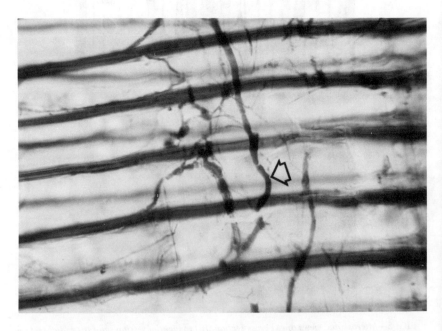

FIG. 6—*Microscopic view of a radial section of wood. The arrow points out one of many strands of hyphae, which indicate the presence of a wood rot fungus.*

2, or Table 3 of ASTM Method for Establishing Clear-Wood Strength Values (D 2555-81). Since we are unable to determine the location where the wood was grown or the exact species of some woods, the lowest value in Tables 1, 2, or 3 of ASTM Method D 2555-81 should be used for the specific strength property. In the case of the example joist, which was determined to be Douglas fir (*Pseudotsuga menziesii*), the value of 46 774 kPa (6784 psi) will be used for the unadjusted clear wood strength in bending with a standard deviation of 6260 kPa (908 psi). These values can be found under "Modulus of Rupture" in Table 1 of ASTM Method D 2555-81. The unadjusted clear wood strength for the strength property in question and its standard deviation must be determined for each member in the random sample and entered under Item 5 on Data Collection Form "A" (Fig. 2).

Assigned Unadjusted Clear Wood Strength Determination

In accordance with ASTM Method D 2555-81, Note 9, the average unadjusted clear wood strength is not to be used for determining the allowable unit stress for the modulus of rupture (bending), for compression parallel to grain, or for shear strength. For these strength properties, an assigned unadjusted clear wood strength value is calculated (this value also is known as the fifth percent exclusion limit). The assigned unadjusted clear wood strength (AUCWS) value is calculated with the following equation:

$$AUCWS = \bar{x} - 1.645\ s$$

where

$\bar{x}$ = estimate of species average unadjusted clear wood strength for a specific property (Item 5, Fig. 2), and

s = estimate of standard deviation of unadjusted clear wood strength for the same species and specific strength property (Item 5, Fig. 2).

The AUCWS value is calculated for each member in the random sample and the values are entered under Item 6 on Data Collection Form "A" (Fig. 2). In the case of the example joist, the AUCWS value was calculated to be 36 473 kPa (5290 psi).

Adjustment Factor Determination

Depending on the strength property in question, the AUCWS value is to be adjusted by the values in ASTM Method D 245-81 (Sections 4.2.5, 6.2, 6.2.1, and Table 9). The adjustment factor for each member is to be entered under Item 7 on Data Collection Form "A" (Fig. 2). Since the example joist is made of a softwood (Douglas fir) and its allowable bending strength is being determined, the adjustment factor used is 1/2.1 (Table 9 of ASTM Method D 245-81 and Fig. 2).

Determination of Allowable Unit Stress of Clear Straight-Grained Wood

The allowable unit stress for a specific property of clear straight-grained wood then is calculated by multiplying the adjustment factor (Fig. 2, Item 7) by the AUCWS (Fig. 2, Item 6). The calculated allowable unit stress for clear straight-grained wood of each member is entered under Item 8 on Data Collection Form "A" (Fig. 2). The allowable unit stress for clear straight-grained wood of each member must now be adjusted and modified by various factors for the actual conditions of each member. These factors are compiled for each member on Data Collection Form "B" (Fig. 3).

Limiting Strength Ratio Determination

The strength ratios for slope of grain, knots, shakes, checks, and splits present in each member are determined as stated in ASTM Method D 245-81 (Sections 5.2, 5.3, 5.4, Tables 1–6, and Figs. 1 and 2). The observation forms (Fig. 1) are used to identify the most severe knots, shakes, checks, and splits on each face as well as the slope of grain. The strength ratios for each characteristic found on a member are listed then on a table similar to Table 1 (this paper). From this type of table, the most limiting characteristic is determined for each member and listed under Item 11, Data Collection Form "B" (Fig. 3). The most limiting characteristic on the example joist is the knot on the centerline of the north side wide face (Fig. 1 and Table 1). The allowable strength ratio for this knot is 37% of the allowable unit stress of clear straight-grained wood. This value is listed under Item 11, Data Collection Form "B" (Fig. 3).

TABLE 1—*Limiting characteristics and related strength ratios for the example joist* (Member No. 25).

Strength Property	Limiting Characteristics	
	Characteristic	Strength Ratio, %
Bending	narrow face knot = 19 mm (3/4 in.)	62
	knot on centerline of wide face = 89 mm (3 1/2 in.) Avg.	37
	knot at edge of wide face = 25 mm (1 in.)	70
	slope of grain = 25 mm (1 in.) in 254 mm (10 in.)	61

Specific Gravity Factor

The allowable unit stresses for the various properties of clear straight-grained wood may be increased by the values given in Table 8 of ASTM Method D 245-81 if the requirements of Section 5.6 of ASTM Method D 245-81 are met. The example joist has four annual rings in 25 mm (1 in.) (Fig. 1) and is therefore classified as medium-grained wood (ASTM Method D 245-81). With four annual rings in 25 mm (1 in.), no increase is allowed under Table 8 of ASTM Method D 245-81. The specific gravity factor is determined for each member and entered under Item 12 on Data Collection Form "B" (Fig. 3). The specific gravity factor for the example joist is 1 and is entered under Item 12.

Size Factor Determination

The allowable unit bending stress for clear straight-grained wood must be adjusted for size by the equation in Section 3 of ASTM Method D 245-81. This equation is

$$F = (2/d)^{1/9}$$

where

$F =$ the size factor, and
$d =$ the actual depth of the member.

The size factor for the example joist was calculated to be 0.89 based on its depth (Fig. 1), and this size factor is listed under Item 13 on Data Collection Form "B" (Fig. 3).

Seasoning Adjustment Factor Determination

Based on the moisture content of each member measured in the field, the allowable unit stress for the various strength properties of clear straight-grained wood can be increased in accordance with ASTM Method D 245-81 (Section 7.1 and Table 11). It should be noted that the increases for 15% moisture content listed in Table 11 of ASTM Method D 245-81 can be used only if the wood was manufactured as 15% moisture content or less (ASTM Method D 245-81, Section 7.1.1). Also, the factors in Table 11 of ASTM Method D 245-81 do not apply to wood which has a moisture content higher than 19%. Since the example joist was found to have a 19% moisture content, a seasoning adjustment factor of 1.25 is used (from Table 11 of ASTM Method D 245-81) and is entered under Item 14 of Data Collection Form "B"

(Fig. 3). Similarly, the seasoning adjustment factor for each member is determined and entered under Item 14 of Data Collection Form "B".

Duration of Load Factor

The allowable unit stress for clear straight-grained wood which was calculated previously by multiplying the assigned unadjusted clear wood strength by an adjustment factor is for normal duration of load only. For other duration of loads, an appropriate load factor must be used to adjust the allowable unit stress for clear straight-grained wood. The correct duration of load factor is determined from Section 7.2 and Fig. 5 of ASTM Method D 245-81. For the example joist, normal duration of load is appropriate, and no factor is entered under Item 15 on Data Collection Form "B" (Fig. 3).

Treatment Factor

Preservatives and fire retardants, if used on wood members, reduce their various strength properties. If preservatives or fire retardants are found in any of the wood members through microscopic inspection, the allowable unit stress of clear straight-grained wood for the member must be reduced as indicated in Section 7.5 of ASTM Method D 245-81. From microscopic inspection, the example joist was found to have no treatments, and, therefore, no factor is entered under Item 16 on Data Collection Form "B" (Fig. 3). If any of the wood members are found to have treatments, an appropriate reduction factor must be entered under Item 16 on Data Collection Form "B".

Multiple Member Factor Determination

In accordance with Section 7.8 of ASTM Method D 245-81, if three or more members such as joists, rafters, studs, or decking are contiguous or are spaced no more than 609.6 (24 in.) and are joined by load distributing elements, a 15% increase in bending stress can be applied. The example joist is one of many which are spaced 406 mm (16 in.) on center and is nailed to decking. Since this joist meets the requirements of Section 7.8 of ASTM Method D 245-81, a factor of 1.15 is entered under Item 17 on Data Collection Form "B" (see Fig. 3).

The allowable unit stress for the strength property in question now can be calculated for each member. The allowable unit stress for each member is calculated by multiplying all of the factors under Items 11 through 17 on Data Collection Form "B" (Fig. 3) by the allowable unit stress of clear straight-grained wood under Item 10 on Data Collection Form "B" (Fig. 3). The calculated allowable unit stress of a specific property for each member is then rounded in conformance with Section 6.1.1 of ASTM Method D 245-81 and entered under Item 18 on Data Collection Form "B" (Fig. 3). For the example joist, the allowable unit stress for bending was calculated to be 8274 kPa (1200 psi) and is listed under Item 18 on Data Collection Form "B" (Fig. 3). Once the allowable unit stress for a given property is calculated for each member, the average ($\bar{x}$) allowable unit stress and the estimated standard deviation (s) for the specific property of all the members of the random sample is calculated. The allowable unit stress for a specific property to be used for structural calculations to determine the allowable load capacity of a structure then is determined by the following equation

$$\text{AUSLC} = \bar{x} - 1.645\ s$$

where

AUSLC = the allowable unit stress of a specific strength property to be used in allowable load capacity calculations,

$\bar{x}$ = the average of the allowable unit stress for a specific strength property of all of the members in the random sample, and

s = the estimated standard deviation of the allowable unit stress for a specific strength property of all of the members in the random sample.

In order to determine the allowable load capacity of an entire structure, the AUSLC for each type of member (that is, column, joist, etc.) and for each type of strength property (that is, bending, compression perpendicular to grain, etc.) on each floor must be determined as previously described in this paper. With all the AUSLC values calculated, the allowable load capacity of the entire structure or portions of the structure can be calculated using standard engineering formulas. The allowable load capacity which is calculated in this manner is based on the assumption that any degraded members are replaced with new members or repaired such that they have similar load-carrying capacities as those in the random sample.

Discussion

The method for determining the allowable strength of in-place wood structural members as discussed in this paper will provide strength values which are considerably more accurate than values which might otherwise be assumed. The strength properties determined by the method described in this paper, however, can be made more accurate if factors are developed for the reduction of the allowable unit stress of clear straight-grained lumber due to the presence of decay, preservatives, and fire retardants in wood. Further research is necessary to determine the relationship between the change in specific gravity of wood due to decay and its change in strength properties. Currently, ASTM D 245-81, under Section 7.4, does not allow the determination of the strength properties of a wood member if decay is present. Further research also is necessary in developing methods for determining the presence of preservatives and fire retardants in wood and their effect on the reduction of strength properties. Currently, ASTM Method D 245-81 in Section 7.5 only indicates a possible range of strength loss due to preservatives and does not indicate any possible loss of strength due to the presence of a fire retardant. It is hoped that this paper will stimulate interest in the development of an ASTM standard specifically for the determination of the allowable strength properties of in-place wood structural members. This standard will have to deal with the problem of viewing all sides of an in-place member, the inability to determine the location where the wood was grown, the inability to separate certain species of wood from one another, as well as the reduction of strength due to the presence of decay, preservatives, and fire retardants in wood members.

Acknowledgments

The author would like to thank John L. Van Ostrand, president of Architectural Investigation and Documentation Services, P.C. for his contributions to the general development of this paper and the method described. The author also would like to thank the staff at the Forest Products Laboratory in Madison, Wisconsin for their help in obtaining information valuable in the preparation of this paper.

Bibliography

Wood Identification

Core, H. A. and Coté, W. A., *Wood Structure and Identification*, 2nd ed., Syracuse University Press, Syracuse, NY, 1979.

Kukachka, B. F., "Identification of Coniferous Woods," Vol. 43, No. 11, Technical Association of the Pulp and Paper Industry (TAPPI), Atlanta, Nov. 1960.

Panshin, A. J. and de Zeeuw, C., *Textbook of Wood Technology, Structure, Identification, Properties, and Uses of the Commercial Woods of the United States and Canada*, 4th ed., McGraw-Hill Book Co., New York, 1980.

Wood, General

"Wood Handbook: Wood as an Engineering Material," Agriculture Handbook No. 72, Forest Products Laboratory, Forest Service, U.S. Department of Agriculture, Madison, WI, revised Aug. 1974.

Wood Strength Properties

Bendtsen, A. and Galligan, W. L., "Deriving Allowable Properties of Lumber (A Practical Guide for Interpretation of ASTM Standards)," General Technical Report FPL 20, Forest Service, U.S. Department of Agriculture, Forest Products Laboratory, Madison, WI.

Wood Decay

Eslyn, W. E. and Clark, J. W., "Wood Bridges—Decay Inspection and Control," Agriculture Handbook No. 557, Forest Service, U.S. Department of Agriculture, Forest Products Laboratory, Madison, WI, Oct. 1979.
Scheffer, T. C. and Verrall, A. F., "Principles for Protecting Wood Buildings from Decay," FPL 190, Forest Service, U.S. Department of Agriculture, Forest Products Laboratory, Madison, WI, revised 1979.

Moisture Meters

James, W. L., "Electric Moisture Meters for Wood," FPL-6, Forest Service, U.S. Department of Agriculture, Forest Products Laboratory, Madison, WI, 1975.

Wood Compression Failures

Pillow, M. Y., "Studies of Compression Failures and Their Detection in Ladder Rails," Report No. 1733, Forest Service, U.S. Department of Agriculture, Forest Products Laboratory, Madison, WI, 1949 (reprinted 1962).

Kenneth B. Kellermeyer[1] and Ian R. Chin[2]

Lessons Learned from Investigations of Over 500 Distressed Masonry and Stone Facades

REFERENCE: Kellermeyer, K. B. and Chin, I. R., **"Lessons Learned from Investigations of Over 500 Distressed Masonry and Stone Facades,"** *Building Performance: Function, Preservation, and Rehabilitation, ASTM STP 901,*G. Davis, Ed., American Society for Testing and Materials, Philadelphia, 1986, pp. 152-164.

ABSTRACT: The authors and their colleagues have investigated over 500 buildings with distressed masonry and stone facades in the last five years. This work has included investigations of distressed conditions in building facades made of brick, concrete block, terracotta, granite, limestone, and marble.

Masonry and stone facades are frequently chosen by designers and building owners for their inherent durability to resist weathering and for their inherent low maintenance costs. When properly designed in accordance with available standards, their performance is normally excellent. However, their performance can be affected by insufficient care in the design of joints and by insufficient care in the design of attachment and flashing systems.

Based upon architectural design principles, knowledge of masonry and stone materials, and experience gained from investigating numerous masonry and stone facade failures, the authors discuss design factors and details that could help designers avoid failures in new masonry and stone facades. The authors also present information that can assist architects, engineers, and building owners rehabilitate and preserve existing facades on buildings.

KEY WORDS: moisture expansion, thermal expansion, shrinkage, expansion joints, relief joints, control joints, differential movements, frame shortening, crazing, spalling, water penetration, cavity walls, single wythe walls, composite walls, flashing, weep holes

Although masonary and stone materials have been used in building wall construction for over 9000 years, the design and construction technology of masonry and stone exterior walls was relatively limited compared to present

---

[1]President, Kellermeyer Godfryt Hart, P. C., Chicago, IL 60602.
[2]Senior consultant, Wiss, Janney, Elstner Associates, Inc., Northbrook, IL 60062.

technology. Historically, masonry exterior walls on buildings were designed as solid load-bearing walls based upon previously established empirical design principles. This design approach resulted in masonry bearing walls, the thickness of which varied up to about 1.83 m (6 ft) at the lower floors of some structures. In the past, these thick, heavy masonry walls were constructed with relatively soft lime mortars and with masonry units having compressive strengths that were adequate for their intended purposes but which were often lower than the compressive strengths of masonry units in use today.

With the advent of structural steel and reinforced concrete skeleton frame construction in the late 1800s and early 1900s, significant changes were made in the design, construction, and behavior of exterior masonry walls on buildings. These changes included the following:

1. The use of thin, nonload-bearing exterior masonry and stone walls which primarily act as curtain walls to protect interior spaces from the weather and to provide fire protection for exterior columns and beams.

2. The use of high-strength, portland cement-based mortars and high-strength bricks to construct walls.

3. The use of cavity and composite masonry walls consisting of brick, stone, and hollow masonry units.

The utilization of stronger masonry units and mortars produced masonry walls with high compressive strengths, and thin walls resulted through optimization and utilization of the increased masonry strengths. However, these thin walls are more brittle, less watertight, and do not possess the flexibility to accommodate movements of the masonry and of the structure to which they are attached without suffering distress, as did the thicker "softer" preskeleton-frame, solid-masonry, load-bearing walls.

This paper discusses the common types of deficiencies and resulting distress that the authors and their colleagues have observed during the course of investigating approximately 500 new and old masonry and stone structures. The vast majority of the distressed conditions observed occurred as a result of the following:

1. The lack of provisions to properly accommodate volumetric changes of the materials used in the construction of the walls.

2. The lack of proper details to accommodate differential movements between the walls and the building structure.

3. The lack of proper details to reduce the entry of water into the walls, which can result in the accelerated deterioration of anchors, ties, and supports.

Clay Brick Facades

Clay bricks, when removed from the kiln after firing, will begin to permanently increase in size as a result of absorption of moisture from rain, snow, and humidity in the air. Published information of research performed on the moisture expansion of fired clay products in the United States, England, and Australia has indicated that the rate of moisture expansion in fired clay products increases linearly with the logarithm of time, and that 100% of the potential moisture expansion will generally occur about 60 to 100 years after the clay products are fired [5]. Accordingly, it is estimated that approximately 40% of the total potential moisture expansion of bricks will occur approximately three months after the bricks have been fired and that approximately 50% of the total potential moisture expansion will occur approximately one year after the bricks have been fired.

The design coefficient for moisture expansion of clay bricks as recommended by the Brick Institute of America is 0.0002 mm/mm (0.0002 in/in.) [1]. However, tests performed by the authors and their colleagues on brick samples removed from distressed brick masonry walls have revealed that moisture expansion coefficients for some bricks are considerably higher than the recommended design coefficient.

In addition to the continuous permanent growth of the clay bricks due to moisture absorption, seasonal reversible expansion and contraction of clay bricks will occur due to changes in the ambient air temperature. It is not uncommon for the exterior surface of a dark colored brick to reach temperatures in excess of 80°C (175°F) on a hot summer day when directly exposed to solar radiation. Likewise, surface temperatures as low as −35°C (−30°F) can be reached due to nocturnal radiation into clear skies. The recommended design coefficient of linear thermal expansion of clay bricks as recommended by the Brick Institute of America is 0.000007 mm/mm/°C (0.000004 in./in./°F [2].

With the use of thin masonry curtain walls, less mass is available to buffer the effects of temperature gradients through the wall construction. Also, less wall mass is available to absorb and distribute stresses resulting from moisture and thermal movements of the clay bricks when such movements are not adequately accommodated.

Investigations of distressed masonry facades performed by the authors and their colleagues have revealed that moisture and thermal expansion of clay brick walls often result in cracking of the masonry units, particularly at building corners and offsets, and at horizontal shelf angles if these movements are not properly accommodated.

Because parapet walls are exposed to the weather on three faces and relatively small compressive stresses exist, dramatic horizontal movement and severe distress can occur in masonry parapet walls when adequate provisions to accommodate horizontal masonry expansion are not provided.

To properly accommodate the anticipated horizontal expansion of the masonry, vertical expansion joints should be provided. Vertical expansion joints should be located in close proximity to building corners and offsets, at locations of changes in the vertical height of the walls, and at regular intervals in long walls. Vertical expansion joints should be extended through the parapet wall construction. Also, it is advisable to provide additional vertical expansion joints in parapet walls midway between the full-height, wall-expansion joints to allow for the greater anticipated expansion of the parapet walls. The vertical expansion joints should be free of mortar and debris and should be properly sized to accommodate the anticipated horizontal expansion of the brickwork, as shown in Fig. 1.

Severe distress to exterior brick walls also can result from the lack of provisions to accommodate the differential vertical expansion of the brickwork and shortening of the structure, particularly in mid-rise and high-rise buildings. Building columns, when loaded, will undergo elastic shortening in the vertical direction. The total change in length due to elastic shortening is dependent upon the magnitude of the axial load, the length and cross-sectional size of the column, and the material of the column. Typically, reinforced concrete columns will experience a greater change in length due to elastic shortening than a comparably designed steel column. In addition, concrete structures decrease in size in the vertical and horizontal directions due to shrinkage and creep after they have been constructed and loaded. Although the greatest amount of shrinkage in concrete structures occurs within the first two to three months after the structure is poured, shrinkage in concrete structures will continue indefinitely in decreasing amounts. Creep is a slower phenomenon continuing for a decade or more.

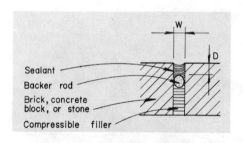

W = width of joint	D = depth of sealant
1/4 in. min	1/4 in.
1/4 to 1/2 in.	1/4 in.
1/2 to 1 in.	$W \div 2$

W = total anticipated movement of masonry $\times$ C
C = compressibility factor of sealant
  = 3 or 4 depending on type of sealant

Sealant shall be compatible with facade material.
Moisture expansion of brick masonry is not reversible.
Thermal expansion of marble is partially reversible.

FIG. 1—*Plan detail of vertical expansion joint.*

Unless provisions are provided to accommodate these movements, compressive forces due to confined frame shortening and vertical brick expansion can result in crushing and cracking of the brick units, as shown in Fig. 2.

To properly accommodate vertical expansion of the brickwork and shortening of the structural frame, horizontal expansion joints are recommended below all horizontal shelf angles that support the wall, as shown in Fig. 3. Horizontal expansion joints should be located intermittently over the height of the building. Some building codes [6] require exterior brick walls that are 10.67 m (35 ft) or greater in height to be supported on horizontal shelf angles attached to the structure of the building at each floor level and a horizontal expansion joint to be located in the brickwork directly below each horizontal shelf angle. Horizontal expansion joints should be properly sized to accommodate the anticipated shortening of the building frame, the anticipated deflection of the shelf angle, and the anticipated vertical expansion of the clay bricks. Flashings and weep holes also should be provided at shelf angles to divert and to drain moisture that penetrates into the walls to the exterior of the building.

Vertical and horizontal expansion joints in brick masonry walls are normally sealed with sealant to prevent the penetration of moisture into the joints. To properly accommodate the anticipated movements at the joints and to ensure that the selected sealant in the joints will last for its expected life,

FIG. 2—*View of cracked and spalled brickwork at horizontal shelf angle.*

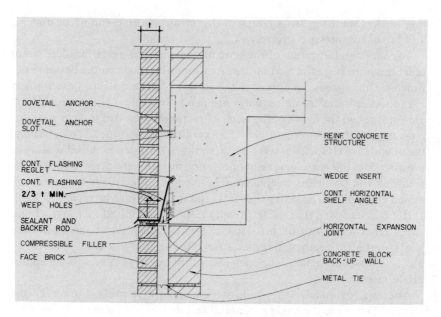

DOVETAIL   ANCHOR

DOVETAIL   ANCHOR
SLOT

CONT.   FLASHING
REGLET

CONT.   FLASHING

2/3 t MIN.

WEEP   HOLES

SEALANT   AND
BACKER   ROD

COMPRESSIBLE   FILLER

FACE   BRICK

REINF.   CONCRETE
STRUCTURE

WEDGE   INSERT

CONT.   HORIZONTAL
SHELF   ANGLE

HORIZONTAL   EXPANSION
JOINT

CONCRETE   BLOCK
BACK-UP   WALL

METAL   TIE

FIG. 3—*Horizontal expansion joint detail.*

the size of the joints normally should be three to four times the anticipated movements depending on the type of sealant used.

During the early stages in the development of masonry curtain wall technology, it was common practice to place the masonry tight against exterior building columns and beams. However, published information recommends that exterior masonry walls should be separated from columns with at least a 19-mm (3/4-in.)-wide space [3]. This recommendation was overlooked by the designers of a number of the buildings in which masonry failures have been investigated. Where masonry is placed tight against the structure, cracking of the masonry often occurs as a result of unaccommodated differential movements between the masonry and the building frame.

Terra-Cotta Facades

Terra-cotta, being a fired clay product, will experience permanent expansion due to moisture absorption and seasonal reversible volumetric changes due to temperature variations. Typically, early terra-cotta buildings were constructed without vertical and horizontal expansion joints, and the terra-cotta on some of these buildings suffered significant distress from forces which developed as a result of unaccommodated terra-cotta expansion.

Vertical expansion of the terra-cotta units and shortening of the building frame also can result in substantial compressive stresses in the units. Crushing, vertical splitting, and spalling of the terra-cotta units can occur under a buildup of compressive stresses.

To obtain an indication of the level of stress in terra-cotta facades, strain relief tests can be performed in situ. At various locations on the building perimeter, strain gages are affixed to the surface of the terra-cotta, as shown in Fig. 4. After initial strain readings are taken, horizontal and vertical joints are cut through the depth of the unit. After a short period of time to allow for relaxation of the test piece, final strain readings are recorded. To determine the modulus of elasticity of terra-cotta, samples are tested in the laboratory in compression. For each increment of compressive load, the associated strain is recorded and the stress calculated. The modulus of elasticity is then determined by graphically plotting the stress and strain for each increment of load.

If it is determined that the terra-cotta cladding is stressed excessively high, stress relief joints can be provided at predetermined locations by cutting joints for the full depth of the units. After allowing the terra-cotta to redistribute the stresses or "relax," the open joints then can be pointed with an appropriate mortar.

After approximately 1915, mild steel anchors were utilized to attach the terra-cotta units to the backup material and structure. In many of these older buildings, some of the metal anchors inspected have been found to be cor-

FIG. 4—*View of strian relief test performed on existing terra-cotta facade.*

roded to such an extent that they no longer provide positive anchorage of the units to the structure. In some instances, forces that developed as a result of confined expansion of corroded anchors have caused external and internal cracks in the units. To determine if existing terra-cotta units are adequately anchored to the building or if they contain internal cracks, the individual units can be "sounded" by gently tapping the face of the units with a hammer. An experienced investigator normally can determine the integrity of the unit by the quality of the sound produced.

To reanchor loose and cracked terra-cotta units to the backup material, stainless steel or brass-threaded pins can be inserted in epoxy in predrilled holes which extend into the backup materials, as shown in Fig. 5.

Another common type of distress found in glazed terra-cotta units is crazing and subsequent spalling of the surface glaze. The different rates of thermal expansion and contraction between the surface glaze and the inner clay body can create tension stresses which can cause crazing of the glazed surface. When the crazing extends through the depth of the glazed finish, water is able to penetrate into the clay body of the unit, and, upon freezing, can cause spalling of the faces of the units.

The delaminated portion of the terra-cotta can be reattached to the facade by pinning in the manner previously described, or the damaged area can be patched with a suitable material. Units which have experienced extensive deterioration may require total replacement with either new terra-cotta, precast concrete, or another suitable substitute material. At locations where visual appearance is not of particular importance, brick or a cementitious material applied over a clay brick backup can be utilized as a method of repair.

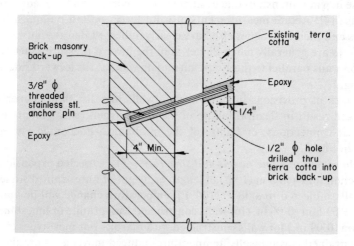

FIG. 5—*Detail to reanchor loose terra-cotta panels.*

Stone Facades

One of the key problems associated with the use of thin stone curtain walls on buildings is the problem of mechanical anchorage of the stone panels to the building frame. Mechanical anchorage related problems arise from stress concentration associated with gravity loads, wind loads, and differential movements between the curtain wall and the structural frame. Additional problems have been experienced in stone curtain walls due to the lack of provisions to accommodate thermally induced movements of the stone panels.

1. *Gravity loads*—If the curtain wall is designed to be constructed with an air space of 25.4 to 50.8 mm (1 to 2 in.) in width between the back of the stone panels and the front face of the structure, the use of ordinary mechanical anchors to carry the weight of the panels will result in extremely large anchors when pins or straps are used due to the eccentricity of the facade relative to the structure. Therefore, it is customary to support the weight of the panels on steel clip angles placed intermittently at floor levels.

If thin, bent metal straps are used to anchor the panels to the structure, excessive bending of the strap can occur if the eccentricity between the horizontal portion of the strap and the fastener is large. This condition can result in unwanted lateral distortion of the strap to a point where its ability to resist wind suction forces is seriously reduced.

2. *Wind loads*—The intensity of wind loads varies with height above the ground. The intensity of wind loads at the upper portions of tall buildings can be as much as three times the intensity of the wind loads at the base of the building.

Wind tunnel studies on structures have indicated that there is a substantial increase in wind intensities due to suction at the corners and roof edges of the buildings [4]. Actual measurements of wind forces on tall buildings by the authors and their colleagues also have clearly indicated that the outward suction forces are generally much higher than the inward pressure. Suction will occur on walls parallel to the airstream and on walls at the leeward side of the building.

The lack of provisions in stone curtain walls to resist these higher wind forces can result in flexural failure of the stone panels, shear failure of the panels at connections, or failure of the mechanical anchorage system, as shown in Fig. 6.

3. *Movement of stone panels and structure*—The expected expansion and contraction for each 3 m (10 ft) of length or height of unrestrained stone curtain walls subjected to a 38°C (100°F) temperature change will be approximately 1.52 mm (0.06 in.) for walls constructed with granite or limestone and 2.30 mm (0.09 in.) for walls constructed with marble. For most types of stone in unrestrained curtain walls, temperature-induced movements are theoretically reversible. However, certain stones, particularly some marbles, undergo

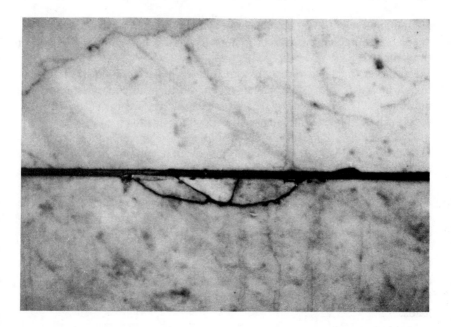

FIG. 6—*View of cracked stone panel at connection.*

a thermal hysteresis phenomenon; wherein, when subjected to a large number of thermal cycles, there is an irreversible expansion in the material amounting to as much as 20% of the total original thermal expansion. Such hysteresis, if not considered in the design, may result in unaccommodated expansion and bowing of thin marble curtain walls.

Compared to the moisture expansion of clay masonry, volume changes due to moisture changes in most stones are relatively small. Swelling and contraction of natural stone associated with water absorbed into the pores of the material has been measured. Generally, it is not a critical item in design.

To prevent unanticipated stresses and associated distress from developing in stone curtain walls attached to structural frames of tall buildings, it is essential that properly sized horizontal expansion joints be located below supporting steel clip angles to allow the structure to shorten and the stone to expand and contract in the vertical direction. If stone curtain walls are constructed without horizontal expansion joints at supporting clip angles, stress concentrations due to stacking of gravity loads or differential vertical movements or both between the stone curtain wall and the structure of the building can cause cracking and spalling of the stone panels. Rigid spacers and leveling devices placed between panels or below supporting clip angles also can cause the panels to crack and spall under similar stress concentrations.

It is also essential that properly sized vertical expansion joints be located at regular intervals in long stone curtain walls to accommodate thermally induced horizontal movements of the stone panels and horizontal movements of the structure.

Cantilever floor and roof slabs can frequently have sizable elastic deflections which can cause stone panels resting on them to undergo undesirable movements. This is especially true if such cantilevers are made from concrete which will be subjected to long-term deflections due to creep.

4. *Blind anchorage techniques*—Blind anchorage techniques were originally developed to attach stone panels to interior partition walls. However, for a time this technique was regularly used to attach stone curtain walls to the exterior of the buildings. To utilize such an anchorage technique to bridge across an air space and to blindly place the anchor in plaster pockets in the concrete or masonry backup has proven to be a very risky procedure as adequate mortar bond is not assured.

5. *Flexible stud channels*—Excessive deflection of flexible steel stud backup members can be transferred to the stone curtain wall and can cause the panels to deflect and crack. Such backup members need to be carefully investigated to determine the deflection they will experience under wind loads.

Water Penetration Through Masonry and Stone Facades

During the design of most types of masonry and stone curtain wall systems, the designer must recognize that a certain amount of water will penetrate through the curtain wall under wind-driven rain conditions, and that, consequently, a second line of defense should be provided in the curtain wall system to collect and divert the water to the exterior.

The results of water permeability tests and related investigations performed on existing masonry facades by the authors and their colleagues, using a field modified ASTM test procedure [Method for Water Permeance of Masonry (E 514-74)] over an area of 1.15 m^2 (12 ft^2) have indicated that a water penetration rate of under 1 L/h can be expected. Water penetration rates between 1 and 5 L/h are significant. However, at this level of water penetration, properly installed flashings and weep holes, together with a proper internal drainage system, usually will perform satisfactorily to divert and drain the water out of the wall system to the exterior. Water penetration rates over 5 L/h are excessive and require special remedy measures.

In order to properly design and properly construct exterior masonry curtain walls on buildings that provide the best resistance to water penetration, the following recommendation are offered:

1. Use either cavity wall construction or a single wythe or solid multiwythe wall with a proper internal drainage system.

2. Install proper flashing in the wall under horizontal sills and copings, at intersections of walls and horizontal surfaces, over heads of openings in walls, and at floor lines. Extend flashing beyond jambs of openings, and turn ends up to form a dam.

3. Extend flashing beyond the exterior face of the wall and turn flashing down to form a drip.

4. Install weep holes immediately above all flashing at a maximum horizontal spacing of 610 mm (24 in.) on centers. Keep weep holes free of mortar drippings. If wicks of 6.35-mm ($1/4$-in.)-diameter fiber glass rope or similar materials are used as weep holes, they should be spaced at a maximum horizontal distance of 406 mm (16 in.).

5. For most installations, use Type N mortar made with portland cement, hydrated lime, and sand.

6. Completely fill all head and bed joints with mortar and tool all exposed mortar joints to a concave or "V" profile.

7. Use materials that conform with applicable ASTM standards.

8. During construction, properly protect all materials and walls from freezing temperatures.

9. Apply a water repellent coating on exterior surfaces of single-wythe, concrete-block masonry walls.

Conclusions

The design and construction of masonry and stone facades on buildings is not simple and requires careful scrutiny and detailing. This paper has presented several factors that should be considered in the design and construction of masonry and stone facades on buildings.

Based upon the results of over 500 investigations of distressed masonry and stone facades on buildings performed by the authors and their colleagues in the last five years, it has been found that the vast majority of the distressed conditions occurred as a result of the following:

1. Inadequate provisions within the facade to accommodate volumetric changes of materials.

2. Inadequate provisions within the facade to accommodate differential movements between the facade and the structural frame of the building to which it is attached.

3. Improper design and installation of expansion and control joints.

4. Inadequate detailing and construction to reduce the entry of water into the facade to acceptable levels and to prevent the entry of water into the interior of the building.

5. The use of wind suction forces in the design of the facade at the upper portions of high-rise buildings that are significantly lower than actual wind suction forces.

Acknowledgments

The work presented in this paper is based upon over 500 investigations of masonry and stone facade failures on buildings performed by Wiss, Janney, Elstner Associates, Inc.

References

[1] "Differential Movement—Cause and Effect," Technical Note 18, *Brick Institute of America*, McLean, VA, April 1963.
[2] "Differential Movement—Expansion Joints," Technical Note 18A, *Brick Institute of America*, McLean, VA, May 1963.
[3] "Differential Movement—Flexible Anchorage," Technical Note 18B, *Brick Institute of America*, McLean, VA, June 1963.
[4] Cohen, E. and Vellozzi, J., "Proposed American Standards Building Code Requirements for Minimum Design Wind Loads," *Proceedings*, Design Symposium, Northwestern University, Evanston, IL, March 23, 1970, pp. 51.
[5] Cole, W. F. and Birtwistle, R., *Ceramic Bulletin*, Vol. 48, No. 12, 1969, pp. 1128.
[6] "North Carolina State Building Code," The North Carolina Building Code Council and The North Carolina Department of Insurance, 1978 ed., Section 1414.5(b).

Richard A. Livingston,[1] *Larry G. Evans,*[2]
Thomas H. Taylor, Jr.,[3] *and Jacob I. Trombka*[4]

Diagnosis of Building Condition by Neutron-Gamma Ray Technique

REFERENCE: Livingston, R. A., Evans, L. G., Taylor, T. H., Jr., and Trombka, J. I., **"Diagnosis of Building Condition by Neutron-Gamma Ray Technique,"** *Building Performance: Function, Preservation, and Rehabilitation, ASTM STP 901*, G. Davis, Ed., American Society for Testing and Materials, Philadelphia, 1986, pp. 165–180.

ABSTRACT: This paper describes a technique for nondestructive, in situ analysis of building condition that involves the use of neutrons from a portable source and the detection of the gamma rays resulting from the interactions of the neutrons with the building materials. Applications of this technique include the mapping of salt and moisture profiles within the walls and the location of voids or inclusions.

The technique uses a californium-252 neutron source (10^6 N/s) for composition measurements and a cesium-137 gamma-ray source for density measurements and energy calibration. Emitted gamma rays are measured with a high-purity germanium detector. The intensity of discrete gamma-ray lines is a function of the concentrations of the various elements encountered within the wall by the neutron flux. Using characteristic gamma-ray energy signatures for materials of interest, a measured gamma-ray spectra can be processed to yield information on the relative elemental distribution of a variety of substances, including water, salt, and building materials such as limestone, brick, and iron reinforcing bars.

Applications of this technique to several common problems of building diagnosis are discussed, including the case of an 18th-century building at Colonial Williamsburg suffering from salt damage.

KEY WORDS: neutron-gamma technique, salt damage, moisture, building diagnosis, nondestructive evaluation, brick, Colonial Williamsburg

A number of investigators in recent years have surveyed nondestructive techniques for application to diagnosis of building deterioration techniques

[1] Research associate, Geology Department, University of Maryland, College Park, MD 20740.
[2] Principal scientist, Astronomy Programs, Computer Sciences Corp., Silver Spring, MD 20910.
[3] Chief architectural conservator, The Colonial Williamsburg Foundation, Williamsburg, VA 23185.
[4] Astrophysicist, Laboratory for Astronomy and Solar Physics, NASA Goddard Space Flight Center, Greenbelt, MD 20771.

[1-3]. Reliable means to diagnose building deterioration are essential to identify both structural flaws that may make the building unsafe and agents of deterioration that increase the maintenance costs of the structure. These considerations are becoming increasingly important with the trend toward restoration of existing structures rather than the construction of new ones. However, existing methods of evaluation are generally limited to visual observations and destructive tests on small specimens. As Noland et al [2] point out, "These methods are limited because visual observations can only reveal gross defects, and testing of a sufficient number of specimens taken from the building may be prohibitive due to cost, time, and aesthetic considerations."

In a recent survey of techniques for assessment of building condition, Lerchen et al [4] found that those nondestructive methods that had the potential to reveal internal details of walls all had severe limitations. Moreover, the methods that were promising for identification of density variations, such as cracks or voids, were not able to provide information about the constituents causing these variations. This is a major drawback because it is important to know what is present within the wall that could be causing the density variations, particularly salts and moisture.

A recent report by a National Academy of Science committee [5] stated that the "dominant factor in deterioration of stone and masonry structures is water and moisture." However, as Stambolov and van Asperen de Boer [6,7] conclude after recent surveys of the literature, there "has been little reported progress in the determination of both relative humidity and moisture content of building materials." Water alone can cause severe deterioration by freeze-thaw cycles and dissolution of building materials [8], but its effects are accentuated by soluble salts [9-11].

The neutron-gamma method described in this paper answers a number of these problems. The diagnosis of building condition by this technique is based on the measurement of the distribution of characteristic elements within the structure under investigation. With the appropriate choice of elements to be characterized, a variety of building condition problems can be studied.

Application of Elemental Analysis to Building Deterioration Problems

Some examples of how elemental distribution patterns can be interpreted are as follows:

1. Identification of Moisture Within Walls

There are at least five different pathways by which water can accumulate within a wall: by rainfall penetration; by capillary rise of ground water; by condensation of humidity in either interior or ambient air; by leakage from plumbing systems; or through maintenance activities such as wall cleaning or shrubbery watering [12]. The correct identification of the source of the moisture is essential to successful elimination of the problem. This can be done only through an assessment of water distribution, both as a function of height and as a function of depth into the interior of the wall. In some situations the fluctuation of the distribution with time also must be analyzed.

A number of possible nondestructive techniques for moisture determination have been surveyed by Facoaru [1]. However, the only quantitative methods now in widespread use are electrical conductivity and neutron thermalization. Under certain conditions, infrared thermography can be used to give a qualitative picture of moisture distribution based on relative differences in surface emission of infrared radiation. Electrical conductivity has two major drawbacks: it only measures moisture at or near the surface and is affected by the presence of salts. The neutron thermalization method is limited to certain flat and shallow surfaces such as roofs and pavement.

With the neutron-gamma technique, the measurement of the distribution of the element hydrogen would be the primary diagnostic for the presence of moisture. The hydrogen gamma ray spectrum has a single, well-defined line, so this element is relatively easy to detect. The building material itself also may contain hydrogen, but this would be a relatively uniform background. Moisture distribution still could be identified as a relative change from point to point.

2. Measurement of Salt Distributions and Desalinization

As with water, salt can get into walls in several ways: from ground water rising by capillary action; from beach sand or stone used in the masonry units, as well as cement or mortar; from road salt splash; from deposition of marine aerosols or air pollution; or from building uses that involve the use of salts, such as pickling or the salt curing of food [9]. The correct identification of the source is essential to eliminating the problem. Common salt, sodium chloride, is a frequent source of damage. Chlorine can be used as the element for characterizing the salt distribution in the neutron-gamma technique since it is usually not present in building materials. Other salts such as magnesium and sodium sulfates also have caused problems [10]. Their distributions also can be characterized by the elemental distributions of magnesium, sodium, or sulfur.

The technique generally used in desalinizing building materials is a wet poultice applied to the wall. This creates a concentration gradient that encourages the salt to diffuse out of the wall and into the poultice. After the poultice is saturated, it is thrown away, and if the salts are not yet entirely removed from the wall, a new poultice is applied. By measuring the initial chlorine distribution through the wall and then its distribution after the poultice is removed, it is possible to obtain a measure of degree of desalinization and hence whether a new poultice needs to be applied.

3. *Effectiveness of Consolidants or Water Repellents*

A major problem for building materials is to find effective ways to preserve surfaces from attack by air pollution or weather or to consolidate crumbling materials. The treatment generally involves one or more chemicals that can be applied in liquid form to penetrate the surface and then be solidified by various means [13]. After more than a century of attempts [14], no completely successful treatment has yet been found [15].

A significant cause of treatment failure is the inability to achieve adequate penetration and dispersal into the material during the process of application. As a result, the treatment is contained just below the surface, creating a thin layer which has different physical properties than the substrate. This layer subsequently may spall off due to the action of thermal cycling or hydrostatic pressure in the material.

The lack of penetration is sometimes due to inadequate preparation of the surface beforehand. It is important to remove salt and moisture from the stone that would otherwise impede the movement of the treatment into the material. The problems of measuring the eliminating moisture and salt distributions have been just described, together with the ways in which a knowledge of elemental distributions can help solve the problem.

Assuming that the material has been correctly prepared, another source of failure during application is the inability to specify precisely the viscosity, driving pressure, hardening time, etc. Currently, these parameters have to be fixed in advance using data from laboratory tests on small samples. However, it may be necessary to adjust these parameters in the field while applying the treatment in order to correct for variations in the material, changing weather conditions, etc. This can be done effectively only if there is some way to measure continuously the rate of penetration of the treatment into the material. This may be done through in situ measurement of the elemental distributions.

One approach involving elemental distributions to evaluate the treatment is to measure the changes in hydrogen distribution during the application process, since most treatments involve either water or organic solvents of known molecular composition. The rate of change versus the rate of neutron thermalization in the hydrogen signal during the application of a fixed quantity of treatment can be interpreted to yield a measure of the rate of penetration. Doping the treatment with trace quantities of an extraneous element such as a rare earth would yield an unambiguous signal of the treatment's distribution.

Neutron-Gamma Technique

The National Aeronautics and Space Agency (NASA) has refined some instrumental systems and techniques, originally designed for planetary geology, that have the capability of measuring in situ and nondestructively the elemental distributions in materials. One technique is neutron-gamma ray spectroscopy. The neutron-gamma ray technique measures bulk average properties to a depth of several tens of centimeters within the material.

Neutron-gamma ray methods for determining elemental composition have been used for many years in such fields as oil well logging [16] and environmental monitoring [17]. In the mid-1960s it was suggested that these methods could be used for in situ geochemical analysis of planetary surfaces [18]. Remote sensing gamma ray spectroscopy was used to map the distribution of elements from lunar orbit during the Apollo program [19,20]. Significant advances in the design of detectors and multichannel analyzers have enabled these neutron-gamma ray methods to be used for many other applications where nondestructive in situ chemical analyses of bulk samples are needed.

The irradiation of material by a flux of neutrons will induce the emission of characteristic gamma radiation. The induced emission can be mainly attributed to three interaction processes: inelastic neutron scatter, neutron capture, or neutron activation. Inelastic neutron scatter occurs when fast neutrons are scattered by the nuclei of the material. Some of the neutron's energy in this scattering process is lost to the nucleus, leaving the nucleus in an excited state. The de-excitation of the nucleus is accomplished by the emission of gamma radiation characteristic of the excited nucleus. This de-excitation occurs typically $10^{-14} - 10^{-12}$ s after the initial event. In conventional notation, the inelastic scatter process can be represented by

$$_{Z}^{A}X + _{0}^{1}n \rightarrow {}^{A*}_{Z}X + _{0}^{1}n'; \qquad {}^{A*}_{Z}X \rightarrow {}_{Z}^{A}X + \gamma\text{-ray}$$

where

X = a nuclide of atomic weight A and atomic number Z;
$_{0}^{1}n$ = the neutron with some initial energy,
$*X$ = an excited state of the nuclide, and
$_{0}^{1}n'$ = the neutron with reduced energy.

Neutron capture occurs when thermal neutrons are captured by the material creating compound nuclei, which are formed in an excited state. De-excitation of the compound nucleus follows with the emission of characteristic gamma radiation with a time period generally about 10^{-12} s. This neutron capture process can be represented by

$$_{Z}^{A}X + _{0}^{1}n \rightarrow {}^{A+1*}_{Z}X \rightarrow {}^{A+1}_{Z}X + \gamma\text{-ray}$$

Following the emission of the prompt gamma ray after the neutron capture, the new nuclear species are usually unstable and can decay with the emission of beta particles and gamma radiation. This decay follows some characteristic half-life of the isotope. It is the measurement of these delayed gamma rays that is usually termed *activation analysis*. The two former processes involve prompt interactions and can offer many advantages over activation analysis for some types of measurements. Prompt interactions usually require much lower neutron fluxes and, therefore, much smaller sources than activation. Also, since the interactions are prompt, only measurements during the irradiation are used for analysis. Furthermore, there is negligible residual radioactivity after the measurement is completed.

The availability of larger high-resolution, high-purity germanimum (HPGe) detectors to replace low-resolution scintillation detectors allows the detection of many more elements and permits the rapid computer processing of the measured spectra. The recent production of "n" type Ge detectors which are more resistant to neutron damage than the old "p" type is another beneficial development for neutron-gamma methods. Neutron fission sources such as californium-252 (^{252}Cf) offer a convenient, trouble-free, and small size for field applications. The only drawback is that the neutron energy spectrum has a maximum intensity at approximately 2 MeV and the neutron intensity for higher energies is relatively low. Portable pulsed 14-MeV neutron generators have been developed for well logging [21] and could be used for other neutron-gamma applications.

Most elements of interest in the area of environmental degradation of building materials can be detected using neutron-capture gamma rays. These include silicon, hydrogen, chlorine, titanium, calcium, aluminum, and iron. Some elements, notably carbon and oxygen, cannot be detected by capture gamma rays and would require the production of high energy (14-MeV) neutrons. In addition, there are a number of elements with neutron capture cross sections[5] orders of magnitude greater than the elements just mentioned. These include cadmium, samarium, and gadolinium and might be useful for certain kinds of diagnostic tests and simulations. For example, tracking the diffusion of water, salt, or monomers used in consolidents in a wall can be accomplished by adding small amounts of one of these elements as a tracer.

Neutron-gamma techniques are particularly well suited for measurements of bulk materials such as building walls because the neutrons can travel through large thicknesses of material before interacting to produce characteristic gamma-radiation. The range of the gamma-radiation is more limited, however, typically on the order of 15 to 20 cm.

This defines the region where the elemental composition can be detected to a hemispheric volume of radius 15 to 20 cm around the detector. However, bulk elemental composition maps of building walls can be obtained by moving a neutron source and detector in tandem over the wall surface and measuring the gamma-ray emission spectrum (Fig. 1). The configuration of the source and the detector must be kept fixed at each measurement location.

---

[5] Neutron capture cross sections are proportional to the probability of a neutron being captured by a nucleus.

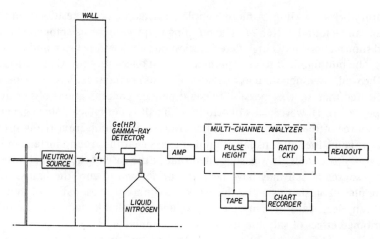

FIG. 1—*Schematic diagram of experimental apparatus for measurement of building walls.*

The gamma-ray spectra are collected using a multichannel analyzer (MCA). High energy resolution is achieved by using a MCA with 8192 channels to cover an energy range of 0 to 10 MeV. The spectra can be recorded on magnetic tape for further processing, and real-time analysis of the spectrum can be accomplished using the video display of the MCA to determine qualitatively the presence of unexpected or erroneous results requiring further measurements. Complete spectra are analyzed using a nonlinear least squares fitting program which determines the peak location and area for the many lines typically found in a spectrum [22].

The presence of a particular spectral line is used for qualitative analysis, and the intensity of the line is used for quantitative analysis. Other factors affecting the intensity of gamma ray are the bulk density of the material, the presence of elements with a large neutron absorption cross section, and the hydrogen content. Partial compensation for the variation in the gamma-ray intensities due to these factors can be achieved by taking ratios of gamma-ray line emission for each element relative to that for a dominant element that remains essentially constant in concentration from position to position. Neutron and gamma-ray transport calculations also have been successfully used to correct gamma-ray line intensities to obtain absolute elemental concentration [23].

Colonial Williamsburg Case Study

To test the feasibility of measuring the distribution of contaminants in building walls, tests were carried out at Colonial Williamsburg in an 18th-century brick building. A more complete discussion of the results from these tests can be found in Ref *24*. The building in question was a smokehouse that had shown abnormally high deterioration rates in both the brick and the mortar. The building had to be repointed at least once every two years. Moisture in the walls was suggested as one possible cause of damage. Visual inspection indicated that another possibility could be high concentrations of salt at the upper levels. However, this distribution of salt is not typical, since generally the source of the salt in building materials is deposition from rising ground water. Thus, the salt is usually found at levels near the ground instead of near the top of the walls. It was suggested that in the case of the smokehouse another source of salt may have been the brine used to cure the hams, which were placed on shelves along the walls. Preliminary investigation of moisture with an electrical resistivity meter produced unreliable data because of the combined effect of salt and moisture on conductivity.[6]

Using a ^{252}Cf and a 120-cm^3 HPGe detector, mapping was successfully done for the water and salt distribution in the walls. A cesium-137 (^{137}Cs) gamma ray source also was used to map the bulk density changes in the wall simultaneously with the spectral measurements. Two characteristic gamma ray pulse height spectra are shown in Fig. 2, and a number of lines from characteristic elements are indicated. The first spectrum is for a region of high chlorine concentration, and the second spectrum is where no chlorine was detected.

In this case, it was not necessary to determine the absolute concentrations of hydrogen and chlorine. Relative differences were sufficient. To compensate for minor variations in brick composition, the data were calculated as ratios of the elemental intensity to that of the silicon line intensity. Typical results for one wall are given in Table 1.

It can be seen that the intensities of hydrogen are highest at the lowest level and decline with height. This is consistent with the pattern of rising ground water. The chlorine intensity, however, is lowest at the bottom and increases with height, implying that there was a source near the top of the building. This tends to support the hypothesis that salt came from the brine. Brick cores taken from two of the measured points are being analyzed to determine the absolute concentration of elements [*24*].

A result from the density measurements was the detection of a void in the wall. This was observed when one point showed an intensity of ^{137}Cs gamma rays, a factor of two higher than the neighboring points. Drilling subsequently confirmed that an 8-cm gap existed inside the wall at this point [*24*].

Finally, the effect of a poultice was investigated. In measurements taken in Jan. 1982, for a certain inside point, the chlorine/silicon ratio was equal to 1.06. Afterwards, a poultice was applied at this point. In July 1982 a measurement gave a chlorine/silicon value of 0.52 at the same point. The significant

[6]Taylor, T., private communication to Protimeter, Inc., Jan. 1982.

decrease in the chlorine intensity was attributed to the effect of the poultice in desalinizing the wall.

Some measure of the level of detection for this technique can be gained from Table 2, which compares the intensity ratios of some elements versus absolute concentrations measured in two samples using X-ray fluorescence. This table indicates the detection limits for some minor elements such as aluminum, potassium, titanium, and iron.

General Considerations

The neutron-gamma technique applied to building diagnoses is still in the prototype stage. Although the apparatus used at Colonial Williamsburg yielded useful results, there are several aspects where improvements are being made:

1. *Portability*—The multichannel analyzer, amplifiers and tape deck were all rack-mount laboratory-type equipment. They are awkward to transport and set up. Miniaturized, portable versions are now commercially available. Similarly, the Ge detector used at Colonial Williamsburg was kept cool by a large liquid nitrogen flask which was heavy to move and to position accurately. Smaller-size flasks are available, as well as solid cryogen equipment, both of which would be much lighter.

2. *Spatial resolution*—As noted, the effective region measured is a hemisphere 15 to 20 cm in diameter. Finer resolution can be obtained through the use of shielding, although at the cost of longer counting times and reduced mobility.

3. *Penetration*—Since the effective range of the emitted gamma rays is on the order of 15 to 20 cm, this is the thickness of material that can be analyzed for a given point. However, since the penetration range of neutrons is much larger, on the order of 60 cm, it is still possible to measure thick walls. The configuration of detector and source needs to be adapted to each specific case. For example, at Colonial Williamsburg, the inside and outside surfaces of a 41-cm-thick wall were measured by switching the placement of the source and the detector. Although the transmission mode, with source and detector on opposite sides of the wall, is the simplest, it is also possible to operate with the source on the same side as the detector. This is the arrangement used in neutron oil well logging.

4. *Alternate building types*—The initial work was done using a brick and mortar structure, but the technique is not limited to this building material. The neutron-gamma technique has been used successfully in oil well logging in limestone and sandstone formations. In each case, the equipment would have been calibrated by testing it on a section of known composition.

5. *Counting times*—The time to count a spectra at a given point is a function of the background radiation, the intensity of the neutron source, and the concentration of the elements under investigation. For example, at Colonial

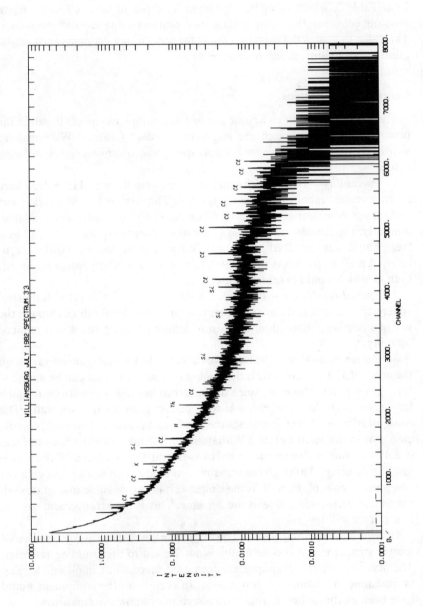

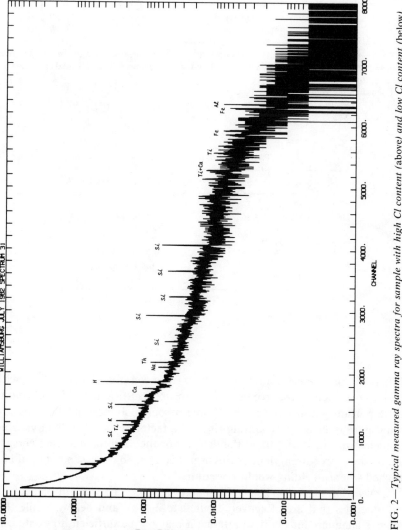

FIG. 2—*Typical measured gamma ray spectra for sample with high Cl content (above) and low Cl content (below).*

TABLE 1—*Williamsburg results (average).*[a]

Vertical Position		H/Si	Cl/Si	[137]Cs
Low	inside	1.64 ± 0.05	0.67 ± 0.02	0.14 ± 0.01[b]
	outside	1.40 ± 0.04	1.00 ± 0.03	0.18 ± 0.01[b]
Middle	inside	1.17 ± 0.03	1.64 ± 0.05	0.21 ± 0.01
	outside	0.89 ± 0.03	1.72 ± 0.05	0.26 ± 0.02
High	inside	1.23 ± 0.04	1.70 ± 0.05	0.30 ± 0.02
	outside	1.04 ± 0.03	1.61 ± 0.05	0.29 ± 0.02

[a] The average is over four points horizontally at each level. The results given are relative intensities and are only meaningful when compared for the same element. The indicated error bars are due to statistical fluctuations only.

[b] Excluding the void region.

TABLE 2—*Elements detected.*

Neutron-Gamma Analysis	X-Ray Fluorescence, Weight %
Aluminum	3 to 6
Silicon	25 to 44
Chlorine	0.3 to >60
Potassium	0.3 to 0.7
Titanium	0.03 to 0.04
Iron	0.4 to 0.8
Tin	. . .[a]

[a] Element could not be measured due to interference with the X-ray target material.

Williamsburg, it was found preferable to use a counting time of 2000 s with the 1 μg ^{252}Cf neutron source in order to ensure a sufficient number of counts for important gamma ray peaks. Using a source strength of 9 μg instead would have reduced the counting time by a factor of three, without causing problems with neutron flux at the detector or the need for shielding personnel. As the source strength increases over this level, however, a point would be reached where shielding would be required.

6. *Neutron sources*—The ^{252}Cf source produces a spectrum of neutron with energies that are effectively limited to 2 MeV and below. While this range is adequate for many situations, it may not be sufficient to excite certain elements by inelastic neutron scatter, such as oxygen or carbon. The alternative is a pulsed neutron generator which produces neutrons with energies of 14 MeV. Portable pulsed neutron generators have been developed for oil well application but have not yet been used for the purpose of building diagnosis.

Prospects for Application of the Neutron-Gamma Method to Building Diagnosis

As noted in the previous section, this technique is still in the development and demonstration phase, and much testing remains to be done to define its potential and limitations. However, experiments thus far have surpassed expectations and have indicated new possibilities.

Generally speaking, the fundamental theory of the method was developed in the field of radiation shielding and has been well-established for over 40 years. Basic physical data such as neutron collision cross sections and mass absorption coefficients have been extensively measured for a variety of materials including steel and reinforced concrete. Furthermore, its application to geological problems has been amply demonstrated in the fields of oil well logging and planetary exploration.

The technique uses commercially available technology and, as demonstrated at Colonial Williamsburg, can be successfully carried out with off-the-shelf components. Some redesign and repackaging of certain parts of the system would be preferable to make the technique more convenient in the field for this particular application and to improve its productivity. However, no major research and development program is required before it can be used routinely for building applications.

Consequently, there appear to be no restrictions on the type of building materials that can be studied with this technique. Certain combinations of materials and building geometries may cause significant interferences or strong attenuation of either neutrons or gamma rays. However, this does not necessarily render the technique unusable in these cases because various parameters such as neutron source strength, system configuration, or counting time can be adjusted to compensate for these conditions.

The range of building problems that can be investigated with this technique is at present limited primarily by the ingenuity of the investigator and his experience in the interpretation of the experimental results. As long as the problem can be defined in terms of the distribution of specified elements, those elements can be measured by the neutron-gamma technique and their spatial distribution used to diagnose building conditions.

Since this technique has been applied just recently to building diagnosis, there has been little opportunity for the building scientists to work with the nuclear scientists to explore potential uses. The nuclear scientists have not been aware of the nature of the building diagnosis problems, and the building scientists have not been familiar with the capabilities of the technique. Thus far, the method has been used to measure interior distributions of moisture, salt, and voids in brick walls three wythes thick. The data suggest that the method also can be used to study the provenance and quality of the bricks. Moreover, it can be used to monitor the effectiveness of rehabilitation measures such as consolidation and desalination. Other possible applications that have been proposed include the location of reinforcing bars in concrete, identification of the type of metals used as clamps to support building facades, the identification of type and distribution of aggregate in concrete domes, and the location of termite nests in masonry walls. With more interchange between the nuclear scientist and the building scientist, it is expected that other applications will be found.

There are some inherent limitations due to the physics of the technique. It generally is not usable for surface layer measurements. It cannot be used to provide information on the chemical bonding of the elements involved. The spatial resolution is presently on the order of 15 to 20 cm. However, this can be improved through the use of more sophisticated software, collimators, and tomographic methods to something on the order of 3 cm, if necessary, for a particular application.

This technique should not be regarded as simply an alternative to a single existing measurement method, such as moisture measurement by electrical resistivity. Instead, it should be viewed as a means of measuring several different variables simultaneously, such as salt distribution and composition, moisture distribution, and density. Furthermore, it can measure things which are beyond the capability of existing methods, such as distributions within the interior of walls.

The cost of the equipment is on the order of $100 000 and, as noted, the components are commercially available. However, it is unlikely that many firms directly involved in building construction or rehabilitation will purchase the equipment outright because, first of all, a license is required from the Nuclear Regulatory Commission to own or use the neutron source, even though the radioactivity involved is very low. Secondly, sensitive electronics are involved, which require skilled technicians to maintain. Thirdly, because each building problem requires some adaption of the method, it is most productive when operated by specialists with a knowledge of nuclear physics. Finally, the most critical part of this technique is the data interpretation, which involves advanced computer software and knowledge of the physics involved in the technique. Consequently, the building industry will probably make use of this technique through the services of specialized consulting firms in the same way that structural or geotechnical engineering firms are used as consultants to diagnose building problems.

It is premature to give precise costs figures, but it is apparent that the costs are determined not so much by the equipment but by the skilled labor involved. The costs of the technique then would be on the order of that for other consulting engineering services. The total costs for using this technique depend upon the nature of the problem under study, number of points to be measured, the size of the building, and other site factors, but again it would be in the ballpark of similar work by engineering consultants. A lower limit of $5000 for the total job would be expected for small buildings and relatively straightforward analyses. These costs should be put into perspective by considering the delays and overruns that can be avoided in the construction or rehabilitation of a building through more accurate knowledge of the condition of the building prior to the start of work.

References

[1] Facoaru, I., "Non-destructive Methods for Moisture Measurements in Buildings," *2nd International Symposium on Moisture Problems in Buildings*, CIB-RILEM, Rotterdam, Holland, 1974.

[2] Noland, J. L., Atkinson, R. H., and Baur, J. C., "An Investigation Into Methods of Non-Destructive Evaluation of Masonry Structure," *Proceedings*, Second North American Masonry Conference, D. W. Vannoy and J. Colville, Eds., University of Maryland, College Park, MD, 1982, pp. 4-2-4-25.

[3] Clifton, J. and Anderson, E., "Nondestructive Evaluation Methods for Quality Acceptance of Hardened Concrete in Structures," NBSIR 80-2613, National Bureau of Standards, Washington, DC, 1981.

[4] Lerchen, F. H., Pielert, J. H., and Faison, T. K., "Selected Methods for Condition Assessment of Structural, HVAC, Plumbing and Electrical Systems in Existing Building," NBSIR 80-2171, Center for Building Technology, National Bureau of Standards, Washington, D.C., 1980.

[5] Baer, N., in *Conservation of Historic Stone Building and Monuments*, National Academy Press, Washington, DC, 1982, pp. 5-6.

[6] Stambolov, T. and van Asperen de Boer, J. R. J., "The Deterioration and Conservation of Porous Building Materials in Monuments: A Review of the Literature," International Centre for the Study of the Preservation and the Restoration of Cultural Property, Rome, pp. 24 and 75, 1976.

[7] Stambolov, T. and van Asperen de Boer, J. R. J., "The Deterioration and Conservation of Porous Building Materials in Monuments: A Literature Review, Supplement 1981," in *Proceedings*, ICOM Committee for Conservation, 6th Triennial Meeting, Ottawa, International Council of Museums, Paris, 1981.

[8] Winkler, E., *Stone: Properties, Durability in Man's Environment*, Springer-Verlag, New York, 1975, pp. 91-101.

[9] Arnold, A., "Soluble Salts and Stone Weathering," in *The Conservation of Stone*, Vol. I, R. Rossi-Manaresi, Ed., Centro per la Conservazione delle Sculture all'Aperto, Bologna, Italy, 1976.

[10] Arnold, A., in *The Conservation of Stone*, Vol. II, R. Rossi-Manaresi, Ed., Centro per la Conservazione delle Sculture all'Aperto, Bologna, Italy, 1981, pp. 13-24.

[11] Charola, A. E. and Koestler, R. J., "The Action of Salt-water Solutions in the Deterioration of the Silico-Aluminate Matrix of Bricks," in *Mattone di Venezia*, Vol. II, 2nd Conference on the Masonry of Venice, Cura Dell'Istituto Studio Della Dinamica Delle Grandi Masse Del CNR, Italy, in press, 1982, pp. 67-76.

[12] Smith, B. M., "Dampness Problems of Historic Masonry Walls: Methods of Diagnosis and Treatment—Draft Preliminary Report," Technical Preservation Services, National Park Service, Washington, DC, 1981, p. 74.

[13] Frohndorff, G. F. and Clifton, J. R., "Stone Consolidating Materials—A Status Report," in *Conservation of Historic Stone Buildings and Monuments*, National Academy of Science Press, Washington, DC, 1981.

[14] Lewin, S., *Art and Archaeology Technical Abstracts*, Vol. 6, No. 1, 1966, pp. 185-277.

[15] Price, C., "The Evaluation of Stone Preservatives," in *The Conservation of Historic Stone Buildings and Monuments*, The National Academy of Sciences Press, Washington, DC, 1981.

[16] Hertzog, R. C. and Plasek, R. E., *IEEE Transactions on Nuclear Science*, Vol. NS-26, 1979, p. 1558.

[17] Failey, M. P., Anderson, D. L., Zoller, W. H., and Lindstrom, R. M., *Analytical Chemistry*, Vol. 51, 1979, p. 2209.

[18] Caldwell, R. L., Mills, W. R., Allen, L. S., Bell, P. R., and Heath, R. L., *Science*, Vol. 152, 1956, p. 457.
[19] Fichtel, C. E. and Trombka, J. I., *Gamma-Ray Astrophysics*, NASA SP-453, U.S. Government Printing Office, Washington, DC, 1981.
[20] Johnson, R. G., Evans, L. G., and Trombka, J. I., *IEEE Transactions on Nuclear Science*, Vol. NS-26, 1979, pp. 1574–1578.
[21] Jensen, D. H., Humphreys, D. R., Stephenson, W. A., Weinlein, J. H., and Birens, H. M., *IEEE Transactions in Nuclear Science*, Vol. NS-28, 1981, p. 1685.
[22] Phillips, G. W. and Marlow, K. W., *Nuclear Instruments and Methods*, Vol. 137, 1976, p. 525.
[23] Evans, L. G., Lapides, J. R., Trombka, J. I., and Jensen, D. H., *Nuclear Instruments and Methods*, Vol. 137, 1982, p. 525.
[24] Evans, L. G., Trombka, J. I., Livingston, R. A., and Taylor, T. H., "Neutron/Gamma-Ray Techniques for Investigating the Deterioration of Historic Buildings," *Nuclear Instruments and Methods*, Vol. A242, 1986, p. 346.

Richard A. Livingston[1]

Evaluation of Building Deterioration by Water Runoff

REFERENCE: Livingston, R. A., **"Evaluation of Building Deterioration by Water Runoff,"** *Building Performance: Function, Preservation, and Rehabilitation, ASTM STP 901,* G. Davis, Ed., American Society for Testing and Materials, Philadelphia, 1986, pp. 181–188.

ABSTRACT: A significant cause of building deterioration is the erosion of surfaces through rainwater runoff, a process which can be accelerated by attack by air pollution, including acid rain. In order to make an accurate diagnosis of the problem, it is necessary to identify which agents of deterioration are present and to estimate the rate at which the material is being lost. This can be done rapidly and directly by measuring the amount of dissolved and suspended material removed in the water runoff and then calculating mass balances.

This paper proposes procedures for performing this type of measurement, including the apparatus required, the major variables and ions to be analyzed, and the interpretation of results. The general approach is to isolate a test area of the building surface so that the water flowing over it can be collected. The water can be either rainfall or distilled water sprayed on the building. If rainfall is the source of the runoff, samples of the incident runoff also must be collected to complete the mass balance. The collected sample is analyzed for concentrations of ions characteristic of the building materials under examination, such as aluminum, calcium, iron, and silicon. In addition, ions related to air pollution—such as sulfates and nitrates—are measured.

KEY WORDS: erosion, stone deterioration, acid rain, runoff, carbonate dissolution, building diagnostics

The selection of the best approach to deal with the deterioration of masonry surfaces requires an estimate of the rate at which the materials are being lost. If the rate is rapid, some emergency measures, such as consolidation, may be called for. If the rate is slow, however, the deterioration may be ignored.

A surface that has been exposed for more than a few years often may have had a complicated history. Over its lifetime, it may have been exposed to major differences in pollution levels. Other events may have included fires or cleaning. The cumulative effect of this past thus may have a significant effect

[1] Research associate, Geology Department, University of Maryland, College Park, MD 20742.

on the deterioration rate currently observed. Therefore, it may be misleading to estimate rate of deterioration based only on current levels of environmental factors.

Furthermore, although significant over the long run, the physical changes in surface dimensions may not be detectable in the short term of a few months [1]. Finally, it is often the case with buildings of cultural significance that it is not permitted to take samples by destructive methods.

The method presented in this paper provides an estimate of the total mass removed during the process of rainwater running over the surface. In humid and temperate climate zones, this usually constitutes the major mode by which material is removed from the surface, although it can be loosened prior to removal by a number of mechanisms including frost and biological activity. The rainwater carries off material either in solution or as suspended solids.

Recently, this deterioration process has received more attention because of the possible incremental effect of acid rain on building deterioration rates [2]. By measuring the concentrations of major ions in the water, along with the suspended material load, it is possible to estimate the total mass of material lost and thus the rate at which surface is being lost. This analysis also will identify the chemical form in which the material is being dissolved and thus give insight into the major agents of attack. This technique is a microscale version of a method that long has been used by geomorphologists to estimate the rate of the lowering of landscapes [3].

Earlier studies following this approach sampled rainwater running off the building material [4,5]. Incident rainfall also was collected and analyzed. Any increases in ionic concentration between the rainfall and the runoff were attributed to material picked up from the surface. While taking advantage of the actual deterioration process, this approach presents some practical difficulties. The most obvious is the necessity to schedule activities around the random timing of rain events. A second drawback concerns the difficulties of collecting representative rain samples and subsequently analyzing them [6]. Hydraulic aspects also are involved because the volume of rain varies from event to event. A sufficient volume of runoff may not occur during light rainstorms, and in intense rainstorms the water may be thrown off the surface rather than flow uniformly over it [7].

The method proposed here attempts to overcome these difficulties. Rather than using rainfall, the measurements are performed with known quantities of distilled water washed across the surface, and a specific area of surface is isolated for the washdown.

Typical ionic constituents in runoff from a fresh marble surface washed by acid rain are presented in Table 1 [8]. It can be seen that Ca^{++} and HCO_3^- dominate, as would be expected given that marble is almost entirely calcite ($CaCO_3$). Also prominent is $SO_4^=$, due to reaction of sulfur dioxide (SO_2), and acid rain containing $SO_4^=$ with the surface [9]. Minor constituents are Mg^{++}, Na^+ and Cl^-, which may come from marine aerosols.

TABLE 1—*Ionic concentrations for marble runoff, mg/L [8].*

Ca^{++}	8.5 to 9.6
Mg^{++}	0.18 to 0.25
Na^+	0.90 to 1.80
K^+	0.28 to 0.42
NH_4^+	...
HCO_3^-	21.35 to 30.50
$SO_4^=$	3.4 to 4.0
Cl^-	2.1 to 5.8
NO_3^-	0.61 to 1.35

The ratio of suspended load to dissolved load depends on several factors. Among them are the mineralogy of the building material, the grain size, the length of time the surface has been exposed, and the rate of water flow over the surface. An example of the rate of surface loss due to suspended versus dissolved loads is given in Fig. 1 for sandstone on Freiburg Cathedral [4]. It can be seen that in this particular case, the suspended load loss rate reaches a level ten times higher than the dissolved load.

Apparatus

The equipment and procedures described in this paper were designed for a study of the rate of deterioration of the Washington Cathedral, which is constructed of oolitic Indiana limestone. Some aspects may vary with other building materials or locations.

The apparatus consists of a 5 to 10-L container which serves as a reservoir for the washdown water, a pump, a spray head, connecting hoses, a 2000-mL

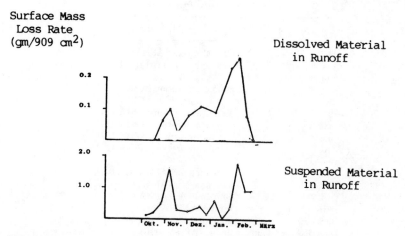

FIG. 1—*Rate of surface loss by dissolved versus suspended load (Freiburg Cathedral sandstone) [4].*

graduate cylinder, a funnel holding a 200-mesh sieve, and a plastic mask with an opening to isolate a test area of the surface. The mask is made of a rigid plexiglass sheet with a rectangular opening on the order of 500 to 1000 cm^2. The long dimension of the opening is in the direction of flow. Around the opening on the side of the mask in contact with the surface is a neoprene O-ring–type gasket to prevent leaks around the opening. The mask is beveled to channel the washdown water into the collection funnel. The mask is clamped into place by a wooden frame with enough pressure on the O-ring gasket to form a tight seal.

A fixed amount (about 5 L) of the distilled water is measured into the reservoir from which it is drawn by the pump at a rate of 1 L/min. The water is directed by the spray head onto the surface under study, which is isolated by the plexiglass mask. The water, after flowing over the surface, is directed into the funnel, which contains the 200-mesh sieve. The filtered water then passes into the 2000-mL plastic cylinder for collection and measurement of volume.

Sample Area Preparation

A sample area 20 by 25 cm is chosen on an upper surface normally exposed to rain. The area should be uniform and as free as possible of joints. It also should have a steep slope for good drainage and should be located above the elevation that could be affected by rising ground water or by other abnormal causes of deterioration such as road deicing salt splashed on the structure by passing traffic.

TABLE 2—*Laboratory analysis.*

Variable	Method
pH	glass electrode (APHA 423)
Conductivity	conductivity cell (APHA 205)
Cations	
Ca^{++}	atomic absorption (APHA 1203)
Mg^{++}	atomic absorption (APHA 1203)
K^+	atomic absorption (APHA 1203)
Na^+	atomic absorption (APHA 1203)
Fe^+	atomic absorption (APHA 1203)
Al^+	atomic absorption (APHA 1203)
Anions	
$SO_4^=$	auto analyzer (APHA 426D)
NO_3^-	auto analyzer (APHA 418F)
CL^-	auto analyzer (APHA 407D)
HCO_3^-	titration (APHA 406B)
Silica	auto analyzer (425 E)
Total dissolved solids	drying (APHA 209B)

Procedure

A measured volume (3 to 5 L) of distilled water, or water of a specified ionic composition, is poured into the reservoir. The pump is turned on and the flow is directed by the spray head over the isolated sample area. When approximately 2000 mL of runoff have been collected in the cylinder, the pump is turned off.

The volume of distilled water remaining in the reservoir is measured and recorded along with the exact volume of runoff water in the collection cylinder. The collected runoff water is measured for temperature, pH, conductivity, and carbonate content and the data recorded. The water is then transferred to a sealed bottle for transport to the laboratory for further analysis. If the laboratory analysis cannot be carried out within 48 h, the samples should be refrigerated at a temperature of 5°C to inhibit changes in ionic composition. The solids on the sieve are washed off by acetone into a glass specimen bottle.

In the laboratory, the water is analyzed according to the tests specified in Table 2. The methods are described in detail in Ref 10. The material collected on the sieve is dried. If sufficient solid is collected, the sample can be weighed and may be analyzed by X-ray diffraction, if desired. Otherwise, the collected particles can be mounted on a glass microscope slide and their volume and composition analyzed using standard petrographic methods [11].

Calculations

The volume of water lost through leakage is computed by

$$V_1 = V_0 - V_f - V_c \qquad (1)$$

where

V_1 = volume of water lost,
V_0 = initial volume in reservoir,
V_f = final volume in reservoir, and
V_c = volume of water collected.

With a good seal, V_1 should be less than 10%.

In the case of erosion of limestone or marble, the original material is essentially pure calcite, $CaCO_3$, plus some calcium nitrate or calcium sulfate formed by reactions with acid rain or sulfur dioxide and nitrogen oxides in the atmosphere. Thus the major ions in the runoff will be: Ca^{2+}, $SO_4^=$, NO_3^-, and HCO_3^-, as shown in Table 1. The bicarbonate rather than carbonate is the ion present in the pH range normally found in runoff water ($3 < pH < 7$) because of reaction with atmospheric CO_2 [12]

$$CaCO_3 + CO_2 + H_2O = Ca^{++} + 2HCO_3^- \qquad (2)$$

The ion balance based on stoichiometry is

$$m_{Ca^{++}} = 0.5 m_{HCO_3^-} + m_{SO_4^=} + 0.5 m_{NO_3^-} \tag{3}$$

where the m_i are molarities. The effect of the minor ions is ignored as a first approximation, and the initial concentrations of Ca^{++}, HCO_3^-, $SO_4^=$, and NO_3^- are assumed to be negligible in the distilled water.

The total mass, $M_{Ca^{++}}$ of dissolved calcium in the runoff is

$$M_{Ca^{++}} = 40.1(V_c m_{Ca^{++}}) \tag{4}$$

Assuming that all the dissolved calcium was originally in the form of calcite, although some of it may have been subsequently altered by air pollution attack, the total equivalent calcite mass dissolved from the surface is

$$M_{cal} = 2.5 M_{Ca^{++}} \tag{5}$$

However, to this must be added the mass of material removed as suspended solids rather than in solution

$$W = M_{cal} + M_{ss} \tag{6}$$

where

W = the total mass removed from the surface, and
M_{ss} = the mass of suspended solids.

The rate of erosion in terms of mass loss per unit area of surface area is then obtained by dividing W by the total area exposed to the washdown

$$E = W/A \tag{7}$$

Note that E is the erosion per runoff event. The annual erosion rate, R, can be estimated by multiplying E by the ratio of annual volume of precipitation, P to V_c, the volume collected in the runoff experiment

$$R = EP/V_c \tag{8}$$

For short-term erosion rates on porous materials, it is best to report erosion rate in mass units. However, an equivalent rate of surface recession can be approximated if the density, ρ, of the material is known. The dimension loss, L, in centimetres per year is

$$L = R/A\rho \tag{9}$$

It will be noted that in calculating R, the only ionic concentration actually used was Ca^{++}. It can be argued, therefore, that it is unnecessary to measure the other ions in the runoff water. This approach in fact was used by Guidobaldi [13] in laboratory studies of marble deterioration rates. One reason for analyzing the other ions is to be able to construct a cation-anion balance (Eq 3) as an error check. As a further check, the conductivity can be calculated by summing the conductivities of the individual ions

$$K_c = \sum_i a_i C_i \qquad (10)$$

where

K_c = calculated conductivity,
a_i = conductivity factor for the ith ion, and
C_i = concentration of the ith ion, in milliequivalents per liter.

If the observed conductivity differs from K_c by more than 2%, the chemical analysis may be in error [14]. The other possibility is the presence of additional ions in the solution that were not analyzed.

Another reason for measuring the other ions is to gain insight into the major mechanisms of deterioration. This comes from examining the relationships of $SO_4^=$ and NO_3^- to HCO_3^-. For example, the results presented by Faugere et al [8] for fresh marble exposed in Bordeaux show that 9 to 40% of the calcite was dissolved by acid in the rain, while the remaining 60 to 91% was dissolved by the karst reaction given in Eq 2. On the other hand, in an experiment on Bowling Green Custom House in New York on a marble statue that had been exposed to high levels of air pollution for 75 years, calcite dissolved in the form of sulfate accounted for 70% of the material lost [15].

Discussion

It should be noted that certain parameters of the procedure may be varied depending on local conditions. For example, the area masked for washing should be as long as possible in the direction of the runoff flow, within the physical constraints of the structure being studied. Flow rates may have to be varied to match local climate. The distilled water volume and flow rate specified in this case were intended to simulate a short but intense summer rainstorm. This could favor erosion by suspended solids. However, the intensity, duration, and frequency of rain events all vary regularly [16]. Slow rains, lasting for long periods, may occur at times. Different flow conditions may affect the rate at which certain chemical species go into solution. For instance, the solution rate of calcite appears to be controlled by surface reactions rather than fluid transport [17] and has a low solubility. Therefore, its measured concentration would not be expected to vary greatly with changes in flow conditions. The opposite would be expected for gypsum, which has a solution controlled by transport conditions. Therefore, it may be desirable to conduct the runoff tests at a number of different flow rates to simulate the range of rain events.

Similarly, the chemical conditions in rain vary seasonally. In most places in the Eastern United States, the acidity in the rain reaches a peak in the summer months [18]. In addition to washdowns with distilled water, it also may be worthwhile to conduct a series of experiments using water with sulfuric and nitric acid added to simulate acid rain. The composition of the simulated acid rain should be based on actual measured values of rain acidity in the vicinity of the structure under study, since the pH and the $SO_4^=/NO_3^-$ ratios vary spatially [19].

References

[1] Trudgill, S., *Earth Surface Processes*, Vol. 2, 1977, p. 251.
[2] Fisher, T., *Progressive Architecture*, July, 1983, pp. 99–105.
[3] Goudie, A., *Earth Science Journal*, Vol. 4, No. 2, 1976, pp. 59–65.
[4] Rönicke, G. and Rönicke, R., *Deutsche Kunst und Denkmalpflege*, Vol. 30, 1972, p. 57.
[5] Livingston, R., Kantz, M., and Dorsheimer, J., "Stone Deterioration Studies at Bowling Green Custom House: Interim Report," National Technical Information Service, Springfield, VA, 1983, p. 15.
[6] Hansen, D. and Hidy, G., *Atmospheric Environment*, Vol. 16, No. 9, 1982, pp. 2107–2126.
[7] Marsh, P., *Air and Rain Penetration of Buildings*, The Construction Press, Ltd, London, 1977, p. 26.
[8] Faugere, J., Derion, J., and Bardy, J., "Action des Nuisances sur les Materiaux en Oeuvre Lessivage par Les Pluies Acids Eaux de Percolation Simulation de Deterioration: Convention de Recherche," No. 80060, Ville de Bordeaux Laboratoire Municipal, Bordeaux, France, 1976, p. 93.
[9] Livingston, R. and Baer, N., "Mechanisms of Air Pollution-Induced Damage to Stone," *Proceedings*, Vol. 3, VIth World Congress on Air Quality, Paris, International Union of Air Pollution Prevention Association, Paris, France, 1983, pp. 33–42.
[10] "Standard Methods for Examination of Water and Wastewater," American Public Health Association, Washington DC, 1981.
[11] Galeshouse, J. in *Procedures in Sedimentary Petrology*, R. Carver, Ed., John Wiley & Sons, New York, 1971, pp. 385–408.
[12] Butler, J., *Carbon Dioxide Equilibria and Their Applications*, Addison-Wesley Publishing Co., Reading, MA, 1982, p. 76.
[13] Guidobaldi, F., "Acid Rain and Corrosion of Marble: An Experimental Approach," in *The Conservation of Stone*, Vol. II, R. Rossi-Manarese, Ed., Centro per La Conservazione delle Soultuve all'Aperto, Bologna, Italy, 1981.
[14] "Standard Methods for Examination of Water and Wastewater," American Public Health Association, Washington, DC, pp. 30–32.
[15] Livingston, R., "Estimation of Mass Balances for the Statue of Phoenicia," unpublished manuscript.
[16] Foster, E., *Rainfall and Runoff*, The Macmillan Co., New York, 1949, pp. 170–232.
[17] Berner, R., *American Journal of Science*, Vol. 278, 1978, pp. 1235–1252.
[18] Miller, J., Pack, D., and Telegadas, K., "The pH of Precipitation in the Washington DC Area: 1975-1981," NOAA Technical Memorandum ERL ARL-118, NOAA Air Resources Laboratory, Rockville, MD, 1983, pp. 4–9.
[19] Olsen, A. and Watson, C., "Acid Precipitation in North America: 1980, 1981, and 1982: Annual Data Summaries, based on the Acid Deposition System Data Base, Pacific Northwest Laboratory, Richland, WA, 1984, pp. 4.11–4.12.

Author Index

Subject Index

A

Acid rain, 181
Administration buildings, 79–81
Aesthetics of buildings, 43, 78
Air
    Circulation (*see also* "Tight building syndrome"), 114–116
    Pollution of, 181
    Quality of, 5, 24, 34–37
Allowable load capacity, wood, 147
Allowable strength properties, wood, 136
Allowable unit stress, wood, 146
Architects, 78
Architecture school building, 39
ASTM standards
    D 245-81, 129, 140, 141, 145–150
    D 2016-74 (1983), 140
    D 2555-81, 129, 145
    D 3737-83*a*, 129
    E 105-58 (1975), 140
ASTM Subcommittee
    E06.24, Building Preservation and Rehabilitation, 1
    E06.25, Overall Performance of Buildings, 1
AUCWS (assigned unadjusted clear wood strength), 145
AUSLC (allowable unit stress load capacity), 149
    ASTM Standard D 245-81, 145–150
Automation equipment
    Demands on building systems, 27

B

Bending stress
    ASTM Standard D 245-81, 145

Brick structures
    Neutron–gamma ray analysis, 165
Bricks, 153–157
Building delivery process, 5, 39
Building performance
    ASTM Subcommittee E06.25, 1
    Diagnostic model, 11, 27
    Diagnostic tools for, 5, 10, 165, 181
    Guidelines for evaluation, 2
    Mandates, 7 (table)
    Monitoring of, 42–43, 45
    New Zealand, 86
    Occupancy analysis, 23, 39, 46
    Ontario, Canada, 111
    Physical descriptors of, 18 (table)
    Rehabilitated buildings, 39, 46, 69
    Scope of studies, 1
    United States, 39, 87, 93, 136
Building preservation (*see* Preservation)
Building rehabilitation (*see* Rehabilitation)
Building stock, 83–84
Business firm
    History of building needs, 74–77

C

Carbonate dissolution, 181
Case studies
    Business firm, 74–78
    Castle, 80–81
    Colonial Williamsburg buildings, 171–173
    Freiburg Cathedral, 183–188
    Government buildings,
        Federal, 30–38
        Regional, 79–81

W

Walls
  Cavity, 162-63
  Clay brick, 153-157
  Composite, 15
  Curtain, 152
  Masonry, 152
  Single wythe, 162-163
  Stone, 160-162
  Terra-cotta, 157-159
Washington Cathedral, 183
Water (*see also* Condensation; Moisture)
  Rain, 181-182
  Repellents, 157, 163, 168
  Runoff, 162-163, 181
  Wall penetration, 152, 163, 165-67
  In wood, 123, 140
Weathering
  Effect on wood, 126
Weep holes, 156, 162-163
Wind
  Effect on curtain walls, 160
Wood
  Chemical preservatives in, 131, 143, 148
  Decay of, 123, 127-128, 140, 144
  Factors affecting durability, 123-127, 140-142
  Fire retardants, 148-150
  Knots, 12, 141, 148
  Lumber grading
    ASTM Standard D 245-81, 129
  Physical properties of, 122-123
  Preservation of, 121
  Strength of, calculation, 145-149
    ASTM standards,
      D 245-81, 145-149
      D 2555-81, 145
  Structures, 121, 136
    Field studies of, 136
    Loading of, 124-125, 136
    Repair of, 131-132
Workbooks
  For inner city rehabilitation, 95, 99, 107-110

Z

Zoning, inner city, 101